A SANSKRIT METHOD

A RAPID SANSKRIT METHOD

George L. Hart

MOTILAL BANARSIDASS PUBLISHERS
PRIVATE LIMITED • DELHI

Reprint: Delhi, 1986, 1989, 1996, 2000, 2006
First Edition: Delhi, 1984

ISBN: 81-208-0173-3 (Cloth)
ISBN: 81-208-0199-7 (Paper)

MOTILAL BANARSIDASS
41 U.A. Bungalow Road, Jawahar Nagar, Delhi 110 007
8 Mahalaxmi Chamber, 22 Bhulabhai Desai Road, Mumbai 400 026
236, 9th Main III Block, Jayanagar, Bangalore 560 011
203 Royapettah High Road, Mylapore, Chennai 600 004
Sanas Plaza, 1302 Baji Rao Road, Pune 411 002
8 Camac Street, Kolkata 700 017
Ashok Rajpath, Patna 800 004
Chowk, Varanasi 221 001

Printed in India
BY JAINENDRA PRAKASH JAIN AT SHRI JAINENDRA PRESS,
A-45 NARAINA, PHASE-I, NEW DELHI 110 028
AND PUBLISHED BY NARENDRA PRAKASH JAIN FOR
MOTILAL BANARSIDASS PUBLISHERS PRIVATE LIMITED,
BUNGALOW ROAD, DELHI 110 007

चलत्कर्णानिलोद्धूतसिन्दूरारुणिताम्बरः ।
जयत्यकालेऽपि सृजन्सन्ध्यामिव गजाननः ॥

Victory belongs to Gaṇeśa, the elephant-faced,
as the wind from his ears blows reddish sindūra powder
from his body, reddening the sky and making
twilight at the wrong time of the day.

शुनः पुच्छमिव व्यर्थं जीवितं विद्यया विना ।
न गुह्यगोपने शक्तं न च दंशनिवारणे ॥

As useless as
the tail of a dog
is life without learning.
It cannot cover
what should be concealed
and it cannot keep off
insects which bite.

PREFACE

The Sanskrit language is perhaps the one thread which binds together the many disparate cultures of Hindu India. That would be reason enough for any student of India to learn it; but there are other reasons which are equally valid.

Sanskrit, or saṃskṛtabhāṣā, "the refined language," evolved from the tongue in which the Vedas were written some time in the later half of the second millennium B.C., a language known as Vedic or Vedic Sanskrit. Sanskrit, which may never have actually been a language spoken by the common people (unlike its forerunner, Vedic), was standardized once and for all by the great grammarian Pāṇini and his predecessors in about the fifth century B.C. From that time until the hegemony of the Moslems, it remained the chief language used in India for communication from one region to another (with the possible exception of the five centuries before Christ, when the use of Prakrit was common). Sanskrit was, moreover, the language used for much of the cultural activity of the subcontinent for nearly two thousand years. It is, like Chinese, Arabic, Greek, and Latin, one of the few languages which has been a carrier of a culture over a long period of time. Thus, the variety of writings in it, and the quantity of those writings, are staggering. An incomplete list of subjects treated in Sanskrit, usually with great prolixity, is as follows :

The four Vedas

The Brāhmaṇas and Āraṇyakas

The Upaniṣads

Grammar (Vyākaraṇaśāstram)

Epic (paurāṇika) literature—including 18 major purāṇas, 18 minor purāṇas, and hundreds of sthalapurāṇas

Classical literature, including hundreds of plays, kāvyas and other classical forms

Buddhist Mahāyāna literature

Works on esthetics (alaṃkāraśāstram)

Works on erotics
Works on medicine
Works on philosophy and theology, comprising six main orthodox Hindu systems, six main heterodox systems, and scores of subsystems
Works on logic
Stotras—devotional hymns
Dictionaries
Works on astronomy and astrology
Works on mathematics
Lawbooks
Works on ritual
Works on Tantrism
Works on architecture
Histories
Panegyrics
Inscriptions
Works on music
Works on sculpture and painting

On most of these subjects, there is an immense literature still extant. Indeed, a rough estimate of the works which will be listed in The New Catalogus Catalogorum yields a total of about 160,000 works still extant in Sanskrit, many so difficult that it would take years of study to properly understand them. And while it would be wrong to suppose that every work in Sanskrit is of great esthetic or scientific value, the fact remains that Sanskrit does have its share of great writers: Kālidāsa ranks with the greatest poets, Pāṇini is without question the greatest pre-modern grammarian, the Mahābhārata ranks with the Iliad and the Odyssey, and the Bhāgavatapurāṇa is among the finest works of devotion ever written, being equalled in my opinion only by other works in Indian languages.

Sanskrit is important for students of linguistics, and especially for Indo-Europeanists, as Vedic is one of the closest languages to Indo-European, the parent of most European and North Indian languages. Pāṇini's system itself has been an object of the study of many modern linguistics students; its discovery has been called the beginning of the modern science of linguistics.

For students of all modern Indian languages (except perhaps Urdu, some knowledge of Sanskrit is essential. Not only are the North-Indian languages descended from Sanskrit (or something close to it); in addition, all of the Indian languages (except Tamil and Urdu) draw on Sanskrit for most of their technical vocabulary, with the result that they have tens of thousands of words taken unchanged from Sanskrit. Indeed, works in Telugu, Kannada, and Malayalam often possess Sanskrit compounds more complex than those normally encountered in Sanskrit literature itself, a state of affairs which, I am told, applies also to some of the North-Indian languages.

Thus an excellent argument can be made that for most students of India an acquaintance with Sanskrit is helpful, and that for many it is essential. Yet I strongly feel that the importance of the other Indian languages should also be pointed out here, if only because so many Indologists in the past have felt that it is enough if students of ancient and medieval India know only Sanskrit. As a student of Tamil with some acquaintance with the other South-Indian languages and literatures, I have been struck by the extent and quality of the classical literature in each of the Dravidian languages. And not only at the extent, but also at the profound difference of the classical literature in each from Sanskrit. Indeed, it seems to me now that any student who knows only Sanskrit, and does not know any South Indian language, cannot hope to fathom accurately any aspect of South Indian history, and that his awareness of classical Indian literature can only be one-sided, like that of a classics student who knows only Latin or only Greek. This is especially true with regard to Tamil literature, which rivals Sanskrit in size and scope as well as quality. Yet a reader of most of the histories of Indian literature, of Indian esthetics, of Indian religion, and of India itself cannot help but be taken aback at how rarely non-Sanskritic sources are even mentioned (much less consulted) by writers on these subjects. The fact is that most authors have written as if Sanskrit and its close relatives constitute the only classical tradition of India, ignoring the fact that all of the Southern languages and many of the Northern languages have classical or medieval literatures which are vitally important for most of the fields investigated by Indologists. Because of this, many areas of Indology need extensive revision, a process which will occupy the attention of Indologists for many years. The student should also keep in mind the fact that Sanskrit, in spite of its size, is a classical language, with no living tradition. To neglect the study of a modern Indian language is to cut oneself off from modern India, to restrict for oneself that access to a living culture which is of great help in the understanding of all aspects of India. Thus I feel that it is essential that Indologists combine with their study of Sanskrit the study of at least one modern Indian language, chosen with their eventual specialization in mind.

A note concerning the use of this book is in order. Before receiving its final form, it was used for a semester at the University of Wisconsin. During that time, many mistakes were corrected, and several explanations which the students found unclear were rewritten. The book is intended to be completed in one semester by a class which meets for three hours a week. The introduction should be completed in a week, after which lessons 1-12 should be covered at the rate of three a week. Thereafter, it is necessary to go slower, spending two classes on each lesson. Each teacher will have to find his own speed, but I feel that it is inadvisable to go slower than this. It may not be possible to finish the entire primer in one semester, but it should be possible to go at least through lesson 27. During the second semester Lanman's Sanskrit Reader should be the text, with between one and two pages covered at each class meeting, so that all (or almost all) of the selections through page 56 (the end of the Kathāsaritsāgara section) are covered. It is not necessary to complete any unfinished lessons of this primer during the second semester, but the students should read over and assimilate the grammatical material in the remaining lessons and the appendix. During the second year, I feel that it is best to read material which is relatively easy—ideally, material from the epics. For example, the entire Gītā may be covered during the first semester of the second year, while material from the epics may be read during the second, at the rate of 20-25 ślokas a class (assuming three classes a week). Then, by the third year, the student should be prepared to begin the study of more technical materials.

For virtually everything which is good in this book I

have Daniel H. H. Ingalls, my teacher and guru, to thank. The method is based ultimately on the way in which he taught me Sanskrit, as are the suggestions for material to be covered in subsequent semesters given above. I can only repeat his advice at this point; that, while class study is essential for a Sanskritist, it is equally essential that he supplement his study with extensive Sanskrit reading on his own after the first year. This means between 10 and 20 hours a week of extra work. The best materials for such outside work I have found are the Mahābhārata and the Kathāsaritsāgara (again, at Ingalls' suggestion).

The ultimate aim of the course of study outlined above is to make the student nearly as fluent in reading Sanskrit as he is in reading his own language. I would stress that no matter what field of Sanskrit a student wishes to investigate, fluency in simple Sanskrit is a prerequisite. I have found that students who cannot read easy Sanskrit with facility simply cannot handle more difficult texts, no matter how much effort they put forth, for they lack an intuitive model for the structure of the language, something which can be acquired only by extensive rapid reading of the sort which cannot be carried on in the more technical subjects. Thus I would strongly advise all students of philosophy or other technical subjects to become fluent enough in simple Sanskrit to read at least 30 (and, ideally, 100) ślokas an hour.

It is a commonplace that valuable endeavors require work and effort. Certainly, as this Preface suggests, the learning of Sanskrit is no exception to this rule. Yet the results of such study are valuable in so many ways that it is impossible to list them all. Suffice it to say that the student will find his entire awareness broadened by the ability to conceive things in a different cultural context which the study of Sanskrit imparts.

अयं निजः परो वेति गणना लघुचेतसाम् ।
उदारचरितानां तु वसुधैव कुटुम्बकम् ॥

CONTENTS

A NOTE OF THANKS

I would like to add a note of thanks to the Sanskrit class with which I first used this primer during the fall semester of 1971-72. They found an enormous number of mistakes and opaque explanations, all of which have been corrected or rewritten in this edition. Special thanks are due to James Solomon who went through this book with special care and found more than his share of mistakes.

INTRODUCTION

THE SANSKRIT ALPHABET

The Sanskrit alphabet is arranged scientifically and can be memorized in a few minutes. The alphabet treats vowels, diphthongs, stops, semivowels, sibilants, and h, while within each of these categories the order is from the back of the mouth to the front.

Vowels : a ā i ī u ū ṛ ṝ ḷ ḹ

Diphthongs : e ai o au

Stops :

Gutturals k kh g gh ṅ
Palatals c ch j jh ñ
Retroflexes ṭ ṭh ḍ ḍh ṇ
Dentals t th d dh n
Labials p ph b bh m

Semivowels :

Palatal y
Retroflex r
Dental l
Labial v

Sibilants :

Palatal ś
Retroflex ṣ
Dental s

Final Letter : h

Vowels : here the order is from the back of the throat (a) to a palatal (i), to a labial (u), to a retroflex (ṛ), to a dental (ḷ). Note that this is different from the order elsewhere, which is guttural, palatal, retroflex, dental, labial. Each category consists of a short vowel followed by a long vowel. A long vowel is pronounced for approximately twice as long as a short one.

a is pronounced like the initial a of America. Ex. api, even.
ā like the a of father. Ex. āgatam, come (neuter past participle).
i like the i of in. Ex. iti, thus. At the end of a word, like -y in Betty.
ī like ee in deep. Ex. pīyate, it is drunk.
u like oo in too, but short and not a diphthong. Ex. umā, name of a goddess.
ū like the oo in too, but long and not a diphthong. Ex. pūrṇam, full.
ṛ like the -er in butter, but rolled. Ex. anṛtam, lie.
ṝ like ṛ, but longer. This letter is rare. Ex. pitṝṇām, of the fathers.
ḷ like -le in little. This letter is rare. Ex. kḷptam, arranged.
ḹ like ḷ, but longer. This letter occurs only in grammatical treatises.

Diphthongs : These letters are formed by the union of vowels, and are always long.

e, formed from a+i, is pronounced like ai in paint. Ex. evam, so.
ai, formed from ā+i, is pronounced like i in kite. Ex. aiśvaryam, power.
o, formed from a+u, is pronounced like o in pole. Ex. osadhi, herb.
au, formed from ā+u, is pronounced like ow in cow. Ex. Kaurava, a proper name.

Stops : These letters are so named because the breath is stopped in pronouncing them (a fact which is not strictly true for the nasals). Gutturals are pronounced in the back of the throat; palatals are pronounced with the tongue against the palate; retroflexes, which do not exist in English, are pronounced with the tongue curled back so that the bottom of the tongue strikes the roof of the mouth; dentals, which are rare in English, are pronounced with the tip of the tongue striking the root of the front teeth; and labials are pronounced with the lips closed. The English stops t and d are alveolar, that is, they are pronounced with the tip of the tongue striking further back than a true dental. Such sounds do not exist in Sanskrit—in fact, English t and d are heard as retroflexes by speakers of Indian languages (with the exception of Malayalam, which has true alveolars). In each category of the stops, the order followed is unvoiced unaspirated, unvoiced aspirated, voiced unaspirated, voiced aspirated, and nasal. Note that in English, unvoiced unaspirated sounds are rare, as are voiced aspirated sounds. The letters k, ch, t, and p are aspirated in English; you will have to practice to pronounce the Sanskrit k, c, ṭ, t, and p correctly. The letters gh, jh, ḍh, dh and bh can be learned more easily.

k is pronounced like k in sky. Ex. kim, what.

kh is pronounced like c in cake. Ex. khalu, indeed.

g like g in gamble. Ex. gacchati, he goes.

gh has no English equivalent, but can be pronounced by saying h and g at the same time. Ex. gharma, warm.

ñ is pronounced like English ng in going. It almost always occurs before another guttural. Ex. añga, limb.

c is pronounced like ch in chain, but unaspirated. Ex. cāru, dear.

ch is pronounced like ch in chain. Ex. châyâ, shadow,

j is pronounced like j in jump. Ex. jagat, world.

jh is quite rare. It is pronounced by saying j and h at the same time. Ex. jhaṭiti, quickly.

ñ is pronounced like ni in onion. It usually occurs before another palatal stop. Ex. kāñcanam, gold.

ṭ is pronounced like t in tank, but is unaspirated and retroflex. Ex. jaṭā, matted hair.

ṭh is pronounced like t in tank, but is retroflexed. Ex. paṭhati, he reads.

ḍ is pronounced like d in doctor, but is retroflexed. Ex. krīḍā, play (n.)

ḍh is pronounced like ḍ, but is aspirated. Ex. līḍha, licked.

ṇ is pronounced like n in earn, but is more retroflexed. Ex. mani, jewel.

t is pronounced like t in start, but is more dental. Ex. tu, but.

th is pronounced like t in tip, but is dental. Ex. atha, then.

d is pronounced like d in dip, but is dental. Ex. dīpa, lamp.

dh is pronounced like d, but is aspirated. Ex. adhara, lower lip.

n is pronounced like n in nose, but is dental. Ex. nāsā, nose.

p is pronounced like p in spark. Ex. api, even.

ph is pronounced like p in path. Ex. phalam, fruit.

b is pronounced like b in bat. Ex. balam, strength.
bh is aspirated b. Ex. bhāryā, wife.
m is pronounced like m in mother, Ex. mātā, mother.

Semivowels : These are consonants which are pronounced without the air being stopped. They are called semivowels because each has a corresponding vowel which becomes the semivowel before another vowel.

y is pronounced like y in yes. Ex. yathā, as.
r is pronounced like the initial r in razor in some English dialects. It should be rolled. Ex. rājā, king.
l is pronounced like l in lip. Ex. labhate, he obtains.
v is pronounced like v in velvet, but is slightly closer to w. Ex. tava, your.

Sibilants : Sanskrit has two *sh* sounds, while English has only one.

ś a palatal, is pronounced like Russian š in širokiĭ—it is more palatal than English sh. Ex. śānti, peace.

ṣ a retroflex, is pronounced like ti in partial, but is a bit more retroflex. Ex. ṣaṭ, six.

s a dental, is pronounced like s in sit. Ex. prasāda, grace.

The final letter.

h is pronounced like h in him. Ex. he, a vocative interjection.

Other sounds. Sanskrit has two other sounds, called visarga and anusvāra.

Visarga : this is written ḥ in transliteration, and is pronounced like hu in hull, after a, ā, u, ū, and o, but it is much shorter. After i, ī and e, it is pronounced like hi in hit, but is much shorter.

Anusvāra : This is written ṃ in transliteration, and is pronounced differently when it appears in different environments. At the end of a word it is pronounced like m. Before a stop inside a word, it becomes the nasal of the group to which the stop belongs. Thus gaṃgā is pronounced gaṅgā; paṃca is pronounced pañca; piṃḍam is pronounced piṇḍam; kāṃtā is pronounced kāntā; and kaṃpati is pronounced kampati. In fact, in these cases, each version is equally acceptable in writing—one may write paṃca or pañca with equal correctness. In the dictionary, the version with anusvāra is found under the nasal (i.e. paṃca is found as its equivalent pañca).

Before a non-stop—that is, before a semivowel, a sibilant, or h, anusvāra is pronounced as a nasal, as and in French quand. Ex. saṃskṛtam, refined, cultivated. When used in this way, the alphabetical position of anusvāra is after the diphthongs and before the stops—thus saṃskṛtam would be found before sakāra.

Exercise : practice pronouncing the words in the writing exercise on page xxiv.

THE DEVANĀGARĪ WRITING SYSTEM

Traditionally, each linguistic region of India used its own writing system to write Sanskrit (with the exception of Tamil Nadu, which used grantha, an alphabet closely related to the Tamil alphabet). Devanāgarī was the name of the writing system used in central northern India. Today, however, Devanāgarī is used for most Sanskrit books printed, though important Sanskrit works are still printed in the regional alphabets as well.

Like the other Indian alphabets, Devanāgarī is a syllabary; that is, in Devanāgarī, a symbol stands for a syllable rather than a phoneme as in European alphabets. The unmodified sign for consonants (that is, for stops, semivowels, sibilants, and h) signifies the consonant followed by -a. The signs for the vowels and diphthongs which you will learn now are used only when the vowel or diphthong is initial. If the vowel or diphthong follows a consonant, the sign for the consonant is modified, as will be shown. If you wish to write a consonant not followed by any letter, a line called a virāma is placed under it. When two consonants come together, their signs coalesce into a ligature. First, learn to recognize and write the following letters. Note that three letters have no line (called a frame) over them—th, dh, and bh. Except for this, dh is identical to gh and bh to m. In the cursive version given here, the letters without a frame begin with a curlicue, so that they may be more easily distinguished from the letters with a frame.

	Printed	How to write
a	अ	
ā	आ	
i	इ	
ī	ई	
u	उ	
ū	ऊ	
ṛ	ऋ	
ṝ	ॠ	
ḷ	ऌ	
ḹ	ॡ	
e	ए	
ai	ऐ	
o	ओ	
au	औ	
ka	क	
kha	ख	
ga	ग	
gha	घ	
ña	ङ	
ca	च	
cha	छ	
ja	ज	
jha	झ or झ	
ña	ञ	
ṭa	ट	
ṭha	ठ	
ḍa	ड	
ḍha	ढ	
ṇa	ण	
ta	त	
tha	थ	
da	द	

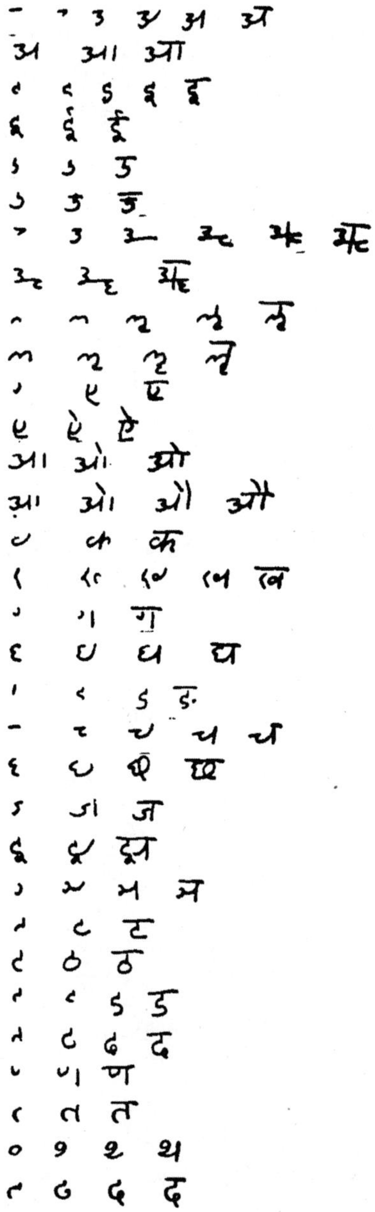

dha	ध
na	न
pa	प
pha	फ
ba	ब
bha	भ
ma	म
ya	य
ra	र
la	ल
va	व
śa	श
ṣa	ष
sa	स
ha	ह

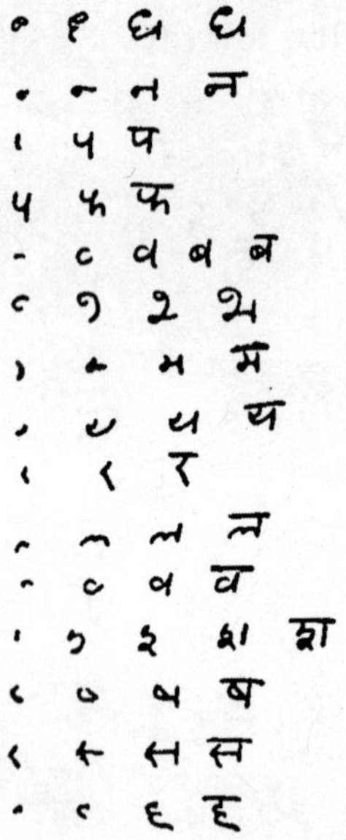

The best way to learn these signs is to put each on a 3/5 card, with its Roman equivalent on the back, and then to go through the cards in random order until you can recognize and write each letter.

In order to write vowels other than -a after a consonant, the sign for the consonant is modified. Study the way in which क is modified for the various vowels. Other consonants are modified in an identical manner, with a very few exceptions.

kā	का
ki	कि
kī	की
ku	कु
kū	कू
kṛ	कृ
kṝ	कॄ
kḷ	क्लृ
ke	के
kai	कै

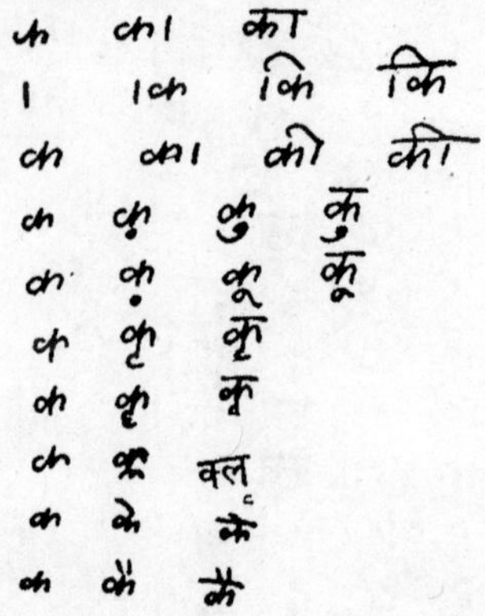

ko को 
kau कौ 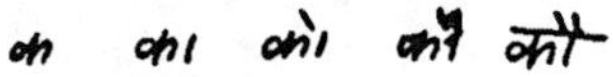

Anusvâra and visarga are written as follows :

kaṃ कं 
kaḥ कः 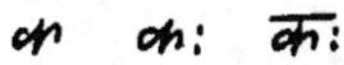

A letter not followed by any other vowel is written with a virâma:

k क् 

On the next page, a chart is given which shows all of the Sanskrit consonants written with all of the vowels after them. The following are formed in special ways :

ru रु 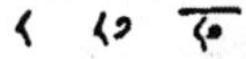
rū रू 
śu शु  (or in the normal way, शु)
śū शू  (or in the normal way, शू)
śṛ शृ  (or in the normal way, शृ)
hṛ हृ 

In this chart, the vowels ṝ, ḷ, and ḹ are omitted because they are rare.

	अ	आ	इ	ई	उ	ऊ	ऋ	ए	ऐ	ओ	औ
क्	क	का	कि	की	कु	कू	कृ	के	कै	को	कौ
ख्	ख	खा	खि	खी	खु	खू	खृ	खे	खै	खो	खौ
ग्	ग	गा	गि	गी	गु	गू	गृ	गे	गै	गो	गौ
घ्	घ	घा	घि	घी	घु	घू	घृ	घे	घै	घो	घौ
(ङ्	ङ	ङा	ङि	ङी	ङु	ङू	ङृ	ङे	ङै	ङो	ङौ)
च्	च	चा	चि	ची	चु	चू	चृ	चे	चै	चो	चौ
छ्	छ	छा	छि	छी	छु	छू	छृ	छे	छै	छो	छौ
ज्	ज	जा	जि	जी	जु	जू	जृ	जे	जै	जो	जौ
झ्	झ	झा	झि	झी	झु	झू	झृ	झे	झै	झो	झौ
(ञ्	ञ	ञा	ञि	ञी	ञु	ञू	ञृ	ञे	ञै	ञो	ञौ)
ट्	ट	टा	टि	टी	टु	टू	टृ	टे	टै	टो	टौ
ठ्	ठ	ठा	ठि	ठी	ठु	ठू	ठृ	ठे	ठै	ठो	ठौ

ड्	ड	डा	डि	डी	डु	डू	डृ	डे	डै	डो	डौ
ढ्	ढ	ढा	ढि	ढी	ढु	ढू	ढृ	ढे	ढै	ढो	ढौ
ण्	ण	णा	णि	णी	णु	णू	णृ	णे	णै	णो	णा
त्	त	ता	ति	ती	तु	तू	तृ	ते	तै	तो	तौ
थ्	थ	था	थि	थी	थु	थू	थृ	थे	थै	थो	थौ
द्	द	दा	दि	दी	दु	दू	दृ	दे	दै	दो	दौ
ध्	ध	धा	धि	धी	धु	धू	धृ	धे	धै	धो	धौ
न्	न	ना	नि	नी	नु	नू	नृ	ने	नै	नो	नौ
प्	प	पा	पि	पी	पु	पू	पृ	पे	पै	पो	पौ
फ्	फ	फा	फि	फी	फु	फू	फृ	फे	फै	फो	फौ
ब्	ब	बा	बि	बी	बु	बू	बृ	बे	बै	बो	बौ
भ्	भ	भा	भि	भी	भु	भू	भृ	भे	भै	भो	भौ
म्	म	मा	मि	मी	मु	मू	मृ	मे	मै	मो	मौ
य्	य	या	यि	यी	यु	यू	यृ	ये	यै	यो	यौ
र	र	रा	रि	री	रु	रू		रे	रै	रो	रौ
ल्	ल	ला	लि	ली	लु	लू		ले	लै	लो	लौ
व्	व	वा	वि	वी	वु	वू	वृ	वे	वै	वो	वौ
श्	श	शा	शि	शी	शु (शु)	शू (शू)	शृ (शृ)	शे	शै	शो	शौ
ष्	ष	षा	षि	षी	षु	षू	षृ	षे	षै	षो	षौ
स्	स	सा	सि	सी	सु	सू	सृ	से	सै	सो	सौ
ह्	ह	हा	हि	ही	हु	हू	हृ	हे	है	हो	हौ

Examples of words written in Devanāgarī :

api	अपि	अपि	katham	कथम्	कथम्
iti	इति	इति	abhavat	अभवत्	अभवत्
kānanam	काननम्	काननम्	viśālaḥ	विशालः	विशालः
apavādaḥ	अपवादः	अपवादः	kīdṛśaiḥ	कीदृशैः	कीदृशैः
pitṝṇām	पितॄणाम्	पितॄणाम्	saṃsāraḥ	संसारः	संसारः
bhojanam	भोजनम्	भोजनम्	mūḍham	मूढम्	मूढम्
kimapi	किमपि	किमपि	mukham	मुखम्	मुखम्
ṛtuḥ	ऋतुः	ऋतुः	kaliyugam	कलियुगम्	कलियुगम्
īśaḥ	ईशः	ईशः	apāraḥ	अपारः	अपारः
madaḥ	मदः	मदः	aliḥ	अलिः	अलिः

Exercise : write the following words in Devanāgarī.

mūlam
yādṛśā
anukaroti
aitihāsika
ṛṣīṇām
bhavatu
kutaḥ
sakhā
kalayati
auṣadhī
kalā
Śiva
Umā
palāyati
pālayet
āgataiḥ
dhārāḥ
gṛhe
upaviśatu
atha
daivikam
narakāsuraḥ
Rāmānujaḥ
rājānam
mahārājāya
vadatu
ṛṣiḥ
yuvānam
īrayati
nadīm
saṃrodhayati
śatāni

Ligatures : When two consonants come together, they are represented by a combination of their two signs. In general, such combinations can be easily remembered, but a few bear little relation to one or both of the letters used to form them and must be memorized with special care. First, ligatures of particular importance which belong to the second category are given. These should be memorized actively now. Then a list of most of the ligatures you are likely to encounter is given. These need not be memorized actively at this time, but you should familiarize yourself with them and with the principles used to form them. The Devanāgarī type used for Sanskrit in these lessons is unable to form some of the ligatures commonly used (e g. ṭtha)—it must form such ligatures by putting a virāma under the t. But even where the type ṭ cannot make the proper ligatures you should employ them in writing your exercises, as they are universally used in writing and printing.

Ligatures to be memorized.

r: when r precedes a consonant, the sign is placed over the consonant. Thus :

rka र्क

rṣa र्ष etc. Note that rkā is र्का, rkaiḥ is र्कैः, rkaṃ is र्कं.

When r immediately follows a consonant, a small line is added to that consonant, as in the following examples:

kra क्र

grā ग्र And so on—see list of ligatures below

kṣa क्ष

jña ज्ञ (pronounced dña)

tta त्त (Use the cursive version)

tra त्र (Use the cursive version)

dya द्य

ṣṭa ष्ट (Use the cursive version)

ṣṭha ष्ठ (Use the cursive version)

Ligatures : an alphabetical list. Familiarize yourself with the principles used in forming these. Always use the cursive version if it is different from the printed one. Difficult combinations are marked with an asterisk.

*kta क्त

*ktva क्त्व

*kya क्य

kra क्र

*kla क्ल

*kva क्व

*kṣa क्ष or

gga ग्ग

gda ग्द

gdha ग्ध

gna ग्न

gma ग्म

gya	ग्य
gra	ग्र
gla	ग्ल
gva	ग्व
ghna	घ्न
ñka	ङ्क
ñkta	ङ्क्त
ñkha	ङ्ख
ñga	ङ्ग
ñgha	ङ्घ
ccha	च्छ
cya	च्य
jña	ज्ञ
jya	ज्य
jva	ज्व
ñca	ञ्च
ñcha	ञ्छ
ñja	ञ्ज
ṭṭha	ट्ठ
ṭhya	ठ्य
ḍḍha	ड्ढ
ḍga	ड्ग
ḍya	ड्य
ṇṭa	ण्ट
ṇṭha	ण्ठ
ṇḍa	ण्ड
ṇḍha	ण्ढ
ṇya	ण्य
*tta	त्त
ttha	त्थ
*tna	त्न
tpa	त्प
tpha	त्फ

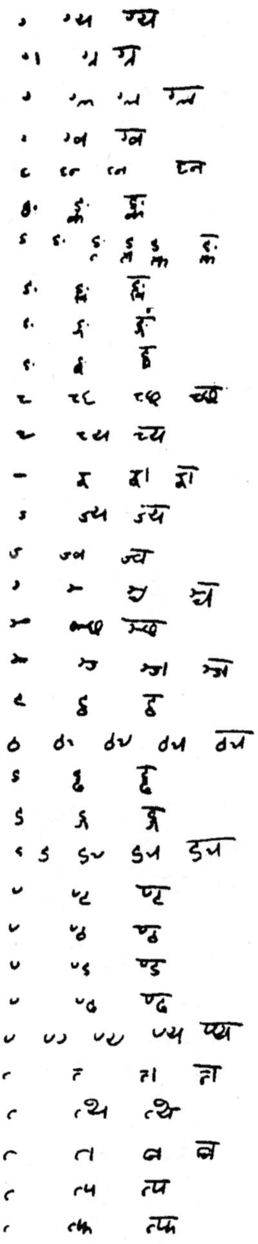

tma	त्म
tya	त्य
*tra	त्र
tva	त्व
tsa	त्स
dga	द्ग
dda	द्द
*ddha	द्ध
ddhya	द्ध्य
ddhva	द्ध्व
dba	द्ब
*dbha	द्भ
*dbhya	द्भ्य
*dma	द्म
*dya	द्य
dra	द्र
dva	द्व
*dvya	द्व्य
dhya	ध्य
dhra	ध्र
dhva	ध्व
nta	न्त
ntra	न्त्र
ntrya	न्त्र्य
ntha	न्थ
nda	न्द
ndha	न्ध
nya	न्य
nva	न्व
nsa	न्स
nha	न्ह
pta	प्त
pya	प्य

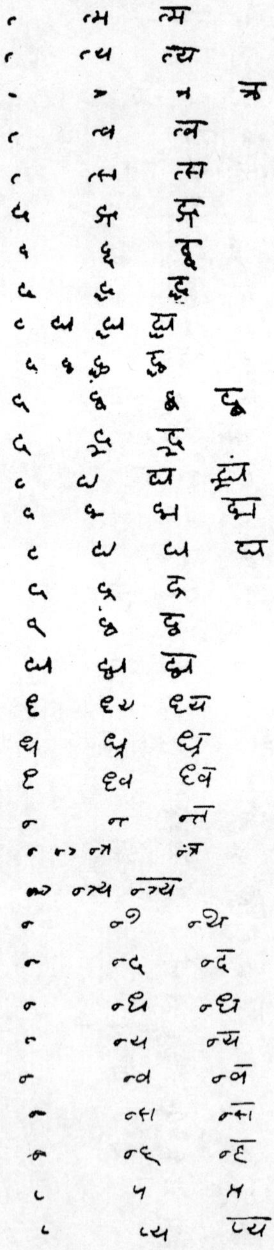

pla	प्ल
psa	प्स
bja	ब्ज
bda	ब्द
bdha	ब्ध
bya	ब्य
bra	ब्र
bhya	भ्य
mya	म्य
mla	म्ल
yya	य्य
rṛ	ऋं (Note this ! Logically, it should be ऋ)
lka	ल्क
lta	ल्त
lpa	ल्प
lma	ल्म
vya	व्य
*śca	श्च
ścha	श्छ
*śna	श्न
*śra	श्र
*ṣṭa	ष्ट
*ṣṭha	ष्ठ
*ṣṭva	ष्ट्व
ṣṇa	ष्ण
sta	स्त
stra	स्त्र
stha	स्थ
sna	स्न
sma	स्म
sya	स्य

sva	स्व
*hna	ह्न
*hna	ह्ण
*hma	ह्म
*hya	ह्य
*hla	ह्ल
*hva	ह्व

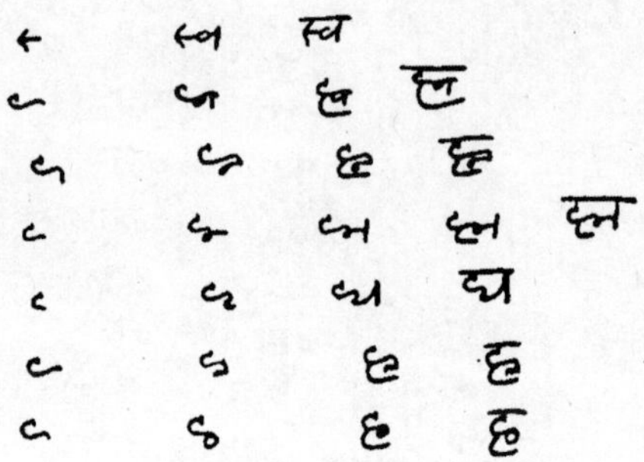

Exercise : Study the way in which the following words are written :

antaḥkaraṇam	अन्तःकरणम्	अन्तःकरणम्	atarkyam	अतर्क्यम्	अतर्क्यम्
prāpnoti	प्राप्नोति	प्राप्नोति	śaknuvanti	शक्नुवन्ति	शक्नुवन्ति
adya	अद्य	अद्य	tiṣṭhatsu	तिष्ठत्सु	तिष्ठत्सु
śatrūṇām	शत्रूणाम्	शत्रूणाम्	dugdham	दुग्धम्	दुग्धम्
dṛṣṭvā	दृष्ट्वा	दृष्ट्वा	jñāpayati	ज्ञापयति	ज्ञापयति
aṣṭau	अष्टौ	अष्टौ	jñātvā	ज्ञात्वा	ज्ञात्वा
kalpaḥ	कल्पः	कल्पः	alpam	अल्पम्	अल्पम्
śraddadhāti	श्रद्दधाति	श्रद्दधाति	laṅkā	लङ्का	लङ्का
pratikṣaṇam	प्रतिक्षणम्	प्रतिक्षणम्	ikṣvākuḥ	इक्ष्वाकुः	इक्ष्वाकुः

Write the following words in Devanāgarī, referring to the list of ligatures wherever necessary.

agram	kalyāṇamitram
arthah	buddhaḥ
jñātvā	aśrūṇi
tadyathā	niścayaḥ
naksatrāṇi	hṛdayasya
prasadah	apatyam
manuṣyah	pratyekabuddhaḥ
ratnāni	indrah

svargam	tātparyam
kṣatriyeṣu	aśvaḥ
netram	cārurūpam
dattāni	cakram
draṣṭavyam	vicitrāṇi
āgacchatsu	śūdraḥ
nirṛtiḥ	vastram

Lesson 1

THEMATIC VERBS

I. Saṃdhi : final -s becomes visarga. In Sanskrit, sounds change according to the environment in which they occur. In lessons 4, 5, and 6, you will learn all of the rules of saṃdhi. For now, you need only learn the rule that final -s becomes visarga (-ḥ) when it occurs at the end of an utterance. Thus the -ḥ given in the forms below in section III stands for -s, and should be so treated when the saṃdhi rules learned later are applied. Note that before initial t-, final -s is unchanged (see sentence 10 in the exercises).

II. Guṇa and Vṛddhi. Vowels often undergo changes as new forms are made. The most common change is for a vowel to be replaced by what is termed its guṇa or vṛddhi equivalent. Memorize the following :

Simple Vowel	a	ā	i, ī	u, ū	ṛ
Guṇa	a	ā	e	o	ar
Vṛddhi	ā	ā	ai	au	ār

(Note that the guṇa of ḷ, which is -al, is found in only one root—kḷp/kalp-; it need not be learned).

III. Thematic verbs, active.

A. Number.

While the persons of the Sanskrit verb are similar to those in other Indo-European languages, the Sanskrit verb (as well as the Sanskrit noun and adjective) has an extra number, called the dual.* Thus, while English has two forms for singular and

*The Indo-European dual has also survived in Homeric Greek and in some fossilized forms in other languages, as the plural of "eye" and "shore" in Russian.

plural, Sanskrit has three forms, for singular, dual, and plural. The singular is used when one thing is the subject of the verb; the dual, when two things are its subject; and the plural, when three or more things are its subject.

B. Thematic versus athematic.

Sanskrit verbs and nouns, like their Greek counterparts, are divided into two broad classes, thematic and athematic. In thematic words, a union vowel (-a- in Sanskrit) is added before the endings. Athematic verbs, which lack this vowel addition, will not be treated until later, as they are more complex than thematic verbs. In this lesson, all of the classes of thematic verbs are treated.

C. The thematic endings.

Note that in the first-person endings, the union vowel -a- has coalesced with the ending (-āmi, -āvaḥ, -āmaḥ).

Person	Singular	Dual	Plural
First	-āmi	-āvaḥ	-āmaḥ
Second	-a-si	-a-thaḥ	-a-tha
Third	-a-ti	-a-taḥ	-a-nti

D. The Classes.

Class I. The endings are added to the guṇated root, i.e. to the root whose vowel has been changed to its guṇa equivalent. If the root ends in the vowel -ī̆ or -ū̆, then the following takes place :

ī̆ → e → ai → ay

ū̆ → o → au → av

Here, the diphthongs e/o have simply been separated into their component vowels, ai/au, and the second of these component vowels has been changed to its corresponding semivowel (y/v). Thus

Root	Form before endings.
bhū, become	bhav-
nī, lead	nay-
ji, vanquish	jay-
pat, fly, fall	pat-
ruh, climb	roh-

Now learn the active present paradigm of bhū, to become :

भवामि	I become	भवावः	we 2 become	भवामः	we become
भवसि	you become	भवथः	you 2 become	भवथ	you (pl) become
भवति	he becomes	भवतः	they 2 become	भवन्ति	they become

Note that in the vocabulary the root, the class, and the third-singular active form are given. There are some important exceptions in each class; therefore, it is best to concentrate on learning the root and its third-singular active form; its class can almost always be told from its 3rd -sg. form while the converse is not true.

Class VI. The endings are added to the weak root, i.e. to the root whose vowel takes neither guṇa nor vṛddhi.

Example : viś, enter.

विशामि	विशावः	विशामः
विशसि	विशथः	विशथ
विशति	विशतः	विशन्ति

Class IV. -y- is added to the unchanged root; the endings are added to the root so augmented.

Example : paś, see,

पश्यामि	पश्यावः	पश्यामः
पश्यसि	पश्यथः	पश्यथ
पश्यति	पश्यतः	पश्यन्ति

Class X. -ay is added to the root, which is guṇated in a light syllable (in which a short vowel is followed by no consonant or 1 consonant), and is unchanged in a heavy syllable (with a long vowel or short vowel followed by 2 consonants). Medial -a is often vṛddhied. Thus cur → corayati; pīḍ, pīḍayati, and taḍ, tāḍayati.

Example : pīḍ, squeeze, afflict, hurt.

पीडयामि	पीडयावः	पीडयामः
पीडयसि	पीडयथः	पीडयथ
पीडयति	पीडयतः	पीडयन्ति

Exceptions : Note that you should actively learn only the words given in the vocabulary. You need only look over the following exceptions and familiarize yourself with the principles involved. Do not memorize them.

a. Some roots of the above classes form the present stem with the suffix -cch :

gam (I), go	gacchati
yam (I), yield, give	yacchati
iṣ (VI), desire	icchati
pracch (VI), ask	pṛcchati

b. Some roots lengthen the vowel -a- :

dam (IV), tame, subdue	dāmyati
kram, step	krāmati

c. Some roots which have a nasal before the final syllable lose it.

daṃś (I), bite	daśati
rañj (IV), become red	rajyati

d. Some roots insert a nasal before the final consonant of the root :

sic (VI), sprinkle	siñcati

e. Some roots are reduplicated. (reduplication will be explained later)

sthā (I), stand	tiṣṭhati
pā (I), drink	pibati

f. Verbs of class VI ending in -ṝ take their present in -ir-

tṝ (VI), cross	tirati

Once again, it is stressed that you should not take time memorizing each class and each exception. Acquaint yourself with the general principles, and then learn the root and 3rd sg. of each verb given in the vocabulary.

VOCABULARY :

कुत्र	kutra	where (interrogative)
गम् (गच्छति)	gam (gacchati)	go (I)
च	ca	and, placed after the last member in series (like Latin -que)
जि (जयति)	ji (jayati)	vanquish, conquer (I)
नी (नयति)	nī (nayati)	lead, convey (I)
पश् (पश्यति)	paś (paśyati)	see (IV)

पीड् (पीडयति)	pīḍ (pīḍayati)	squeeze, afflict, hurt (X)
प्रच्छ् (पृच्छति)	pracch (pṛcchati)	ask (VI)
भू (भवति)	bhū (bhavati)	become (I)
विश् (विशति)	viś (viśati)	enter (VI)
स्था (तिष्ठति)	sthā (tiṣṭhati)	stand (I)
स्मृ (स्मरति)	smṛ (smarati)	remember (I)

TRANSLATE the following into English : Your translations need not be written, but you should be prepared to read each sentence in class.

पश्यामि जयामि च ॥१॥ कुत्र गच्छसि ॥२॥ स्मरतः ॥३॥ नयामः ॥४॥ तिष्ठथ पीडयथ च ॥५॥ कुत्र तिष्ठन्ति पृच्छन्ति च ॥६॥ गच्छति नयति च ॥७॥ जयथः ॥८॥ स्मरावः ॥९॥ पृच्छामस्तिष्ठन्ति च ॥१०॥

TRANSLATE the following sentences into written Sanskrit, using the Devanāgarī alphabet: 1. I stand and see. 2. You two ask. 3. They enter and remember. 4. Where do they two go ? 5. We conquer. 6. We two afflict. 7. You (pl.) go and enter.

Lesson 2

I. Saṃdhi. Before an initial consonant beginning the next word, final m becomes anusvāra. Thus "I see the god" is देवं पश्यामि । (see below for devam). Note that final anusvāra is pronounced -m.

II. Nouns and adjectives. Like other ancient Indo-European languages, Sanskrit is inflected : the endings of words are modified according to their function in the sentence, as you have already seen with regard to verbs. For nouns and adjectives, there are eight cases for each of the three numbers. Each case expresses a grammatical function, as explained immediately below. Sanskrit nouns and adjectives have three genders, like their German counterparts. As in German, the gender of a word is not necessarily correlated with its meaning (moon is masculine : army is feminine; fruit is neuter). With a few exceptions, however, it is possible to tell the gender of a noun from its declension and the form in which it is cited. Thus nouns cited ending in -a are masculine; in -am, neuter; and in -ā and -ī, feminine.

III. The Cases. The names used in this text for the cases are those generally used in Western works. In Sanskrit, the cases are named according to the numerical place they occupy in the traditional listing : nominative is "the first" (प्रथमा), accusative is "the second" (द्वितीया), instrumental is "the third" (तृतीया), etc. (But vocative is not the eighth; rather it is called संबोधनम्).

In the following discussion, remember the primary uses of each case, which are flush with the left-hand margin. Other uses, which you need not remember at present, are given for future reference and are indented. Note that this list is not exhaustive, and that other uses of the cases will be encountered, to be explained at the appropriate time.

Nominative :

Used for the subjects of verbs, and for predicate adj.'s and nouns.

Accusative :

Used for the direct objects of verbs. Also used to express motion to a place—i.e. to translate "to" in the sense of motion, as "he goes to the city."

Other use : extended time, as "for many years."

Instrumental ;

Used to express instrumentality by which the action of the verb is accomplished—in other words, it expresses "by means of." For example, "This work is done *by me*," "I write *with a pen*."

Dative :

Used for the indirect object, as "He gave the book *to me*."

Note : in classical Sanskrit, this case, while still common, is often replaced by the genitive. It also expresses "for the sake of."

Ablative :

Used to express place from which, as "He comes *from the city*." This case is also used to express reason on account of which, as "One learns *from practice*."

Other use : to express the object of comparison, as "He is taller *than I*."

Genitive :

Used for possession or intimate relation, expressed by English "of" as "This is the house *of father*." The Sanskrit genitive precedes the word modified, as does the English possessive in 's —see sentences 4 and 5 in the Sanskrit exercises. Note that the genitive may not be used to translate an English genitive of identity ("This is the town *of Rome*.")—such a sentence must be translated with a karmadhāraya compound ("Rome-town").

Other uses : the genitive is sometimes used instead of the dative for indirect objects. For the logical subject of a passive verb, it may be used instead of the instrumental ("This is done *by me*"). There also exists a construction called a "cosmic genitive" where the genitive is construed with the sentence as a whole—"*For all men*, this is an auspicious time."

Locative :

Used to express the place in which a thing is or in which an action occurs, as well as to express the place into which the action of the verb takes place. "He is *in the city*"; "He goes *into the city*."

Other uses : To translate English "among" and to express time within which: "He is *among friends*"; "*in one moment....*"

Vocative :

Used for address : "*Mother*, give me some food."

IV. The Declensions of deva, god, and phalam, fruit. These must be memorized. Note that deva is masculine (as are all nouns cited ending in -a), while phalam is neuter (like other nouns cited ending in -am). The declension of these nouns is identical except in the nominative, accusative, and vocative of all three numbers. Note that except for the singular of deva, the vocative is identical with the nominative.

Case	Singular	Dual	Plural
Nom.	devaḥ/phalam	devau/phale	devāḥ/phalāni
Acc.	devam/phalam	devau/phale	devān/phalāni
Inst.	devena/phalena	devābhyām/phalābhyām	devaiḥ/phalaiḥ
Dat.	devāya/phalāya	,, ,,	devebhyaḥ/ phalebhyaḥ
Abl.	devāt/phalāt	,, ,,	,, ,,
Gen.	devasya/phalasya	devayoḥ/phalayoḥ	devānām/phalānām
Loc.	deve/phale	,, ,,	deveṣu/phaleṣu
Voc.	deva/phala	devau/phale	devāḥ/phalāni

Other points to note : like all other neuter nouns, phalam has the same nom. and acc. in all numbers. All nouns and adjectives have in the dual identical forms for the nom. and acc.; for the inst., dat., and abl.; and for the gen. and loc.

Now study the declension of deva in Devanāgarī.

Nom.	देवः	देवौ	देवाः
Acc.	देवम्	देवौ	देवान्

Inst.	देवेन	देवाभ्याम्	देवैः
Dat.	देवाय	देवाभ्याम्	देवेभ्यः
Abl.	देवात्	देवाभ्याम्	देवेभ्यः
Gen.	देवस्य	देवयोः	देवानाम्
Loc.	देवे	देवयोः	देवेषु
Voc.	देव	देवौ	देवाः

VOCABULARY :

अश्व	aśva	horse
काक	kāka	crow
क्षत्रिय	kṣatriya	kṣatriya, the second varṇa; the warrior class
गज	gaja	elephant
गृहम्	gṛham	house
जलम्	jalam	water
देव	deva	god
नगरम्	nagaram	city
फलम्	phalam	fruit
पुत्र	putra	son
मित्रम्	mitram	friend

TRANSLATE into English :

अश्वान्पीडयति ॥१॥ गृहं गच्छामि ॥२॥ काकौ कुत्र तिष्ठतः ॥३॥ क्षत्रियस्य पुत्रं पश्यथ ॥४॥ क्षत्रियस्य पुत्रस्य गजौ नयामः ॥५॥ पुत्रस्य फले कुत्र तिष्ठतः ॥६॥ गृहात्पश्यतः मित्रे ॥७॥ जले गच्छन्ति गजाः ॥८॥

NOTE ON WORD ORDER : As you do the following sentences, remember that the normal word order is subject, object, verb. Adverbs are normally before the object or directly before the verb, but they may be put elsewhere. Since you have not yet had certain saṃdhi combinations, in some of the following sentences the words are numbered to show you what order to write the words in to avoid combinations which you have not yet had. Even where the order differs from the normal one, the sentence does not seem excessively abnormal in Sanskrit (though the emphasis may be changed).

TRANSLATE into Sanskrit in Devanāgarī : 1. Where[2] do the two friends[1] stand[3] ? 2. The gods[2] vanquish[1]. 3. I remember the city of the son of the kṣatriya (use sentence 5 above as a model). 4. He goes[2] to the house[1] from the city[3]. 5. We two see[2] two friends[1]. 6. You (pl.) enter[6] the city[5] of the horses[1], crows[2], and[4] elephants[3].

Lesson 3

THE MIDDLE

In lesson I, you learned the present active endings. Like Greek, Sanskrit possesses another set of endings, called the middle, which you will learn in this lesson.

Originally, the middle indicated that the action of the verb is carried out for the sake of the subject, in the subject's interest, a distinction which can still be observed in some verbs in classical Sanskrit (especially in the epics). However, by the time of classical Sanskrit, the use of the endings had become rigid for the most part, so that a particular verb could take only active or middle endings. In this course, a verb will be assumed to take only active or middle endings. Which set of endings a verb takes can be determined by the third-singular form given in the citation of the verb (active in -ti; middle in -te).

Learn the present middle conjugation of labh. Other thematic middle verbs are conjugated in the same way.

	Singular	Dual	Plural
1st pers.	labhe	labhāvahe	labhāmahe
2nd pers.	labhase	labhethe	labhadhve
3rd pers.	labhate	labhete	labhante
	लभे	लभावहे	लभामहे
	लभसे	लभेथे	लभध्वे
	लभते	लभेते	लभन्ते

VOCABULARY : from now on, verbs are cited with only their present 3rd sg. form and the root; classes are not given.

इदानीम्	idānīm	now
एव	eva	only (placed after the word modified—see sent. 8), indeed.
कथम्	katham	how, interrogative

जन् (जायते)	jan, jāyate	be born
तत्र	tatra	there
न	na	not
न वा	na vā	or not (see sent. 1)
मन् (मन्यते)	man, manyate	think
लभ् (लभते)	labh, labhate	acquire, obtain
वा	vā	or (like ca, placed after the last member of the series)
वृत् (वर्तते)	vṛt, vartate	be
वृध् (वर्धते)	vṛdh, vardhate	grow (intransitive)

TRANSLATE into English :

इदानीं तत्र गजमश्वं च पश्यसि न वा ॥१॥ गृहे कुत्र वर्तेते ॥२॥ कथं जलं लभसे फलात् ॥३॥ जायते पुत्रः ॥४॥ पुत्रं मित्रं न मन्यसे ॥५॥ क्षत्रियौ फले लभेते ॥६॥ देव कुत्र गच्छन्ति गजाः ॥७॥ जलमेव नयामि गृहात् ॥८॥

TRANSLATE into Sanskrit in Devanāgarī : 1. Two crows[2] are born[1]. 2. How[1] does he vanquish[3] the kṣatriya[2] ? 3. I remember[2] the god[1] and[4] grow[3]. 4. They two obtain[3] only[2] a fruit[1]. 5. There[1] in the city[2] are[4] two friends[3]. 6. The crow[4] thinks[3] the horse[1] an elephant[2]. (see sent. 5 above.)

LESSON 4

SAMDHI OF FINAL VOWELS

You have already learned two samdhi rules, namely that final -s becomes -ḥ at the end of an utterance and that final -m becomes anusvāra before an initial consonant. Every language has such rules; Sanskrit is unusual in that virtually all such changes are written. Thus in English, we pronounce "the" differently before a vowel and a consonant, while we commonly say, "Put 'em on the table" (but write "them"). In the following three lessons, you will learn all of the rules for combining sounds in Sanskrit; in this lesson, rules for changing final vowels are given.

1. Final vowel + similar initial vowel. When two similar vowels, short or long, come together, they are replaced by a similar long vowel.

-a or -ā+a- or ā- →-ā-	Ex. na+api → nāpi नापि
-i or -ī +i- or ī- →-ī-	Ex. hi+iti → hīti हीति
-u or -ū+u-or ū- →-ū-	Ex. sādhu+uktam→sādhūktam साधूक्तम्

2. -a or -ā + dissimilar vowel. When final -a or -ā comes together with an initial dissimilar vowel, short or long, both are replaced by the guṇa of the dissimilar vowel.

-ă̄+ĭ̄→ -e-	Ex. ca+iha→ ceha चेह
-ă̄+ŭ̄→ -o-	Ex. ca+uktam→coktam चोक्तम्
-ă̄+ṛ→ -ar-	Ex. ca+ṛṣiḥ→carṣiḥ चर्षि:

3. -a or -ā+diphthong. When final -a or -ā comes together with an initial diphthong, both are replaced by the vṛddhi of the diphthong's second element. Note that the second element of e (and of ai) is i (since e can be broken down into ai), while that of o (and of au) is u. Thus the replacing letter is ai and au respectively.

-a + e- → -ai-   Ex. ca+eti → caiti चैति
-ā + o- → -au-   Ex. sā+oṣadhiḥ → sauṣadhiḥ सौषधिः
-ā̆+ai- → -ai-   Ex. senā+aiśvaryam→senaiśvaryam सेनैश्वर्यम्
-ā̆+au- → -au-   Ex. iha+aunnatyam→ihaunnatyam इहौन्नत्यम्

4. Vowels (not ā̆) + dissimilar vowel or diphthong. When vowels, long or short, other than ā̆ come together with a dissimilar vowel or diphthong, the vowel is replaced by its corresponding semivowel.

-ī̆+V- → -y V-   Ex. yadi+api→yady api यद्यपि
-ū̆+V- → -v V-   Ex. bhavatu+evam→bhavatv evam भवत्वेवम्
-ṝ̆+V- → -r V-   Ex. hotṛ+oṣadhiḥ→hotroṣadhiḥ (a compound) होत्रोषधिः

5. -e and -o + a-. Before initial a-, final e- and o- are unchanged, but the initial a- is elided, to be replaced by an avagraha (written with an apostrophe in Roman transliteration, and by the sign ऽ in Sanskrit. The avagraha is not pronounced).

-e+a- → -e '   Ex. vane+api →vane 'pi वनेऽपि
-o+a- → -o '   Ex. so+api →so 'pi सोऽपि

6. -e and -o + Vowel (not a). Before vowels or diphthongs other than -a, e and o are replaced by a, and the hiatus remains.
-e+v̆̄ → -a v̆̄-   Ex. vane + āgaccha—vana āgaccha वन आगच्छ
-o+v̆̄ → -a v̆̄-   Ex. prabho+ehi—prabha ehi प्रभ एहि

7. ai and au + Vowel. Before all vowels and diphthongs, ai becomes -ā, and the hiatus remains; au becomes -āv.

-ai+v̆̄- → -ā v̆̄-   Ex. kasmai + api ←kasmā api कस्मा अपि
-au+v̆̄- → āv v̆̄-   Ex. devau + api → devāv api देवावपि

EXCEPTION : ī, ū, and e as dual endings of nouns and verbs are unchanged before initial vowels. Thus phale atra, the two fruits are here. (Also exceptional in this regard is the final vowel of an interjection, as he aśva, "O horse !") These vowels are called pragṛhya.

VOCABULARY :

अपि	api	even, also, though—placed after the word it goes with
क्लृप् (कल्पते)	kḷp/kalpate	be fit for (+ dat.)

ग्राम	grāma	village
नृप	nṛpa	king
मनुष्य	manuṣya	man
भयम्	bhayam	fear
भोजनम्	bhojanam	food
मुखम्	mukham	face, mouth
वनम्	vanam	forest

EXERCISE : write in Devanāgarī the following combinations, applying the correct saṃdhi :

senā+āgacchati	kākau+iti
nadī+api	vane+api
mahā+ṛṣiḥ	vane+āgaccha
bhāno+atra+ehi	gacchati+iti

TRANSLATE into English :

नैव पश्यामि देवम् ॥१॥ वर्धन्ते ऽश्वाः ॥२॥ न कल्पन्ते फलान्यश्वानां भोजनाय ॥३॥ पुत्रास्तत्र ग्रामेऽप्यश्वान्पीडयति मनुष्यः ॥४॥ भयात्क्षत्रियस्य मुखं पश्यति नृपः ॥५॥

(Sentence 4 is tricky. First determine the subject of the verb; then determine the cases of the other words.)

TRANSLATE into Sanskrit in Devanāgarī : 1. Only[3] two crows[2] are[4] there[1]. 2. Horses[2] are born[1]. 3. Forests[1] also[2] are[4] there[3]. 4. In fear[1] (abl.), the warrior[4] asks[2] the king[3]. 5. The king[4] is fit[3] only[2] for the village[1].

LESSON 5

SAṂDHI OF -as, -ās, -s, -r

8. -as before voiced consonants. Before all voiced consonants (including h-), -as → -o. Ex. devaḥ + gacchati → devo gacchati; nṛpaḥ + viśati → nṛpo viśati.

9. -as before a-. Before a-, -as becomes -o and the a- becomes avagraha. devaḥ + atra → devo 'tra. देवोऽत्र

10. -as before all vowels and diphthongs, except a- loses final s. Ex. devaḥ + eva → deva eva; nṛpaḥ + āgaccha → nṛpa āgaccha.

11. -ās before all vowels, diphthongs, and voiced consonants (including h) loses final s. Before vowels, the hiatus remains. Ex. devāḥ + viśanti → devā viśanti; devāḥ + api → devā api; nṛpāḥ + hi → nṛpā hi.

12 -s and -r become -ḥ before k-, kh-, p-, ph-, ś-, ṣ-, and s-, and at the end of an utterance. Ex. devaḥ + kutra → devaḥ kutra; devaḥ + phalam → devaḥ phalam; nṛpaḥ + smarati → nṛpaḥ smarati; punar + kutra → punaḥ kutra; āgaccheḥ + khalu → āgaccheḥ khalu.

13. -s, -r before c, ch, ṭ, ṭh, and t, th are assimilated to the class of those letters (i. e. before c, s becomes palatal, etc.). Thus -s or -r + c-, ch- → -ś c-, -ś ch-. nṛpaḥ + carati → nṛpaś carati (the retroflex case is very rare and need not be learned).

-s or -r + t-, th- → -s t-, -s th- (here -s is unchanged). Ex. nṛpaḥ + tiṣṭhati → nṛpas tiṣṭhati; punar + tiṣṭhanti → punas tiṣṭhanti.

14. Except after a, and ā, -s becomes -r before all vowels, diphthongs, and voiced consonants (including h). Ex. putrayoḥ + hi —putrayor hi; gaccheḥ + api — gaccher api.

VOCABULARY :

अत्र	atra	here
आगम् (आगच्छति)	āgam/āgacchati	come (this is gam prefixed by ā; almost all roots may take such prefixes.)
पुनर्	punar	again
वद् (वदति)	vad/vadati	speak, say (Used with a double acc., of the thing said and the person addressed).
सह	saha	with (placed after its object, which is in the instrumental, e.g. kākena saha, with the crow). Saha translates with of accompaniment, not of instrumentality.

Note on pracch/pṛcchati : this verb takes a double accusative —the person asked and the thing asked about or inquired after. Pracch does not translate "ask for."

EXERCISE : write the following combinations in Devanāgarī, applying saṃdhi :

nṛpaḥ + vadati	manuṣyāḥ + smaranti
nṛpāḥ + vandanti	vā + api
nṛpayoḥ + eva	phale (dual) + atra (careful)
nṛpāḥ + eva	vardhate + api
āgaccheḥ + iti + atra	punar + tiṣṭhataḥ
nṛpaḥ + ca	vadantu + api
kākaḥ + atra	devaiḥ + āgaccha
kākāḥ + atra	tatra + eva + upaviśa
kākau + atra + eva	tatra + ṛṣiḥ + vasati

TRANSLATE into English :

क्षत्रियस्याश्वस्य भोजनं कुत्र ॥१॥ अत्र क्षत्रिया गृहेभ्य आगच्छन्ति ॥२॥ काको ऽश्वश्च तत्र वने वर्तेते ॥३॥ क्षत्रिय इदानीं ग्राममागच्छति ॥४॥ गजस्य मुखं न

पश्यत्यश्वः ॥५॥ नृपस्य नगरेभ्य आगच्छन्त्यश्वाः ॥६॥ न लभतेऽत्र क्षत्रियो जलम् ॥७॥ पुनरपि नगरं विशतः ॥८॥ नृपो मित्रस्य नगरं क्षत्रियं पृच्छति ॥९॥ नगर आगच्छतो गजावत्र ॥१०॥ तत्रैव गृहे वर्ततेऽश्वस्य भोजनम् ॥११॥ क्षत्रियैः सहागच्छति नृपः ॥१२॥

TRANSLATE into Sanskrit in Devanāgarī : 1. The crow and the horse come into the city. 2. Even in the forest, there are (vṛt) water and food. 3. They ask the man about the village (see sent. 9 above). 4. Now the kṣatriyas vanquish the two elephants.

Lesson 6

SAṂDHI, CONTINUED

15. Final -r before initial r-. Final r, whether original or derived from -s according to rule 14, disappears before initial r-. If the vowel before the final -r is not long, it is lengthened. Ex. nṛpatiḥ + ramate → nṛpatī ramate; putrayoḥ + rathah → putrayo rathaḥ; punar + rāmaḥ → punā rāmaḥ.

Final -n :

16. Before j- and ś-, -n becomes -ñ. If ś- is the initial letter of the next word, it is replaced by ch-. Ex. devān + jayati → devāñ jayati; sarvān + śūdrān — sarvāñ chūdrān.

17. Before l-, n becomes nasalized -l. Thus tān + lokān — tāṃl lokān, written ताँल् लोकान् or, less often तांलोकान्.

18. Before unvoiced palatal and dental stops (c-, ch-, t-, th-,), a sibilant of those classes (i.e. ś, s) is inserted after -n, and -n becomes anusvāra. Ex. devān + ca → devāṃś ca; nṛpān + tatra → nṛpāṃs tatra.

Final -t :

19. Before any voiced sound (vowel, diphthong, voiced consonant, h-), -t becomes -d. If the initial letter of the next word is h-, the h- becomes dh-. Ex. etat + hi → etad dhi; avadat + eva—avadad eva. (Note : similarly, p→b, and -k→ -g; but these are rare as finals). But 20-23 are exceptions to this rule.

20. Before l-, -t becomes -l. mukhāt + labhate—mukhāl labhate.

21. Before c-, ch-, and ś-, -t becomes -c. If the next letter is ś-, the ś becomes ch-. Ex. vṛksāt + chāyā→vṛksāc chāyā; tasmāt + ca→tasmāc ca; nṛpāt + śamaḥ—nṛpāc chamah.

22. Before j-, -t becomes -j. gṛhāt + jalam→gṛhāj jalam.

23. Before nasals, -t becomes -n. gṛhāt + nayati→gṛhān nayati.

-n- Inside a word :

24. Dental -n- when immediately followed by a vowel or by -n-, -m-, -y-, or -v- becomes a retroflex -ṇ- if preceded in the same word by ṛ, ṝ, r or ṣ, unless there intervenes a palatal (except y), a retroflex, or a dental. Note : this is a rather difficult rule; it will help you to remember it if you think that a retroflex sound puts the tongue in a certain retroflex position; unless a sound occurs which changes the retroflex position of the tongue, -n- occurring in the same word is pronounced without the tongue changing its retroflex position and so is retroflex.

Ex. The inst. sg. of grāma is grāmeṇa; the gen. pl. of śūdra and manuṣya are śūdrāṇām and manuṣyāṇām; the inst. sg. of kṣatriya is kṣatriyeṇa. But : the inst. sg. of ratha is rathena (while of nṛpa it is nṛpeṇa).

Miscellaneous Rules. Do not memorize these rules at this time.

25. -n occurring as a final after a short vowel is doubled before an initial vowel. Ex. tiṣṭhan + atra—tiṣṭhann atra. tasmin + api—tasminn api.

26. In general, ch is not allowed to stand after a vowel but becomes cch. Thus sā + chāyā→sā cchāyā.

27. Non-final s becomes ṣ if immediately preceded by any vowel except a or ā, or if preceded by k or r, unless the s is final or followed by r. Thus the reduplication of sthā is tiṣṭhati. The loc. pl. of senā is senāsu (see lesson 7) while of deva it is deveṣu.

VOCABULARY :

आनी (आनयति)	ānī/ānayati	bring (this is nī prefixed by ā-)
तु	tu	but (placed after the word with which it is construed)
रथ	ratha	chariot
रत्नम्	ratnam	jewel
लोक	loka	world; mankind, people (used as a collective)
शूद्र	śūdra	a śūdra, a member of the 4th varṇa

EXERCISES : Write the following in Devanāgarī, applying saṃdhi :

krama, inst. sg.	ratnam, gen. pl.
śūdra, gen. pl.	manuṣya, inst. sg.
ratha, gen. pl.	kutaḥ + api
putrayoḥ + rathaḥ	nayet + jalam
nṛpān + ca	gṛhāt + śūdraḥ
nṛpān + tu	tat + jñātvā
vadan + loke	phalāt + ca
devāt + lokaḥ + eva	bhaveyuḥ + ratnāni
patiḥ + ratnam	devān + jayati
bhavet + api	mukhāt + hi

TRANSLATE into English :

नृपस्य रत्नानि शूद्रस्य गृहे वर्तन्ते ॥१॥ नृपाँस्तत्रैव जयति ॥२॥ अत्रागच्छन्ति शूद्राणां रथाः ॥३॥ अश्वाँल् लभेते नृपौ ॥४॥ क्षत्रियांस्तत्र पश्यामि देवांस्तु न पश्यामि ॥५॥ पुना रत्नानि लभन्ते ॥६॥ नृपस्य नगराज्जलमत्र नयामः ॥७॥ अत्र लोके मनुष्याः कुत्र वर्तन्ते ॥८॥ गजाञ्छूद्रा आनयन्ति ॥९॥ ग्राम आनयति शूद्रोऽश्वम् ॥१०॥ तत्र काका एव । गजानश्वांश्च न पश्यामः* ॥११॥ तिष्ठन्ति रथेषु क्षत्रिया गजाञ्जयन्ति च ॥१२॥

TRANSLATE into Sanskrit in Devanāgarī : 1. Again he sees the chariot. 2. From the forests śūdras lead their horses to the cities. 3. Does the kṣatriya get food or not ? 4. They two carry water from the town. 5. From fear of the elephant, the śūdra enters the city. 6. The king thinks the world of men (is) the world of the gods.

---

*The line in the middle of this sentence is called a daṇḍa (stick) and is equivalent to a period.

Lesson 7

AGNI, KĪRTI, SENĀ

Memorize the declensions of agni (m.), kīrti (f.), and senā (f.). Note that it is not possible to tell from the citation form whether agni is masculine or feminine. Most nouns in -i are masculine; therefore, such nouns will not be marked in the vocabulary; but feminine nouns in -i will be followed by "f." in the vocabulary.

Note that the only cases in which agni is different from kīrti are the instrumental singular and the accusative plural.

	Singular	Dual	Plural
Nom.	agniḥ	agnī	agnayaḥ
Acc.	agnim	,,	agnīn
Inst.	agninā	agnibhyām	agnibhiḥ
Dat.	agnaye	,,	agnibhyaḥ
Abl.	agneḥ	,,	,,
Gen.	,,	agnyoḥ	agnīnām
Loc.	agnau	,,	agniṣu
Voc.	agne		
Nom.	kīrtiḥ	kīrtī	kīrtayaḥ
Acc.	kīrtim	,,	kīrtīḥ
Inst.	kīrtyā	kīrtibhyām	kīrtibhiḥ
Dat.	kīrtaye	,,	kīrtibhyaḥ
Abl.	kīrteḥ	,,	,,
Gen.	,,	kīrtyoḥ	kīrtīnām
Loc.	kīrtau	,,	kīrtiṣu
Voc.	kīrte		
Nom.	senā	sene	senāḥ
Acc.	senām	,,	,,
Inst.	senayā	senābhyām	senābhiḥ

Dat.	senāyai	,,	senābhyaḥ
Abl.	senāyāḥ	,,	,,
Gen.	,,	senayoh	senānām
Loc.	senāyām	,,	senāsu
Voc.	sene		

Note that both senāyai and senāyāḥ before a word beginning with a vowel become senāyā.

VOCABULARY :

अग्नि	agni	fire
अतिथि	atithi	guest
अरि	ari	enemy
कथा	kathā	story
कवि	kavi	poet
कीर्ति f.	kīrti, f.	glory, fame
छाया	chāyā	shadow
ब्राह्मण	brāhmaṇa	
भूमि f.	bhūmi, f.	ground, earth
सेना	senā	army

TRANSLATE into English. Note that in Sanskrit, unlike English, a question need not have special word order. Sentence 7 below is a qestion.

तत्र गजैः सहागच्छति नृपस्य सेना ॥१॥ तत्र च्छायायां तिष्ठति ब्राह्मणः कथां वदति च (see saṃdhi rule 26) ॥२॥ कीर्त्यैव देवानां लोकं लभन्ते क्षत्रियाः ॥३॥ ग्रामं विशति क्षत्रियोऽरिं पश्यति च ॥४॥ अत्रेदानीं फले लभेते मित्रे ॥५॥ सेनया कीर्त्या च सह नृपो नगरं विशति ॥६॥ अत्र कथायां क्षत्रियो नृपो वा भूमिं जयति ॥७॥ न देवा भूमौ तिष्ठन्ति ॥८॥ पुनरपि रथे तिष्ठतः क्षत्रियावरीञ्जयतश्च ॥९॥ ब्राह्मणो गृहाद्वनं गच्छति ॥१०॥ वनेऽप्यतिथयो जलं भोजनं च लभन्ते ॥११॥ नृपस्यारीणां भयान्नगर एव तिष्ठन्ति कवयः ॥१२॥

TRANSLATE into Sanskrit : 1. The king sees jewels in the village and leads his armies there. 2. The king stands in the shadow of jewels and sees his army. 3. Brāhmaṇas with Śūdras obtain water and food from the village. 4. In the army of the king, there are elephants, horses, chariots and Kṣatriyas. 5. The king vanquishes and guests come to the world of the gods. 6. The Śūdra leads the horses from the fire.

Lesson 8

THE IMPERFECT ACTIVE

I. The imperfect active. This tense, used for past action, is formed on the same stem as the present (see lesson 1). It is made by prefixing the augment a- before the stem, and then by adding the imperfect active endings given below to the stem. Note that the augment is added *before* the stem, but *after* any prefixes which the verb may have, as will be shown below. Learn the imperfect active endings (here added to bhū) :

	Singular	Dual	Plural
1st pers.	abhavam	abhavāva	abhavāma
2nd pers.	abhavaḥ	abhavatam	abhavataḥ
3rd pers.	abhavat	abhavatām	abhavan
	अभवम्	अभवाव	अभवाम
	अभव:	अभवतम्	अभवत
	अभवत्	अभवताम्	अभवन्

When the augment is added to a prefixed verb, any saṃdhi required is employed according to the rules you have already learned. For example, āgam means "come." āgacchati means "he comes." "He came" is ā (prefix) +a (augment)+gacchat→ āgacchat (see Saṃdhi rule 1). "He brought" is ānayat (ā+a+nayat). ni-vas means "live, dwell." "He dwelt" is ni+a+vasat →nyavasat. Upaviś means "sit." "He sat" is upa+a+viśat—upāviśat.

II. Learn saṃdhi rule 25 on page 20 : -n occurring as a final after a short vowel is doubled before an initial vowel. Thus abhavan+atra—abhavann atra.

III. An interrogative is changed into an indefinite by adding cit after it. Thus :

kutra cit	somewhere
kathaṃ cit	somehow
kadā cit	sometime: once (upon a time) (kadā means when).

By putting api after an interrogative, an indefinite is also formed. This indefinite, however, is generally used as a universal with a negative.

na kutrāpi	nowhere, not anywhere
na kathamapi	not in any way, under no circumstances
na kadāpi	never

Similarly, cana can be added like api for the same meanings. But the universality implied by cana is weaker than that implied by api.

na kutra cana	nowhere
na kathaṃ cana	not in any way, under no circumstances
na kadā cana	never

VOCABULARY :

अपि	api	see III above; even, also, though
उपविश् (उपविशति)	upaviś/upaviśati	sit down (viś prefixed by upa)
कदा	kadā	when (interrogative)
चन	cana	see III above
चित्	cit	see III above
नश् (नश्यति)	naś/naśyati	perish, be lost
निवस् (निवसति)	nivas/nivasati	live, dwell (vas prefixed by ni)
मुच् (मुञ्चति)	muc/muñcati	loose, release, free
यम् (यच्छति)	yam/yacchati	yield, give, bestow
वस् (वसति)	vas/vasati	live, dwell
वह् (वहति)	vah/vahati	pull, drag
शंस् (शंसति)	śaṃs/śaṃsati	praise

TRANSLATE into English :

न कुत्रापि न्यवसन्नरयो नृपस्य ।।१।। अरिभ्यः क्षत्रियानमुञ्चन्नृपः ।।२।। मित्रे रथं कुत्रावहतम् ।।३।। न कदा चनाशंसन्नृपस्यारीन्कविः ।।४।। कदा चिद्वनेऽवसच्छूद्र इदानीं तु नगरे ब्राह्मणैः सह वसति ।।५।। कवीनां कथाः कीर्तये कल्पन्ते ।।६।।

भयादुपाविशन्नरयो ऽश्वान्गजान्रथाँश्चामुञ्चन् ॥७॥ वनस्य च्छायायामतिष्ठत्क्षत्रियो ऽरीणां सेनामपीडयच्च ॥८॥ ग्रामाद्गृहं कवये जलमानयद्ब्राह्मणः ॥९॥ नृपो ब्राह्मणेभ्यः कविभ्यश्च रत्नानि यच्छति ॥१०॥ न कदापि मनुष्यैर्वदन्ति देवाः ॥११॥ कथं चिच्छूद्रयोरश्वौ रथं नगरमवहताम् ॥१२॥

(Note on sentence 11 : the instrumental by itself may mean "with," "in the company of," "together with," as well as the instrumental followed by saha.)

TRANSLATE into Sanskrit : 1. The poets lived in the villages of the king of the earth. 2. The two friends stood on the chariot and freed the elephants from the enemies' army. 3. Once, guests came here to the village, but now not even a crow comes. 4. From fear of his enemies, the king did not even look at (paś) his food. 5. The kṣatriya brought the two horses to his house and gave (them) food. 6. They went by chariot to the city of the enemies and perished.

LESSON 9

THE IMPERFECT MIDDLE : USE OF ITI

I. The imperfect middle. Like the other tenses you have learned and will shortly learn (present, imperfect, optative, imperative), the imperfect middle is built on the present stem, which you learned to form in lesson 1. Like the imperfect active, it takes an augment. Verbs which are middle in the present are also middle in the imperfect and other tenses. Learn the following forms :

	Singular	Dual	Plural
1st pers.	alabhe	alabhāvahi	alabhāmahi
2nd pers.	alabhathāḥ	alabhethām	alabhadhvam
3rd pers.	alabhata	alabhetām	alabhanta
	अलभे	अलभावहि	अलभामहि
	अलभथाः	अलभेथाम्	अलभध्वम्
	अलभत	अलभेताम्	अलभन्त

II. The use of iti. In English, we use what is called indirect discourse to report direct speech (when we do not quote directly). Thus we commonly use sentences such as "He said that he would come tomorrow", "He asked where the table was." In Sanskrit, there is no indirect discourse; all such English sentences must be translated by turning the indirect discourse into direct discourse, that is, by putting the utterance reported into quotes. When this is done, the word iti is placed after the utterance, and the main verb of the sentence with its subject and object after that. For example, "He said that the Brāhmaṇa came" would be translated "The Brāhmaṇa came," iti he said," that is, ब्राह्मण आगच्छदित्यवदत्.

Before you translate a sentence with indirect discourse into Sanskrit, always put the indirect discourse into quotes (i.e. make it into direct discourse) so that you know what tenses and forms to use. Thus "He said that you should come here" would be rendered," " 'Come here,' iti he said." (You will have the imperative in a future lesson, at which time sentences of this type will be practiced.) The iti construction may also be used, of course, to report direct discourse. For example, "The Brāhmaṇa asked, 'Where has he gone?'" would be rendered, कुत्रागच्छदित्यपृच्छद्ब्राह्मणः.

In English, iti sentences can be translated either by direct or by indirect discourse, whichever seems more appropriate. The Sanskrit sentence 2 lines above, for example, might be translated "The Brāhmaṇa asked where he went."

There is another use of the iti construction which you need not learn actively now, but which you should be acquainted with. An iti clause may be used to signify what a person thinks, and hence his reason or intention. For example, "He did not come because the Brāhmaṇa was there" might be translated, "The Brāhmaṇa was there' iti he did not come."

VOCABULARY:

आचार्य	ācārya	teacher, preceptor
इति	iti	thus—see section II above
पुस्तकम्	pustakam	book
युद्धम् (युद्धम्)	yuddham	war, battle
वृक्ष	vṛkṣa	tree
शिष्य	śiṣya	pupil
सदा	sadā	always
सेव् (सेवते)	sev/sevate	serve, honour; frequent (as animals a woods)
हि	hi	for (conjunction). e.g. "For Brutus is an honourable man." Placed after word, like tu.

TRANSLATE into English:

शिष्या हि सदाचार्यान्सेवन्त इति ब्राह्मणोऽवदत् ॥१॥ नृपस्य कवयः कीर्तेः फलमलभन्त ॥२॥ देवानां लोके वृक्षेषु फलानि सदा वर्तन्ते मनुष्याणां लोके तु कदाचिदेव ॥३॥ युद्धेऽरी अनश्यताम् ॥४॥ वनाद्ध्यागच्छद्गजो नगरमविशच्च ॥५॥ कुत्रारयोऽश्वान्रथांश्चालभन्तेत्यपृच्छन्नृपः क्षत्रियान् ॥६॥ वृक्षस्य च्छायायां मित्रे आचार्यमपश्यतां तत्रागच्छतां पुस्तकान्यलभेतां च ॥७॥ नृपस्य ग्रामे ऽजायत शूद्रैर्युद्धम् ॥८॥ शूद्रात्पुत्रोऽजायतेत्यवदद्ब्राह्मणः ॥९॥ युद्धे कथं जयामीति नृप

आचार्यमपृच्छत् ॥१०॥ कवीनां मुखेष्वजायन्त नृपस्य कीर्तेः कथाः ॥११॥ सेनयापि नाजयन्नृपो ऽरीणां नगरमित्यवदच्छिष्यानाचार्यः ॥१२॥

(For sentence 12, remember that vad takes a double accusative).

TRANSLATE into Sanskrit: 1. The boy (putra) said that the teacher is coming. 2. The king stood in the shadow of the tree and saw the battle of (his) kṣatriyas with the enemy (pl. use simple instrumental without saha). 3. In the woods, the students obtained two fruits and brought (them) to (their) friend's house. 4. "For the books of the poets were fit (kḷp) for glory," said the teacher. 5. The fame of the army grew in the world (loka). 6. From the mouths of poets were born the stories of the gods.

VERSE: beginning with this lesson, an unaltered verse from a Sanskrit book will be given. You will not be required to be able to read these verses for examinations and you will not be held responsible for the vocabulary in them. If you have time, study them so that you can read them in class the day the lesson is discussed. You may wish to memorize them.

को देशः कानि मित्राणि कः कालः कौ व्ययागमौ ।
कश्चाहं का च मे शक्तिरिति चिन्त्यं मुहुर्मुहुः ॥

क who, what (interrog.)	शक्ति power, ability
देश place, home place	मे my, of me
काल time	चिन्त्यम् it is to be pondered
व्ययागमौ expenditure and income	मुहुर्मुहुः again and again
अहम् I	

LESSON 10

DECLENSIONS OF NADĪ AND PAD

I. Learn the declension of nadī, river:

	Sing.	Dual	Plural
Nom.	nadī	nadyau	nadyaḥ
Acc.	nadīm	,,	nadīḥ
Inst.	nadyā	nadībhyām	nadībhiḥ
Dat.	nadyai	,,	nadībhyaḥ
Abl.	nadyāḥ	,,	,,
Gen.	,,	nadyoḥ	nadīnām
Loc.	nadyām	,,	nadīṣu
Voc.	nadi		

This is the declension of all nouns and adjectives in -ī of more than one syllable. All such words are feminine.

II. Consonantal Stems—pad. Many Sanskrit nouns and adjectives end in consonants. Such stems often distinguish between strong and weak forms, a distinction, made by a difference in the quantity of the stem vowel (long/short) or, as will be seen in future lessons, by the presence of a nasal (strong) or its absence (weak). For masculine and feminine words, the first five cases going horizontally are strong, the rest weak. That is, the sg. nom-acc, dual nom-acc, and pl. nom. are strong. In neuter stems (to be exemplified later), only the plural nom -acc. are strong. Endings beginning with a consonant are treated as new discrete words when they are added to a consonant stem and are therefore called the pāda (word) endings. They are: dual inst-dat-abl. (bhyām), pl. inst. (bhiḥ), pl. dat-abl. (bhyaḥ), and pl. loc. (su). When these endings are added, the saṃdhi rules you have learned are applied to the combination.

In Sanskrit, a voiced non-nasal stop cannot stand at the end of an utterance; it must be converted to its unvoiced equivalent. Hence the nom. sg. of pad is pāt. Learn the declension of pad, m., foot:

	Singular	Dual	Plural
Nom.	pāt	pādau	pādaḥ
Acc.	pādam	pādau	padaḥ
Inst.	padā	padbhyām	padbhiḥ
Dat.	pade	,,	padbhyaḥ
Abl.	padaḥ	,,	,,
Gen.	,,	padoḥ	padām
Loc.	padi	,,	patsu

With the exception of the declensions ending in -an, in -ṛ, and in -ant, which you will learn in the next few lessons, few consonantal stems distinguish between strong and weak in classical Sanskrit. Pad is the only one you will have in these lessons. Other consonantal stems are no different in the strong cases than in the weak ones.

The following material on final consonants should *not* be memorized. Look it over and become acquainted with the principles involved.

Permitted final consonants in Sanskrit. It will have been seen that at the end of the nom. sg. of consonantal stems, there is a consonant which must be changed to conform to certain rules. In addition, before the pāda endings such changes are made (though they cannot be discerned in pad), and they occur in other places. In the following discussion, final consonant means that consonant which may occur at the end of an utterance or at the end of a word before saṃdhi is applied (and before the pāda endings).

Permitted final consonants are quite restricted. The following may not occur:

sibilant; semivowel; voiced non-aspirate series; palatal; any aspirate (including h).

It is easier to specify what is permitted. Rare letters, which for all practical purposes may be ignored, are given in parentheses:

-k	(-ñ)		
-ṭ	(-ṇ)		
-t	-n		
-p	-m	(-l)	visarga

There are no other permitted final consonants. Which of these sounds the final consonant of a consonant stem becomes is often straightforward, as the final is the closest related sound to that of the final consonant of the stem (e.g. pāt from pād). In some cases, however, a final consonant may become either -k or -ṭ, depending on its heredity (i.e. on what it was in Indo-European). In general,

-c→ -k
-j→ -k or -ṭ
-ś→ -k or -ṭ
-ṣ→ -ṭ
-h→ -k or -ṭ.

Examples: vāk→ vāc; vaṇij→vaṇik; virāj→virāṭ; diś→dik; viś→viṭ; prāvṛṣ→prāvṛṭ; -duh→ -dhuk; havyavāḥ→havyavāṭ.

Saṃdhi of -k and -ṭ. Before a nasal, -ṭ→ -ṇ; -k→ -ñ. Thus virāṭ+na→virāṅ na; vāk+me→vāñ me. Before voiced sounds, -ṭ→ -ḍ, -k→ -g. vaṇik+dadāti→vaṇig dadāti; havyavāṭ+āgacchati→havyavāḍ āgacchati. Before h-, -ṭ→ḍ, -k→ -g, and h- becomes ḍh- and gh- respectively. Ex. prāvṛṭ+hi→prāvṛḍ ḍhi; vaṇik+hi→vaṇig ghi.

Grassmann's Law: In the examples given immediately before the above paragraph, you will notice that -duh→ -dhuk. In late Indo-European, there was a phonetic law that two aspirated consonants could not occur in the same syllable (i.e. in the same word with only one vowel intervening). If such a juxtaposition did occur, the aspiration of the first occurring consonant was lost. In some environments, however, (e.g. the nominative singular), the aspiration was lost before Grassmann's rule could be applied; in such environments, therefore, the first aspiration was retained. For example, the Greek word for hair is thriks. Here, both consonants were originally aspirated. In the nominative, thriks, the aspiration of the -k- has been lost before -s of the nom. sg. In the genitive, however, no such rule operates, and so Grassmann's law comes into play, making the form trikh-os. In Sanskrit, this rule produces a few strange forms. The two most commonly involved roots are dah (burn) and duh (to milk). In compounds using these two roots to form consonantal stems, we find n. sg. -dhāk, acc. sg. dagham;

n. sg. -dhuk; acc. sg. -dugham. Also involved are the present forms of the root dhā (see page 95).

VOCABULARY : From now on, vocabulary is given in Devanāgarī only.

त्वच् (f. nom. sg. त्वक्)	skin
देवी	goddess
नदी	river
पत्नी	wife
पद् (m.; nom. sg. पात्)	foot
वणिज् (m.; nom sg. वणिक्)	merchant
वाच् (f; nom sg. वाक्)	speech; words (as "spoke these words")
वापी	tank (Indian usage—i.e. artificial pond)
स्पृश् (स्पृशति)	touch

TRANSLATE into English:

वाप्या जलं पत्न्यै ब्राह्मण आनयति ॥१॥ देव्या वाचं सदा मनुष्याः सेवन्त इति शिष्योऽवदत् ॥२॥ युद्धे नृपस्य त्वचमपि नास्पृशन्नरयः ॥३॥ वणिग्भिः सह नृपो रत्नान्यपश्यत् ॥४॥ देवानां लोके गङ्गाया* जलं देवस्य पादौ स्पृशतीत्यवदच्छूद्रं ब्राह्मणः ॥५॥ न कदापि शिष्य आचार्यस्य पत्न्या मुखमपश्यत्पादावेव तु ॥६॥ शिवस्य पत्नीमुमेति वदन्ति (break: "patnīm 'umā' iti...") ॥७॥ न देवानां पादो भूमिं कदापि स्पृशन्ति ॥८॥ अत्र वृक्षाणां छायासु वणिज उपाविशन्ब्राह्मणेभ्यश्च पुस्तकान्ययच्छन् ॥९॥ सदैव हि वर्धन्ते कवीनां कीर्तय इति देवीमवदच्छिवः ॥१०॥ शिष्यः पुस्तकं पदास्पृशदिति शूद्र आचार्यमवदत् ॥११॥ अत्र फलान्यश्वानां भोजनायैव कल्पन्त इत्यमन्यत वणिक् ॥१२॥

TRANSLATE into Sanskrit: 1. The god came to the river with the goddess. 2. The pupil touched the feet of the poet and said, "I remember always the words of (my) teacher." 3. The merchants brought jewels from the city for (their) wives. 4. The kings perished in war and (their) wives became shadows in the stories of poets. 5. Again the Śūdras bring water from the tank in the city of the merchants. 6. "How does the merchant always bring jewels ?" the king asked the Brāhmaṇa.

---

*Gaṅgā—the Ganges.

VERSES:

लोभात्क्रोधः प्रभवति लोभात्कामः प्रजायते ।
लोभान्मोहश्च नाशश्च लोभः पापस्य कारणम् ॥
लोभात्क्रोधः प्रभवति क्रोधाद्द्रोहः प्रवर्तते ।
द्रोहेण नरकं याति शास्त्रज्ञोऽपि विचक्षणः ॥

लोभ	greed
क्रोध	anger
प्रभू	proceed, arise (pra+bhū)
काम	desire
प्रजन्	be born (pra+jan)
मोह	delusion, folly
नाश	destruction, ruin
पाप	sin, evil
कारणम्	cause
द्रोह	treachery
प्रवृत्	proceed (pra+vṛt)
नरकम्	hell
याति	(he) goes—same meaning as gacchati
शास्त्रज्ञ	a knower of the śāstras
विचक्षण	wise, clever

LESSON 11

DECLENSIONS OF DĀTṚ, RĀJAN

I. Rājan/nāman. Stems of this class are masculine or neuter. Memorize the declension of rājan (masculine), noting where the forms of nāman (neuter) differ (where they are italicized).

	Sing.	Dual	Plural
Nom.	rājā/*nāma*	rājānau/*nāmnī*	rājānaḥ/*nāmāni*
Acc.	rājānam/*nāma*	,, ,,	rājñaḥ/*nāmāni*
Inst.	rājñā/nāmnā	rājabhyām/nāmabhyām	rājabhiḥ/nāmabhiḥ
Dat.	rājñe/nāmne	,, ,,	rājabhyaḥ/nāmabhyaḥ
Abl.	rājñaḥ/nāmnaḥ	,, ,,	,, ,,
Gen.	,, ,,	rājñoḥ/nāmnoḥ	rājñām/nāmnām
Loc.	rājñi/nāmni	,, ,,	rājasu/nāmasu
Voc.	rājan/nāman		

Note that the masculine noun is strong in the first cases going horizontally (as described in the last lesson), while nāman, the neuter, is strong only on the plural nom-acc. In the weak cases (except for those with pāda endings), the -n- which immediately follows -j- in rāja is palatalized, a rule which is followed whenever -n follows j. In nāman, there is no need to palatalize the -n-, since it follows -m- and the combination -mn- is permissible. In the word ātman, m., self, an -a- is inserted between the -tm- and the -n- in the weak non-pāda cases, since the combination -tmn- cannot occur in Sanskrit. Thus the inst. sg. is ātmanā, the dat. sg. ātmane, etc. (but the dual inst. ātmabhyām).

II. The declension of dātṛ, giver. -tṛ is the suffix used to form agent nouns, like English -er, to which it is related. In general, -tṛ is added to the guṇated root (e.g. kartṛ, doer, from kṛ, do); however, you need not be able to form an agent noun from a root, though you should be able to recognize them. Note that as with rājan, dātṛ makes a ditsinction between strong, weak, and pāda cases. All nouns in -tṛ are masculine, with the exception of those nouns of relationship which happen to be feminine (e.g. mother).

	Sing.	Dual	Plural
Nom.	dātā	dātārau	dātāraḥ
Acc.	dātāram	,,	dātṝn
Inst.	dātrā	dātṛbhyām	dātṛbhiḥ
Dat.	dātre	,,	dātṛbhyaḥ
Abl.	dātuḥ	,,	,,
Gen.	,,	dātroḥ	dātṝṇām
Loc.	dātari	,,	dātṛṣu
Voc.	dātar		

Note that pitṛ, mātṛ, and other words of relationships (except svasṛ, sister) are declined with -ar- rather than -ār- in the strong forms.* Thus

Nom.	pitā	pitarau	pitaraḥ
Acc.	pitaram	,,	as with dātṛ

The other cases are declined in the same manner as dātṛ

VOCABULARY:

दातृ	giver
धर्म	dharma (untranslatable). law; religious or moral merit; duty; justice; piety; morality
नामन् (neuter)	name
पठ् (पठति)	read, recite
पितृ	father; (dual) parents; (pl.) manes
भ्रातृ	brother
मातृ (feminine)	mother
मृग	deer; any wild beast
राजन्	king
स्वसृ (feminine)	sister

*Note that the endings of the feminine nouns in-ṛ are the same as the masculine endings, except in the accusative plural, where the feminine nouns take-ṝḥ.

TRANSLATE into English:

राज्ञः पितरं रथेऽपश्यन्कवयः ।।१।। अश्वानां दातॄणां नामान्यपृच्छद्राजा ।।२।। वने राजानो मृगानपीडयन्निति ब्राह्मणा अवदन् ।।३।। इदानीं भ्रात्रा पत्न्या च सह वनं विशामीत्यवदद्रामः ।।४।। तत्र भ्रातोः पुत्राणां युद्धे धर्मोऽप्यनश्यत् ।।५।। दातॄन्सदा सेवन्ते देवा इति पुस्तके ब्राह्मणोऽपठत् ।।६।। राज्ञो भ्रातुः पुत्रा वृक्षस्य च्छायायामुपाविशन्मृगस्य कथामपठंश्च ।।७।। धर्मस्यारयोऽनश्यन्युद्ध इति राज्ञः कवयोऽवदन् ।।८।। माता पुत्रं नगरमानयत्तत्र च न्यवसत् ।।९।। कवीनां पुस्तकेषु पुत्राः सदा पितरौ सेवन्ते मनुष्याणां लोके तु कदा चिदेवेत्याचार्यः शिष्यानवदत् ।।१०।। राजन्नरय इदानीमागच्छन्तीत्यवदद्ब्राह्मणः ।।११।। लोकस्य पितरावुमा शिवश्चेति कालिदासस्य पुस्तके शिष्योऽपठत् ।।१२।।

TRANSLATE into Sanskrit: 1. The son of the king's brother entered the fight and perished. 2. The poets recited the names of the god. 3. The teacher said that on the earth, dharma does not always grow. 4. The king Bharata entered the forest, touched the feet of this brother, Rāma, and went again to the city. 5. The water of the river Gaṅgā touches the feet of Hari in the world of the gods. 6. Because elephants frequent the river, the Brāhmaṇa did not go there (use iti construction for the "because" clause).

VERSES:

दुरारोहं पदं राज्ञां सर्वलोकनमस्कृतम् ।
स्वल्पेनाप्यपचारेण ब्राह्मण्यमिव दुष्यति ।।

दुरारोह	hard to attain	अपचार	fault, improper act
पदम्	position	ब्राह्मण्यम्	Brahminhood
सर्व	all	इव	like
नमस्कृत	honored	दुष् (दुष्यति)	be spoiled
सर्वलोकनमस्कृत	honored by all the world		
स्वल्प	small		

धनानि भूमौ पशवश्च गोष्ठे भार्या गृहद्वारि जनः श्मशाने ।
देहश्चितायां परलोकमार्गे कर्मानुगो गच्छति जीव एकः ।।

धनम्	money, wealth
पशु (nom. pl. पशवः)	cow
गोष्ठ	corral
भार्या	wife

गृहद्वार्	door (dvār) of the house
जनः	people. Here, one's people, i.e. relatives and friends
श्मशानम्	cemetery, burning ground
देह	body
चिता	pyre
पर	other
मार्ग	way
परलोकमार्ग	path into the other world
कर्म	karma, one's previous actions which determine rebirth
अनुग	following
कर्मानुग	followed by karma, accompanied by karma
जीव	soul; transmigrating body
एक	one, alone

LESSON 12

DECLENSIONS OF AHAM, TVAM, SA

The words aham, tvam, and sa are respectively the first, second, and third person pronouns. Aham (I) and tvam (you) have the same forms for all three genders, but sa (he, she, it, they) has different forms in different genders. Memorize the following declensions. Where two forms are given, they may be used interchangeably, except that the latter form (mā, me, nau and naḥ; tvā, te, vām, and vaḥ) may not be used at the beginning of a sentence or before the particles ca, eva, or vā.

	Singular	Dual	Plural
Nom.	अहम्	आवाम्	वयम्
Acc.	माम्/मा	आवाम्/नौ	अस्मान्/नः
Inst.	मया	आवाभ्याम्	अस्माभिः
Dat.	मह्यम्/मे	,, /नौ	अस्मभ्यम्/नः
Abl.	मत्	,,	अस्मत्
Gen.	मम/मे	आवयोः/नौ	अस्माकम्/नः
Loc.	मयि	,,	अस्मासु
Nom.	त्वम्	युवाम्	यूयम्
Acc.	त्वाम्/त्वा	युवाम्/वाम्	युष्मान्/वः
Inst.	त्वया	युवाभ्याम्	युष्माभिः
Dat.	तुभ्यम्/ते	,,/वाम्	युष्मभ्यम्/वः
Abl.	त्वत्	,,	युष्मत्
Gen.	तव/ते	युवयोः/वाम्	युष्माकम्/वः
Loc.	त्वयि	,,	युष्मासु

The following is the masc. of sa.

Nom.	सः	तौ	ते
Acc.	तम्	तौ	तान्
Inst.	तेन	ताभ्याम्	तैः
Dat.	तस्मै	ताभ्याम्	तेभ्यः
Abl.	तस्मात्	,,	,,

Gen.	तस्य	तयोः	तेषाम्
Loc.	तस्मिन्	,,	तेषु

The feminine of sa is as follows:

Nom.	सा	ते	ताः
Acc.	ताम्	,,	,,
Inst.	तया	ताभ्याम्	ताभिः
Dat.	तस्यै	,,	ताभ्यः
Abl.	तस्याः	,,	,,
Gen.	,,	तयोः	तासाम्
Loc.	तस्याम्	,,	तासु

The neuter of sa differs from the masculine only in the nom. and acc.

Nom.	तत्	ते	तानि
Acc.	,,	,,	,,

Note that the form saḥ (nom. masculine sg.) loses the final -s before *all* consonants. Thus sa gacchati, *not* so gacchati, he goes. But so 'gacchat, he went, since saḥ does not lose final -s before vowels and diphthongs.

Note that the third person pronoun may be used as a pronoun (as English he, she, it, they) and also as an adjective to modify nouns and other pronouns with a meaning roughly corresponding to the English adjective "that" (though weaker). Thus tat phalam, that fruit: sa śiṣyaḥ, that pupil. When used to modify another pronoun, sa is best not translated. Thus so 'ham "I" (literally, "that I," "I, who am the contextual subject").

THE WORD SAKĀŚA:

In Sanskrit, there are several words meaning "vicinity," "nearness," "presence." These words are used in a peculiar way:

tasya sakāśāt: from him (i.e. from his presence).
tava sakāśe: near you (i.e. in your presence)
tava sakāśam: to you (i.e. to your presence).
In each case, this construction can be used only when the English may be replaced by the literal meaning of the Sanskrit.

VOCABULARY:

अहम्	I (see above in the lesson)
इव	like (placed after the word it governs)

गिरि	mountain
तस्मात्	therefore (lit. "from that")
त्वम्	you (see above)
पत्/पतति	fall, fly
पा/पिबति	drink (the present stem is reduplicated)
स	he, she, it, they (see above in lesson)
सकाश	vicinity, nearness, proximity, presence (see lesson).

TRANSLATE into English:

स राजारीनजयत्ते च तस्माद्गिरेरपतन्ननश्यंश्च ॥१॥ स मनुष्यो गङ्गाया जलमपिबद्देवानां लोकमलभत च ॥२॥ राज्ञः सकाशाद्ब्राह्मण आगच्छत्पुत्राय च पुस्तकान्ययच्छत् ॥३॥ अहं हि राजा । मम सकाशे ब्राह्मणा अपि तिष्ठन्तीत्यवदत्तवारिरिति ब्राह्मणो राजानमवदत् ॥४॥ नाहं तव पत्नीति दमयन्ती* तं शूद्रं भयादवदत् ॥५॥ त्वद्भयान्मनुष्या युद्धे न नश्यन्ति गृहेषु तु तिष्ठन्त्येवेत्यपठद्राज्ञः सकाशे कविः ॥६॥ वृक्षे फलानीव तस्य पितुः पुत्रा अवर्धन्त ॥७॥ राज्ञः पत्नीव शूद्रस्य पत्न्यप्यग्नावनश्यत् ॥८॥ मातुस्ते सकाशादहं तत्फलमानयामीति मम पत्नीमवदत्स कविः ॥९॥ तवारीणां कीर्तयस्तेषां कवीनां मुखेष्वेव वर्तन्ते ॥१०॥ गजस्य च्छायामपश्यद्राजा गिरिः पततीत्यमन्यत च ॥११॥ न कदापि शूद्राणां सकाशे जलं पिबामीति ब्राह्मणस्तान्वणिजोऽवदत् ॥१२॥

TRANSLATE into Sanskrit: 1. "I saw the mountain of your father and came to you," said the kṣatriya. (for "to you," use "to your presence"). 2. In no way do men grow like the shadows of trees said the king to the poet. 3. In the forest on the mountain of the Brāhmaṇas, deer and crows drink water. 4. In my presence, the voice of the goddess said, "Your father has come to the world of Indra." (Be sure to get the order correct for this sentence.) 5. Again he read the names of Śiva before (in the presence of) our (dual) son. 6. That god, the giver of dharma, entered here into the world.

VERSES:

विदेहमुक्तिविषये तस्मिंश्चित्तलयात्मके ।
चित्तनाशे विरूपाख्ये न किं चिदपि विद्यते ॥
न गुणा नागुणास्तत्र न श्रीर्नाश्रीर्न लोलता ।

---

*A proper name.

न चोदयो नास्तमयो न हर्षामर्षसंविदः ॥

न तेजो न तमः किं चिन्न संध्यादिर्न रात्रयः ।

न सत्ता नापि वासत्ता न च मध्यं हि तत्पदम् ॥ लघुयोगवासिष्ठः

वि	prefix: without
देह	body
मुक्ति (cf. मुच्)	release (from saṃsāra); salvation
विषय	realm, subject, object
विदेहमुक्तिविषय	whose scope is the salvation which comes from having no body (i.e. no consciousness of body)
चित्तम्	mind; mental faculty
लय	dissolution
आत्मक	characterized by (lit. whose very self is)
चित्तलयात्मक	characterized by dissolution of the mental faculty
नाश	destruction
चित्तनाश	destruction of the mental faculty
रूप	form
आख्या	name; appearance
विरूपाख्य	whose appearance is formless
किम्	what (interrogative, nom. neut. sg.)
विद्यते	there is
गुण	guṇa—there are 3 guṇas or strands
अ-	alpha privative, corresponding to "un-" in English. Not-.
श्रीः	wealth; splendour or beauty which comes from wealth
लोलता	tremulousness, unsteadiness
उदय	rising, success
अस्तमय	setting, disappearance, failing
हर्ष	joy, elation
अमर्ष	non-endurance, impatience
संविद्	knowledge, awareness
हर्षामर्षसंविद्	awareness of elation and impatience
तेजः	brilliant, warlike splendour
तमः	darkness; the guṇa tamas
संध्या	twilight
आदि	first; at end of compound: etc. (lit. "of which x is first")

संध्यादि	twilight etc.
रात्रि	night
सत्ता	existence, being (lit. "that-which-is-ness")
मध्य	middle. Here, the middle between the two extremes, i.e. partaking of both of them.
पदम्	condition, state
तत्पदम्	the condition of that; or, as sa is used in this lesson, that condition.

LESSON 13

AYAM AND ASAU; RELATIVES

I. Ayam and asau. These words are demonstrative pronouns. ayam means "that" or "this," while asau signifies a more remote relation and is translated "that." They are most commonly used when things are pointed out, as "This is my house." But they may also be used wherever the English pronoun or adjective this or that is found. Memorize the declension of ayam. Do not memorize asau, but look at its declension so that you are able to identify its forms.

The declension of ayam is as follows:

Masculine:

	Sing.	Daul	Plural
Nom.	अयम्	इमौ	इमे
Acc.	इमम्	,,	इमान्
Inst.	अनेन	आभ्याम्	एभि:
Dat.	अस्मै	,,	एभ्य:
Abl.	अस्मात्	,,	,,
Gen.	अस्य	अनयो:	एषाम्
Loc.	अस्मिन्	,,	एषु

Feminine:

Nom.	इयम्	इमे	इमा:
Acc.	इमाम्	,,	,,
Inst.	अनया	आभ्याम्	आभि:
Dat.	अस्यै	,,	आभ्य:
Abl.	अस्या:	,,	,,
Gen.	,,	अनयो:	आसाम्
Loc.	अस्याम्	,,	आसु

Neuter:

Nom.	इदम्	इमे	इमानि
Acc.	,,	,,	,,

The other cases are the same as the masculine.

The declension of asau is as follows:

Masculine:

Nom.	असौ	अमू	अमी
Acc.	अमुम्	,,	अमून्
Inst.	अमुना	अमूभ्याम्	अमीभिः
Dat.	अमुष्मै	,,	अमीभ्यः
Abl.	अमुष्मात्	,,	,,
Gen.	अमुष्य	अमुयोः	अमीषाम्
Loc.	अमुष्मिन्	,,	अमीषु

Feminine:

Nom.	असौ	अमू	अमूः
Acc.	अमूम्	,,	,,
Inst.	अमुया	अमूभ्याम्	अमूभिः
Dat.	अमुष्यै	,,	अमूभ्यः
Abl.	अमुष्याः	,,	,,
Gen.	,,	अमुयोः	अमूषाम्
Loc.	अमुष्याम्	,,	अमूषु

Neuter:

Nom.	अदः	अमू	अमूनि
Acc.	,,	,,	,,

The other cases are the same as the masculine.

II. Other words declined like sa.

A. Words declined exactly the same.

eṣa (m.); eṣā (f.), etat (n.), this. See saṃdhi rule 27 for retroflexing of the s.

B. Words declined like sa, except that final -s is not dropped before consonants in the nom. masc. sg.:

1. Words whose neuter nom. -acc. is same as for sa:
   ya, the relative pronoun "who" (see below)
   anya, other.

2. Words whose neuter nom. -acc. ends in -am.
   sarva, all
   viśva, all

3. Word with special nom.-acc. neuter:
   ka, "who?" (interrogative). nom-acc. neut. is kim.

Note: there are some other words which also follow the declension of sa. These are given for reference only and need not be memorized. Under B. 1. belong katara, "which of two," katama "which of many," anyatara, "one of two," and anyatama, "one of many." Optionally under B. 2. are the words para, "chief," and pūrva, "first."

III. Relatives in Sanskrit. Like English, Sanskrit has words called relatives meaning "who," "which," "where," "if," etc. The Sanskrit usage of these words is distinguished by the fact that each must be accompanied by a correlative (e.g. "there" for "where.") Thus in Sanskrit, one must express "Where the king lives I saw him" as "Where the king lives, *there* I saw him," that is, yatra rājā vasati tatra tam apaśyam. A list of the most common relative words with their correlatives follows:

Word	Correlative
yadi, if	tadā, then (also tarhi, tataḥ)
yadyapi, even if, even though	tathāpi, still
yadā, when, if	tadā, then
yatra, where	tatra, there
ya, who (see below)	sa, he, she, it, they; also ayam, asau.
yathā, as, since	tathā, so, therefore

This construction is relatively straightforward, except for the use of ya, who. First, in Sanskrit, the subordinate "who" clause is placed before the independent clause (or, rarely, after it), never as in English is it inserted into it. Second, in English, the antecedent of "who" is put directly before the subordinate clause, as "The boy who comes is a Brāhmaṇa." In Sanskrit, the English antecedent must be put either after the relative word "who" with which it agrees, or after the inserted correlative "he" etc. with which it agrees. Thus one may say either "Who boy comes, he is a Brāhmaṇa," or "Who comes, he boy is a Brāhmaṇa," that is, yo bāla āgacchati, sa brāhmaṇaḥ, or ya āgacchati, sa bālo brāhmaṇaḥ. (Bāla means boy). The case of "who" is determined by its function in the subordinate clause, while the case of "he" is determined by its function in the main clause. Thus, to translate "I see the king who conquers," first say, "who king conquers, him I see," or "who conquers, him king I see." Note that "who" is the subject of "conquers," and so must be nominative, while "him" is the direct object of "see" and so is accusative. The antecedent "king" is nominative or accusative depending on whether it is placed next to "who" or "him" respectively. Thus, yo jayati tam rājānaṃ paśyāmi, or yo rājā jayati taṃ paśyāmi. Note that if the English antecedent is the third-person pronoun, the correlative sa is sufficient antecedent. Thus "He who comes is my father," is rendered "who comes, he is my father," that is, ya āgacchati sa mama pitā. Study the following sentences:

The king sees the mountain on which I stand.
यस्मिन्गिरौ तिष्ठामि तं नृप: पश्यति
यस्मिंस्तिष्ठामि तं गिरिं नृप: पश्यति
The poet to whom I gave a chariot came.
यस्मै कवये रथमयच्छं स आगच्छत्
यस्मै रथमयच्छं स कविरागच्छत्
He led the horse to the village from which I came.
यस्माद्ग्रामादागच्छं तमश्वमानयत् (or तत्राश्वमानयत्)
यस्मादागच्छं तं ग्राममश्वमानयत् (or तत्र ग्रामम् ०००)
I saw the kṣatriya by whose horse we conquer.
यस्याश्वेन जयामस्तं क्षत्रियमपश्यम्
यस्य क्षत्रियस्याश्वेन जयामस्तमपश्यम्
I saw the horse by which we conquer.
येनाश्वेन जयामस्तमपश्यम्
येन जयामस्तमश्वमपश्यम्

A relative word and optionally its correlative may be doubled, in which case the meaning becomes indefinite—"whoever," "whatever," "wherever," etc. Thus yatra yatrāgacchat tatra vanāny eva, "wherever he went, there were only forests." Yad yad alabhata tat taj jalam iva "whatever he obtained, that was like water."

Occasionally, relatives are used without correlatives. In such cases, the correlative can generally be regarded as having been omitted for meter or other such purpose. When ya is used without a correlative, however, its meaning changes, and the clause which it controls becomes universal. Thus, atra kṣatriyā ye ca brāhmaṇā vasanti, "Here kṣatriyas, and whoever are Brāhmaṇas, live." You need not control this usage actively.

When followed by an interrogative made indefinite by adding api. cit, or cana, ya becomes extremely indefinite. Thus yatra kutrāpi, "anywhere at all," yaḥ ko 'pi, "anyone at all," yat kiṃ cit, "anything." In such cases, ya does not control a subordinate clause and needs no antecedent.

VOCABULARY:

अन्य	other. Declined like sa—see II above.
अयम्	this, that. See I above.
असौ	that, see I above.
क	who (interrogative)
तथा	so; in that way. tathāpi means "still," "nevertheless." It is used as the correlative of yady api and of yadāpi.
तदा	then. Correlative of yadi and yadā.
य	who, relative. See III above.
यत्र	where, relative.
यदा	when, since. yadāpi means even though.
यदि	if. yady api means even if, even though.
सर्व	all, each, Declined like sa—see II above. Note that in the singular this word generally means each, while in the plural or dual it means all.

TRANSLATE into English:

यो वणिग्वाप्या जलं पिबति स मम पत्न्या भ्राता ॥१॥ यानानयन्राज्ञोऽश्वास्तै रथैर्युद्धेऽजयन्क्षत्रियाः ॥२॥ यानि यानि देवस्य नामानि तानि सर्वाण्यपठद्ब्राह्मणः ॥३॥ यद्यपि सर्वे क्षत्रिया अनश्यंस्तस्मिन्युद्धे तथाप्यजयामेत्यमन्यत राजा ॥४॥ ये राजानो धर्मं न सेवन्ते ते सर्वेऽस्मिन्युद्धेऽनश्यन्निति कविरवदत् ॥५॥ अयं मे ग्राम इदं च मे गृहमित्यवददतिथिं शूद्रः ॥६॥ ये लोके कीर्तिमलभन्त ये च कवीनां वाक्ष्वविशंस्ते सर्वेऽनश्यन्न चास्मिल् लोक इदानीं वर्तन्ते ॥७॥ येभ्यो येभ्यो गिरिभ्यो नद्यः पतन्ति तांस्तान्मृगाः सेवन्ते ॥८॥ यदा यदाचार्यः शिष्याणां सकाशे तिष्ठति तदा तेऽपि तिष्ठन्तीत्यपश्यद्वणिजः पुत्रः ॥९॥ येषां मनुष्याणां पुत्रा जायन्ते तेषां धर्मोऽपि वर्धते ॥१०॥ येभ्यः कविभ्यः स गजानश्वांश्च यच्छति ते

सर्वे तं राजानं शंसन्ति ॥११॥ यत्र यत्र रामस्य पादौ भूमिमस्पृशतां तत्र तत्रेदानीममुं देवं सेवन्ते मनुष्याः ॥१२॥

TRANSLATE into Sanskrit: 1. In the village where the merchants were born now the pupils sit in the presence of the teacher. 2. The man who never entered the houses of Śūdras now comes to the village of Śūdras. 3. "Even if you do not give the horses to my father, we will somehow come to the battle," said the kṣatriya to the king. 4. "Who is this one?" asked my brother. 5. In the shadows which we saw on the mountains, animals drink water. 6. We saw the men with whom he came.

VERSES:

प्रसादो निष्फलो यस्य यस्य क्रोधो निरर्थकः ।
न तं राजानमिच्छन्ति षण्ढं पतिमिवाङ्गनाः ॥

प्रसाद	grace, favor
निष्फल	fruitless (nis = without)
क्रोध	anger
निरर्थक	meaningless, arbitrary (artha, object)
इष् (इच्छति)	wish, desire
षण्ढ	eunuch
पति	lord, husband
अङ्गना	woman

किं कुलेन विशालेन शीलमेवात्र कारणम् ।
कृमयः किं न जायन्ते कुसुमेषु सुगन्धिषु ॥

किम्	followed by inst.: "What's the use of..." In the 2nd line, kim merely makes the sent. interrogative and need not be translated.
कुलम्	family
विशाल	large: eminent
शीलम्	nature; character
कारणम्	cause. Here: cause or standard for judging someone
कृमि	worm
कुसुम	flower
सुगन्धिन् (loc. pl. सुगन्धिषु)	fragrant

किं विद्यया किं तपसा किं योगेन श्रुतेन च ।
किं विविक्तेन मौनेन स्त्रीभिर्यस्य मनो हृतम् ॥

किम्	followed by inst.: "What's the use of..."
विद्या	knowledge
तपस्	(consonant stem): austerity, asceticism
योग	yoga
श्रुतम्	scripture
विविक्त	secluded
मौनम्	silence
स्त्री	woman
मनस्	(consonant stem): mind
हृत	taken (supply "is")

LESSON 14

THE OPTATIVE ACTIVE: NOUNS IN -U

I. The optative active. Like the present and imperfect, the optative is formed on the present stem and has an active and middle. The optative expresses wish ("may he receive long life"), request ("Would you come ?"), what is desirable or proper ("Men should perform dharma"), and what may occur ("He may come"). There exists also a gnomic optative, used to describe things the way they should be ("All men honor Brāhmaṇas"). Learn the optative active:

	Sing.	Dual	Plural
1st pers.	भवेयम्	भवेव	भवेम
2nd pers.	भवेः	भवेतम्	भवेत
3rd pers.	भवेत्	भवेताम्	भवेयुः

II. Declension in -u. This declension need not be memorized, but you should be able to recognize its forms. Most words in this declension are masculine, fewer are neuter, and a very few are feminine.

śatru (masc.): enemy.

Nom.	शत्रुः	शत्रू	शत्रवः
Acc.	शत्रुम्	,,	शत्रून्
Inst.	शत्रुणा	शत्रुभ्याम्	शत्रुभिः
Dat.	शत्रवे	,,	शत्रुभ्यः
Abl.	शत्रोः	,,	,,
Gen.	,,	शत्र्वोः (śatrvoḥ)	शत्रूणाम्
Loc.	शत्रौ	,,	शत्रुषु
Voc.	शत्रो		

Of course the -n- in the instrumental singular and genitive plural ending is retroflexed only if required by saṃdhi. Dhenu (fem.), cow, is declined like satru except in the instrumental singular (dhenvā) and the accusative plural (dhenūḥ).

madhu (neuter): honey.

Nom.	मधु	मधुनी	मधूनि
Acc.	,,	,,	,,
Inst.	मधुना	मधुभ्याम्	मधुभिः
Dat.	मधुने	,,	मधुभ्यः
Abl.	मधुनः	,,	,,
Gen.	,,	मधुनोः	मधूनाम्
Loc.	मधुनि	,,	मधुषु
Voc.	मधो		

VOCABULARY:

ऋषि	seer, sage
एक	one, alone (declined like sa; neuter sg. nom. -acc, ekam).
कोप	anger
धनम्	money, wealth (used in sg. and pl.)
तीरम्	shore
धेनु f.	cow
मधु n.	honey
शत्रु m.	enemy
समुद्र	ocean
सूर्य	sun

TRANSLATE into English:

कोपादृषिर्ग्रामादगच्छदस्मिन्ग्रामे सर्वे नश्येयुरित्यवदच्च ॥१॥ यदि देवानां मधु पिबेयुर्मनुष्यास्तदा तेऽपि न नश्येयुः ॥२॥ य आचार्यस्य सकाश उपविशेयुस्ते न किमपि वदेयुः ॥३॥ शत्रूणां कोपाद्देवा अपि युद्धेऽपतन् ॥४॥ यदि मम धनानि सर्वाणि शत्रवो लभन्ते तदाहं नश्येयमित्यवदन्नृपः ॥५॥ यद्यद्धि भवेन्मनुष्यस्तदेव भवति ॥६॥ यदा नद्यास्तीरे धेनूरपश्यद्वणिक्तदा कथं ता ग्राममानयेयमित्यमन्यत सः ॥७॥ यदि न कस्मिन्नपि मनुष्ये कोपो विशेत्तदास्मिंल् लोके युद्धानि न भवेयुः ॥८॥ येऽत्र ब्राह्मणानां पुस्तकानि पठेयुस्ते सर्वे मम नगरमागच्छेयुरित्यवदन्नृपः ॥९॥ यदा समुद्रस्य तीरेऽतिष्ठज्जलमपश्यच्च तदा देवानां लोकेऽविशमित्यमन्यत वणिक् ॥१०॥ यदा ब्राह्मणाः सूर्यादन्येषां *देवानां नामान्यपठंस्तान्देवानशंसंश्च

*the ablative followed by anya means "other than"

तदा सूर्यं एकोऽस्माकं देवो येऽन्येषां देवानां नामानि पठेयुस्ते नास्मिन्नगरे निवसे-युरित्यवदद्राजा ।।११।। न पुनः कदापि सूर्यं पश्येत्स मम शत्रुरिति कोपादवद-त्क्षत्रियः ।।१२।।

TRANSLATE into English: 1. "The enemies of the king fell in battle," the poets said. 2. I would give my money to who (ever) would stand before (in the presence of) my enemies and free the cows. 3. The king saw the anger of the seer and said in fear, "My wealth is yours." (for "yours" use gen. of you followed by eva). 4. A Brāhmaṇa who sits on the shore of the Gaṅgā, sees the sun, and perishes, will come to the world of the gods. (Use opt. for all verbs—this is the gnomic optative). 5. "There is no shore of this ocean," said the sage to his pupil. 6. If men defeated the gods in battle, then they would be gods, and gods men.

VERSES:

त्यजेदेकं कुलस्यार्थे ग्रामस्यार्थे कुलं त्यजेत् ।
ग्रामं जनपदस्यार्थे ह्यात्मार्थे पृथिवीं त्यजेत् ।।

त्यज् (त्यजति)	abandon, renounce
कुलम्	family
अर्थे	for the sake of (preceded by genitive of the word governed)
जनपदम्	country
आत्मन्	self; Self
आत्मार्थे	(compound) for the sake of Self
पृथिवी	earth

धनिकः श्रोत्रियो राजा नदी वैद्यस्तु पञ्चमः ।
पञ्च यत्र न विद्यन्ते न तत्र दिवसं वसेत् ।।

धनिक	rich man
श्रोत्रिय	a Brāhmaṇa well-versed in sacred learning
वैद्य	a physician
पञ्चम	fifth
पञ्च	five
विद्यन्ते	(they) are
दिवस	day

शैले शैले न माणिक्यं मौक्तिकं न गजे गजे ।
साधवो न हि सर्वत्र चन्दनं न वने वने ।।

शैलम्	mountain. Repetition gives the sense of "every mountain"
माणिक्यम्	blue sapphire
मौक्तिकम्	pearl (in Sanskrit and Tamil, elephants produce pearls)
साधु	good man
सर्वत्र	everywhere
चन्दनम्	sandalwood

अपत्यदर्शनस्यार्थे प्राणानपि या त्यजेत् ।
त्यजन्ति तामपि क्रूरा मातरं दारहेतवे ।।

अपत्यम्	offspring, child
दर्शनम्	seeing
अर्थे	for the sake of (preceded by the genitive of the word governed)
अपत्यदर्शनम्	seeing one's child
प्राण	(usually plural): breath, life
त्यज् (त्यजति)	forsake, abandon
क्रूर	cruel
दार	wife
हेतु	cause
दारहेतवे	for the sake of a wife

LESSON 15

THE OPTATIVE MIDDLE: NOUNS IN -S

I. Learn the Optative Middle:

	Singular	Dual	Plural
1st Person	लभेय	लभेवहि	लभेमहि
2nd Person	लभेथाः	लभेयाथाम्	लभेध्वम्
3rd. Person	लभेत	लभेयाताम्	लभेरन्

II. Nouns in -s. There are many Sanskrit nouns which end in -as, -is, or -us, and which take the consonantal endings, like pad (with a few exceptions). They do not distinguish, however, between strong and weak cases. The majority of these words is neuter and differs from pad in the nom. and acc. The singular acc. is in -as (like the sing. nom.), while the dual nom.-acc. is in -ī and for the plural, the final vowel is lengthened and -ṃsi added. For words in -is and -us, the -s is retroflexed in many cases, according to saṃdhi rule 27 (note that this includes the loc. pl.). Study the following paradigms of manas, mind, havis, oblation, and dhanus, bow, all neuter. Do not memorize these declensions, but familiarize yourself with them so that you can identify forms.

	Singular	Dual	Plural
Nom.	मनः/हविः/धनुः	मनसी/हविषी/धनुषी	मनांसि/हवींषि/धनूंषि
Acc.	,, ,, ,,	,, ,, ,,	,, ,, ,,
Inst.	मनसा/हविषा/धनुषा	मनोभ्याम्/हविर्भ्याम्/धनुर्भ्याम्	मनोभिः/हविर्भिः/धनुर्भिः
	etc., as for pad.		
Loc.	मनसि/हविषि/धनुषि	मनसोः/हविषोः/धनुषोः	मनःसु/हविःषु/धनुःषु

Note that the pāda endings are treated as new words when added to the stem, and the saṃdhi rules you learned are applied. Thus inst. pl. manobhiḥ, but havirbhiḥ. (The pāda endings are those which begin with a consonant—review section II on page 30).

Masculine and feminine nouns in -s (which are not numerous, except for compounds) are declined like pad, with the exception of nouns in -as. Such nouns are irregular in that they form the nom. sg. in -âs (while the voc. sg. is in -as). Thus sumanas, favourably minded, well-disposed, m. or f. depending on whether the antecedent is masculine of feminine:

	Sing.	Dual	Plural
Nom.	सुमनाः	सुमनसौ	सुमनसः
Acc.	सुमनसम्	सुमनसौ	सुमनसः

etc. as with pad.

III. Note on adjectives. Sanskrit adjectives may also serve as nouns. Sādhu, for example, may mean either "good" or "a good man." You have already seen this characteristic of the language in the word sa. Most Sanskrit adjectives are declined like deva in the masc., phalam in the neut., and senā in the fem. A very few are declined like deva, phalam, and nadī. There is also a fair-sized group declined like śatru in the masc., madhu in the neut., and nadī in the fem. (e.g. the feminine of bahu, many, is bahvi). Other declensions are found in compound adjectives formed with nouns as their last members, as you will learn when you study compounds. There are also a few non-compound adjectives which take other declensions.

VOCABULARY:

अर्थ	meaning; wealth; goal
अर्थे	for the sake of (preceded by the genitive of the word governed)
कन्या	girl, daughter; an unmarried girl; a virgin, maiden
क्रीड् (क्रीडति)	play
चक्षुस् n.	eye
चुर् (चोरयति)	steal
दह् (दहति)	burn; to be painful, to cause pain. (Both trans. and intrans.)
धनुस् n.	bow (the weapon)
पयस् n.	milk
प्रजा	subject (of a king); offspring, progeny; creature
बहु (fem. बह्वी)	much, many

TRANSLATE into English:

यस्मात्त्वं रथान्गजांश्च लभेथाः स राजेदानीमत्र तिष्ठतीति कविः कविमवदत् ।।१।। ये राजानो न मे प्रजा वर्धेरन्न च धर्मो वर्धेतेति मन्येरंस्ते सर्वे इदानीमेव नश्येयुरित्यमन्यत ब्राह्मणः ।।२।। मम कन्या न कदापि मदन्यान्मनुष्यानपश्यन्नित्यवदन्नृपः ।।३।। यदा यदा देवानां चक्षूंषि दमयन्त्यामपतंस्तदा तदा तत्रैवातिष्ठंस्तानि ।।४।। ये धनं मे चोरयेयुस्ते सर्वे मम सकाशे गजानां पद्भिर्नश्येयुरिति राजावदत् ।।५।। यस्मिन्गिरौ स राजा जले पत्नीभिः सह क्रीडति तत्र न कोऽप्यागच्छेत् ।।६।। वनं दहतीत्यपश्यद्ब्राह्मणो ये च मृगास्तत्र न्यवसंस्तान्सर्वांस्तस्माद्वनादानयत् ।।७।। अस्य पुस्तकस्यार्थः क इत्याचार्यं शिष्योऽपृच्छत् ।।८।। मम कन्या सदा मधुना सह पयोऽपिबदिदानीं तु तेन क्षत्रियेणैका वने गच्छति यज्जलं मृगास्तत्र पिबन्ति तज्जलं सापि पिबतीति मातामन्यत ।।९।। यदेकं मित्रं तेन धनुषैव सहास्माकं गिरिं स आगच्छतीति कन्यामन्यत ।।१०।। येषामर्थे वणिजोऽदो वनमगच्छंस्ते गजा सर्वेऽग्नावनश्यन् ।।११।। सा कन्याग्निरिव मां दहतीत्यवदन्मित्रं स क्षत्रियः ।।१२।।

TRANSLATE into Sanskrit: 1. The girl for whose sake I came to this city may not come out said the kṣatriya. (out: bahiḥ.) 2. Whoever would touch my feet, let him come into my presence. 3. The king saw that his wives and daughters played in the water of the tank and he entered the water like an elephant. 4. In whose words there is anger, they may not live in this forest the Brāhmaṇa said. 5. Whose books are these the pupil asked. 6. No (one) other (use pl.) than kṣatriyas (abl.) perished in battle.

VERSES:

प्रत्यहं प्रत्यवेक्षेत नरश्चरितमात्मनः ।
किं नु मे पशुभिस्तुल्यं किं नु सत्पुरुषैरिति ।।

प्रत्यहम्	daily
प्रत्यवेक्ष् (प्रत्यवेक्षते)	examine
नर	man
चरितम्	conduct, deeds
आत्मन्	self, oneself
किम्	here, indicates the sentence is interrogative
नु	particle meaning "well,"—untranslatable
पशु	cow
तुल्यम्	equal (+inst. of thing to which equality is expressed)

सत्पुरुष	good man

शत्रुर्दहति संयागे वियोगे मित्रमप्यहो ।
उभयोर्दु:खदायित्वं को भेद: शत्रुमित्रयो: ।।

संयोग	joining, being together with
वियोग	separation
अहो	untranslatable—"alas!"
उभय	both (usually in the dual)
दु:खम्	sorrow, suffering
दायित्वम्	giving-ness, nature of giving
दु:खदायित्वम्	nature of giving sorrow
भेद	difference
शत्रुमित्रे	(dual): friend and enemy

उपदेशो हि मूर्खानां प्रकोपाय न शान्तये ।
पय: पानं भुजंगानां केवलं विषवर्धनम् ।।

उपदेश	instruction, teaching
मूर्ख	fool
प्रकोप	anger
शान्ति	peace, calmness
पानम्	drinking
पय:पानम्	drinking of milk
भुजंग	snake
केवलम्	only
विष	poison
वर्धन	increasing, causing to grow
विषवर्धन	poison-producing.

Lesson 16

THE IMPERATIVE ACTIVE; TATPURUSA COMPOUNDS

I. The imperative active. This tense, like the present, imperfect, and optative, is added to the present stem of the verb. It is used for commands. In the second person, it may be translated by the English imperative ("Come."); in the third person, it may be translated by "Let him..." (or "Let her..., etc.); while in the first person, it may be translated by "May I," "May we." Actually, the first person is quite rare and is an invention of the Sanskrit grammarians, who used Vedic subjunctive forms for the first-person imperative—the subjunctive has completely disappeared in classical Sanskrit, except for a few fossilized expressions. Learn the imperative active:

	Singular	Dual	Plural
1st person	भवानि	भवाव	भवाम
2nd person	भव	भवतम्	भवत
3rd person	भवतु	भवताम्	भवन्तु

II. Tatpuruṣa compounds. Sanskrit has four classes of compounds: tatpuruṣa, bahuvrīhi, dvandva, and avyayībhāva. In this lesson, the first of those classes is explained.

All compounds are formed in the same general way. One simply takes the stem forms of nouns and adjectives and puts them together, applying saṃdhi to the combinations where they come together. Only the last member of the compound is declined. In general, the stem form is the form cited in the vocabulary (e.g. deva, pad, śatru, agni, kartṛ, manas). Exceptions are nouns in -am and -an, whose stem forms end in -a.* Learn the stem forms of the pronouns:

*You will have several other declensions in future lessons. The stem forms of words in -in is in -i; of words in -ant, in -at.

Pronoun	Stem form
aham	mat
vayam	asmat
tvam	tvat
yūyam	yuṣmat
sa (he, she, it, they)	tat (used for all genders and numbers of sa)

Special rule: when the last member of a tatpuruṣa is a word in -an (like rājan), its declension changes to that of deva or phalam, depending on its gender. Thus kavirāja, king of poets. Occasionally, other stems also revert to the -a declension (Whitney 1315)

Tatpuruṣa compounds are those in which the first member of the compound is in some case relationship with the second member. The first member may be interpreted as either singular or plural, depending on context. The relationship may be that of any case, as illustrated below:

Nom. rājarṣi, from rājan+ṛṣi, a sage who is a king.
nīlotpala, from nīla blue and utpala, waterlily, a blue waterlily.

Acc. dhanadātṛ, from dhanam+dātṛ, money-giver. (Here, dātṛ, giver, is thought to keep the ability of the verb dā from which it is formed to have a direct object).

Inst. agnipāka, from agni+pāka, cooking, cooking by fire.

Dat. prajāhita, from prajā+hita, good, good for (one's) subjects.

Abl. gajabhayam, from gaja+bhayam, fear of the elephant, fear of elephants (fear takes the ablative in Sanskrit).

Gen. nadītīram, from nadī+tīram, the shore of the river.

Loc. girinadī, from giri+nadī, the river on the mountain.

Note that the relationship of the first member of the compound to the second and the number of the first member are not specified.

Tatpuruṣa compounds in which the relationship is nominative are put in a special class and are called karmadhārayas. Thus rājarṣi and nīlotpala are both tatpuruṣas and karmadhārayas. When you name such compounds, it is best to use the more specialized name, karmadhāraya.

Pronouns may also be the first member of tatpuruṣas, as the following examples show: maddhanam, my money; tattīram, the shore of that; tvaccakṣus, your eye; asmacchatru, our enemy.

When compounds are used in a sentence, they are considered one word and the last member alone is declined. Thus "on the shore of the river" is nadītīre.

Compounds may consist of more than two component words. In such cases, the compound should be analyzed piecemeal: first, consider all but the last component word as one compound word to be construed with the last component word; then repeat the process with the compound consisting of all elements but the last, etc. For example, nadītīragrāma should first be analyzed as nadītīra+grāma, that is a locative tatpuruṣa meaning "the village on the river-shore." Next, nadītīra should be analyzed as a genitive tatpuruṣa meaning "the shore of the river." The entire compound thus means "the village on the shore of the river." More involved examples, using tatpuruṣas and other types of compounds will be exemplified later.

VOCABULARY:

एष	this (declined exactly like sa. Thus fem. nom. eṣā, neut. nom. -acc. etat).
तथापि	still, yet, even so. From tathā and api
धाव् (धावति)	run
बाल	boy, fool
बाला	girl
राज्यम्	kingdom
वीर	fighting man, warrior; virile man
हृदयम्	heart

TRANSLATE into English:

न राजराजोऽपीदं नगरं जयेत् ॥१॥ स गच्छतु। मद्धृदये सदा तिष्ठत्येव ॥२॥ येऽन्यराज्यानि गच्छेयुस्तेभ्यश्चार्थानानयेयुर्न तेषां पत्न्यो मित्राणि वेत्यवदत्सा बाला ॥३॥ जयानि बह्वनां चैतेषां राज्यानामेको राजा भवानीत्यवदद्राजा ॥४॥ त्वदर्थेऽहमागच्छं त्वदर्थेऽहं युद्धेऽजयमिदानीं तु गच्छेत्येव वदसीत्यवदद्वीरो राजानम् ॥५॥ अस्मिन्युद्धे ममारयो जयन्तु। मम वीरा नश्यन्तु। यद्भवेत्तत्सर्वं भवतु। तथापि मम राज्याद्वनं न गच्छामीति नृपोऽवदत् ॥६॥ वीराणां चक्षूंषि चोरयतेति कन्या मातावदत् ॥७॥ यत्र कुत्रापि धावन्त्वेते वनगजास्तथापि

कथमपि राजनगरमेकमानयामीत्यमन्यत शूद्रः ॥८॥ युद्धभूमावपतद्वीरः । तमपश्यद्राजा देवानां लोकं गच्छत्विति चावदत् ॥९॥ नदीजलसकाशेऽतिष्ठंस्ता बाला अक्रीडंश्च ॥१०॥ अस्माकं हृदयेषु सदा वसति स राजेत्यवदंस्तस्य पत्न्यः ॥११॥ शत्रुराज्यनगरेष्विदानीमग्निमेव पश्याम इति कवयोऽवदन् ॥१२॥

EXERCISE: make the following compounds:

the city of the enemy
the glory of the king
the mountain river
the city of the enemies of the gods

TRANSLATE into Sanskrit, putting the italicized phrases into compounds. 1. Let the boys play *on the shore of the sea.* 2. "Come and see the *enemy city,*" said the *king's wife* to the poet. 3. Never *in the shadows of the trees of our city* (all one compound) do boys play with girls said the Brāhmaṇa. 4. Let my sons steal my wealth; let them come into my city; still out of anger I will not go *to the field of battle.* 5. *The words of the poet* entered into the hearts of the citizens. (prajā means citizen) 6. "Let the guests sit here," said the sage.

VERSES:

कारुण्यं संविभागश्च यस्य भृत्येषु सर्वदा ।
संभवेत्स महीपालस्त्रैलोक्यस्यापि रक्षणे ॥

कारुण्यम्	mercy, compassion
संविभाग	sharing
भृत्य	dependent
सर्वदा	always
संभू	(from sam and bhū) to be able, to be competent (with the loc. of what one is capable of)
मही	earth
पाल	protector (Note: an earth-protector is a king)
त्रैलोक्यम्	the three worlds (heaven, hell, and this world)
रक्षणम्	protection

यथा धेनुसहस्रेषु वत्सो विन्दति मातरम् ।
तथा पूर्वकृतं कर्म कर्तारमनुगच्छति ॥

यथा	just as (correlative: tathā)
सहस्रम्	thousand

वत्स	calf
विद् (विन्दति)	find
पूर्व	former. Here: former birth
कृत	done
कर्मन्	karma
कर्तृ	doer
अनुगम्	follow (from anu and gam)

रक्षन्ति कृपणाः पाणौ द्रव्यं क्रव्यमिवात्मनः ।
तदेव सन्तः सततमुत्सृजन्ति यथा मलम् ॥

रक्ष् (रक्षति)	protect
कृपण	wretched, miserly
द्रव्यम्	goods, wealth
क्रव्यम्	flesh
आत्मन्	self, oneself

सत् (nom. pl. सन्तः) good, good person

सततम्	always
उत्सृज् (उत्सृजति)	get rid of; defecate
यथा	like
मलम्	excrement

LESSON 17

THE IMPERATIVE MIDDLE; DVANDVA COMPOUNDS

I. The Imperative Middle. Learn this conjugation:

	Sing.	Dual	Plural
1st person	लभै	लभावहै	लभामहै
2nd person	लभस्व	लभेथाम्	लभध्वम्
3rd person	लभताम्	लभेताम्	लभन्ताम्

II. Dvandva compounds. This type of compound is simply an enumeration of its elements in a series. It is translated by naming the elements and putting "and" before the last element. It is formed in the way described in the previous lesson under tatpuruṣa. There are two kinds of dvandva compounds:

A. Itaretara dvandva. In this compound, the last member is put in the dual if two things are involved, in the plural if more than two are involved. Its gender is the normal gender of its last component word. Thus,

Rāma and Kṛṣṇa	rāmakṛṣṇau
Horses, crows, and elephants	aśvakākagajāḥ
Gods, Gandharvas, and men	devagandharvamanuṣyāḥ

Note that an itaretara dvandva consisting of two elements may be either dual (if two things are meant) or plural (if more than two things are meant). Thus rāmakṛṣṇau, Rāma and Kṛṣṇa, but devamanuṣyāḥ, gods and men. "The god and the man" would be devamanuṣyau. Itaretara dvandvas of three or more component words are always plural.

B. Samāhāra dvandva. (Samāhāra means "composite"). This type of dvandva is always singular and neuter. The series of things is generally referred to as a composite unit. For example:

pāṇipādam, from pāṇi, hand, and pāda, foot. Hands and feet, used as a unit, as, e.g., "They fought with hands and feet."

āhāranidrābhayam, from āhāra, food, nidrā, sleep, and bhayam. "Food, sleep, and fear" as a unit, that is, "animal life".

VOCABULARY:

उद्यानम्	garden
काल	time
धूम	smoke
पुष्पम्	flower
विषम्	poison
सिंह	lion
स्वर्ग	heaven, paradise
हस्त	hand; trunk (of an elephant)

TRANSLATE into English:

ये राजानो मन्मित्राणि तेषां कीर्तिर्वर्धतामित्यवदन्नृपः ।।१।। यत्र यत्र धूमस्तत्र तत्राग्निरित्यवदच्छिष्यमाचार्यः ।।२।। अस्मिन्पयसि विषं भवेदित्यमन्यत राजा न च तदपिबत् ।।३।। अस्मिन्वने सिंहगजा वसन्तीति स वणिगमन्यत भयेन च तदविशत् ।।४।। नगरोद्यानेषु राजबाला अक्रीडन्नुद्यानवृक्षाणां पुष्पाणि गृह्मानयंश्च ।।५।। तत्र वने सूर्यो गजहस्तानपि पीडयति । ये नश्येयुस्त एव तद्विशेयुरिति वणिजमवदत्पत्नी ।।६।। ये स्वर्गं गच्छेयुस्ते सर्वेऽस्मिँल् लोके कीर्तिं लभन्ताम् ।।७।। येषां गजानां हस्तैः सिंहा अनश्यंस्ते सर्वेऽग्नावधावन्ननश्यंश्च ।।८।। यः सिंहो वनराजस्तेन सह काकगजौ न्यवसताम् ।।९।। समुद्रतीरेऽपश्यत्क्षत्रियो देवलोकवृक्षपुष्पाणि किमेतदित्यमन्यत च ।।१०।। न बालोऽपि तथा मन्येतेति कोपाच्छिष्यमवददाचार्यः ।।११।। सर्वकालेषु तव राज्ये पुष्पाणि वृक्षेषु वर्तन्तामित्यवददृषिः ।।१२।।

TRANSLATE into Sanskrit, putting the italicized phrases into componuds. 1. The king thought, "Let *my enemies* get my kingdom; still, I will not enter the fight." 2. *On the shore of the ocean* stood a *Brāhmaṇa and a Kṣatriya*. 3. The king looked at his warriors and thought, "Even in some* flowers there is poison." 4. When he saw the *smoke of the fire*, the poet said to the king, "May your fame always grow as now." (use imperative). 5. In *other kingdoms* also (api) kings afflict their

*Use kaścit for some, making it agree with "flowers."

subjects the Brāhmaṇa thought. 6. Even in paradise, men say in anger, "May your enemies flourish," the Brāhmaṇa thought. (use vṛdh for flourish).

VERSES:

काकस्य गात्रं यदि काञ्चनस्य माणिक्यरत्नं यदि चञ्चुदेशे ।
एकैकपक्षे ग्रथितं मणीनां तथापि काको न तु राजहंसः ॥

गात्रम्	limb
काञ्चनम्	gold
माणिक्यम्	blue sapphire
चञ्चु	beak
देश	vicinity;
एकैक	each
पक्ष	wing
ग्रथितम्	ornament
मणि	jewel, gem
राजहंस	flamingo (haṃsa means goose)

न स्वप्नेन जयेन्निद्रां न कामेन स्त्रियं जयेत् ।
नेन्धनेन जयेद्वह्निं न पानेन सुरां जयेत् ॥

स्वप्नम्	sleep
निद्रा	sleepiness, sloth
काम	desire, lust
स्त्री (acc. sg. स्त्रियम्)	woman
इन्धनम्	kindling; fuel for a fire, firewood
वह्नि	fire
पानम्	drinking
सुरा	liquor

लालनाद्बहवो दोषास्ताडनाद्बहवो गुणाः ।
तस्मात्पुत्रं च शिष्यं च ताडयेन्न तु लालयेत् ॥

लालनम्	indulgence
बहु	many (declined in masc. like śatru)
दोष	fault
ताडनम्	beating
गुण	excellence

तड् (ताडयति) beat
लल् (लालयति) indulge

अर्धमात्रालाघवेन पुत्रोत्सवं मन्यन्ते वैयाकरणाः ।

अर्ध half
मात्रा syllable (actually, the length of time taken up by a short vowel)
लाघवम् lightness; here, lessening, shortening
उत्सव festival; here, birth
वैयाकरण grammarian

तृप्त्यर्थं भोजनं येषां सन्तानार्थं च मैथुनम् ।
वाक्सत्यसेवनार्थाय दुर्गाण्यतितरन्ति ते ॥

तृप्ति satisfaction
–अर्थम्, –अर्थाय (at end of compound) for the sake of
सन्तानम् offspring, continuing one's line
मैथुनम् sexual intercourse
सत्यम् truth
सेवनम् resorting to, observing
दुर्गम् difficulty, trial, tribulation
अतित (अतितरति) cross over

LESSON 18

BAHUVRĪHI COMPOUNDS

I. Neuter nouns in -i. This declension is not very common, but it does occur with some frequency in bahuvrīhi compounds, the subject of this lesson. Do not memorize it, but look at it so that you can identify its forms. The word used as an example is dadhi, neuter, curds, yogurt.

	Sing.	Dual	Plural
Nom.	दधि	दधिनी	दधीनि
Acc.	,,	,,	,,
Inst.	दधिना	दधिभ्याम्	दधिभिः
Dat.	दधिने	,,	दधिभ्यः
Abl.	दधिनः	,,	,,
Gen.	,,	दधिनोः	दधीनाम्
Loc.	दधिनि	,,	दधिषु
Voc.	दधे		

II. Feminine nouns in -ū. As with dadhi, do not memorize the declension of vadhū, wife, but familiarize yourself with it:

Nom.	वधूः	वध्वौ	वध्वः
Acc.	वधूम्	,,	वधूः
Inst.	वध्वा	वधूभ्याम्	वधूभिः
Dat.	वध्वै	,,	वधूभ्यः
Abl.	वध्वाः	,,	,,
Gen.	,,	वध्वोः	वधूनाम्
Loc.	वध्वाम्	,,	वधूषु

III. Bahuvrīhi compounds.

The Sanskrit grammarians analyze all Sanskrit compounds

in terms of what is termed the prādhānyam, that is, the syntactical predominance, which is different for each of the four main types of compounds. For tatpuruṣas, the prādhānyam is on the second element. Thus in the compound rājakopa, the anger of the king, the word kopa is clearly syntactically predominant. In dvandva compounds, the prādhānyam is on all elements equally, as in devagandharvamanuṣyāḥ, "gods, Gandharvas, and men."

A third type of compound, which is not as important as the others and which you need not learn actively, is called avyayībhāva, "having an unchanging nature." Such compounds are invariant, that is, they are not declined. They function as adverbs. Examples are upakumbham, from upa, a prefix expressing nearness, and kumbha, pot, meaning "in the pot," and antargiri, from antar, inside, and giri, meaning "inside the mountain." In such compounds, the prādhānyam is on the first member, that is in the examples cited on upa and antar.

The fourth type of compound is quite important and is called bahuvrīhi. In it, the prādhānyam lies *outside* the compound itself on an antecedent either present or implied. An example is dhanurhasta, from dhanus and hasta, meaning literally "bow-hand." The compound means "who has a bow in his hand," or "the man with the bow in his hand," depending on whether the antecedent of the compound is actually expressed. A bahuvrīhi must agree with its antecedent *in gender, in case, and in number*. If the antecedent of this compound were feminine and nominative singular, it would become dhanurhastā; if it were neuter nominative singular, it would become dhanurhastam, declined like phalam. If the antecedent were tasyai ("to her"), then its form would be dhanurhastāyai, "to her with a bow in her hand." Note that the gender (like the case and number) of a bahuvrīhi is determined only by the antecedent, and is not at all influenced by the original gender of the last word in it. Nor is the number influenced by the singularity or plurality of elements inside the compound; only by the number of the antecedent. Thus vīramitro rājā could mean either "the king whose friend is a hero" or "the king whose friends are heroes." In either case, vīramitrah must be singular to agree with rājā.

Let us call the first element of a bahuvrīhi A and the second element B. Then for the bahuvrīhi AB, the most common meaning is "whose B is A" (or "whose B's are A's" or "whose B's are A," etc.). Some of the possible meanings are given below, with examples. Remember that in each case, both B and A may be either singular or plural.

Whose B is A. vīramitra, whose friends are heroes.

By whom B is A. hatagaja, by whom an elephant is killed (hata).

To whom B is A. dattadhana, to whom money was given (datta). (or, by whom money was given)

For whom B is A. putradhana, for whom (his) money is sons.

And so on, with "who" in various other cases.

Similarly, B may be put in various cases after "whose." This is expressed in English as follows:

In whose B is A. dhanurhasta, in whose hands is a bow.

Or A may be in various cases:

Whose B is for A. putrakāma, whose desire is for sons.

Whose B is of A. puṣpatira, whose shore is of flowers.

In general, the interpretation which best accords with common sense is the correct one.

When the first member of a bahuvrīhi is a prefix, the bahuvrīhi cannot be analyzed by the above scheme. Common prefixes are a-, nis-, sa- and saha-, su-, and dus-, plus a few other less common ones. Note that a- becomes an- before a word beginning with a vowel. Nis- and dus- follow the saṃdhi rules before all sounds except k, kh, p, and ph, before all of which they are changed to niṣ- and duṣ- respectively. That is to say, final -s of nis- and dus- changes to -ḥ before sibilants, -r before all vowels, diphthongs, and voiced consonants, and to -ṣ before k, kh, p, and ph.

a/an- means -less when used as part of a bahuvrīhi. Thus aputra, "sonless." Note that in a karmadhāraya, this prefix means "un-" or "non-," as in adharma, non-dharma, the opposite of dharma.

dus-. This is the antonym of su-. As the first element of a bahuvrīhi it means "having bad B," "having difficult B." An example is duṣkarman, "having bad deeds [karman]." As the first element of a karmadhāraya, it means "bad" or "difficult."

nis- means "without," "devoid of," "lacking in" when used as the prior member of a bahuvrīhi. Thus niṣpuṣpam udyānam, "a garden without flowers."

sa- and saha- both mean "accompanied by," "in the company of," "possessing," or "with" when used as element A in a bahuvrīhi. Thus savīro rājā and sahavīro rājā both mean "the king with his fighting men," "the king accompanied by his fighting men," "the king with fighting men."

su- as the first element of a bahuvrīhi means "having lovely B," "having easy B," "having good B." It is the opposite of dus-. An example is sukarman. "one whose deeds [karman] are good," "having good deeds." As the first element of a karmadhāraya, this prefix means "lovely," "very," "easy," "good."

Since bahuvrīhis take the gender (as well as the case and number) of their antecedents, it is necessary to know what declension to use for each gender of each bahuvrīhi. The masculines and neuters are relatively simple, but the use of the feminine comprises one of the true arcana of Sanskrit, in whose use even Kālidāsa occasionally is mistaken.* For most words, the following rules apply:

a. For bahuvrīhis whose last word normally ends in -a, -am, or -ā, the masculine, neuter, and feminine respectively end in -a, -am, and -ā (or rarely -ī). These of course follow the declensions of deva, phalam, and senā (or nadī).

b. Bahuvrīhis whose last member normally ends in -i have their masculine, neuter, and feminine all in -i (but a few have their feminine in -ī).

*Kālidāsa writes karabhoru, meaning "a woman whose thighs resemble the back of the forearm" in *Śakuntalā* 3.20, instead of karabhorū, required by Pāṇini 4.1.69. The rules regarding the feminines of bahuvrīhis are given in Pāṇini 4.1.3-81. I am grateful to Daniel Ingalls for help in this matter.

c. Bahuvrīhis whose last word normally ends in -u have their masculine, neuter, and feminine all in -u (but a few have their feminine in -ū).

d. Bahuvrīhis whose last member is a consonant stem use that consonant stem in the masculine, neuter, and feminine.

e. Bahuvrīhis whose last member ends in -ī, -ṛ, or -ū have their masculine, neuter, and feminine in -ka, -kam, and -kā respectively. These endings are added to the stem (the form which appears as the prior member in a compound). Thus sapatnīka from patnī; sadātṛka from dātṛ; savadhūka from vadhū.

f. Bahuvrīhis whose last member normally ends in -an either add -ka, -kam, and -kā to the stem, or are declined like rājan in the masculine, nāman in the neuter, and like nadī (ending -nī) in the feminine. Thus the masculine, neuter, and feminine of sa plus rājan are respectively sarājaka, sarājakam, and sarājakā; or sarājan, and sarājñī.

It is also permissible to make any bahuvrīhi, no matter what declension its last member belongs to, by adding -ka, -kam, and -kā to the stem of the last member for the masculine, neuter, and feminine respectively (Pāṇini 5.4.154).

Note that there are a few bahuvrīhis in English—for example, "Blue-beard." Bahuvrīhis are common in American Indian names, for example "red-horse," "swift-foot." Note that all of these examples are the most common type of bahuvrīhi, "Whose B is A." Study the following examples of bahuvrīhis:

dīrghakeśa, from dīrgha, long, and keśa, hair, "long-hair" "he whose hair is long." The feminine dīrghakeśā would mean "she whose hair is long"

mahābāhu, from mahā, great, and bāhu, arm. "Great-arm," "he whose arm is great."

anyarūpa, from anya and rūpa, form. "other-form," "having another form."

sumanas, from su and manas. mind. "good-mind," "well-disposed."

apraja, from a- and prajā, offspring, "childless."

cāracakṣus, from cāra, spy, and cakṣus eye. "spy-eye," "having spies for eyes."

rāmanāman, or rāmanāmaka, "Rāma-name," "he whose name is Rāma."

Note that most bahuvrīhis may also be interpreted as tatpuruṣas (in which case, of course, their meaning changes). If the words listed above were tatpuruṣas, their meanings would change as follows: dīrghakeśa would mean "long hair"; mahābāhu would mean "a great arm"; anyarūpa would mean "another form": sumanas would mean "a good mind," "favorable mind"; aprajā is meaningless as a tatpuruṣa and so cannot be interpreted in that way; cāracakṣus would mean "the eye of a spy"; and rāmanāman would mean "Rāma's name." Tatpuruṣas must take the normal gender of their last member, while bahuvrīhis take the gender of their antecedent. Thus rāmanāman must be neuter if it means "the name of Rāma," while it is masculine if it means "he who is named Rāma." It is usually an easy matter to determine from context whether an ambiguous compound is in fact a tatpuruṣa or a bahuvrīhi.

Long Compounds: Look over this section and become acquainted with the general principles involved. When you encounter a long compound, you must analyze it in accordance with common sense. The general rule is to read the compound from the back. First, consider all but the last component word as one compound word to be construed with the last word; then repeat the process with the compound consisting of all elements but the last, and so on. The only real difficulty comes in dertermining how large each last component word should be. In some cases, it is necessary to make the last component word a compound itself. For example, the compound sarvabhūmirājarājakīrticchāyā should be analyzed as follows: 1. sarvabhūmirājarājakīrti and chāyā, a genitive tatpuruṣa meaning "The shadow of the all-earth-king-king-glory." 2. sarvabhūmirājarāja and kīrti, a genitive tatpuruṣa meaning "The glory of the all-earth-king-king." 3. rajā and rāja, a genitive tatpuruṣa meaning "the king of kings." 4. sarvabhūmi and rājarāja, a genitive tatpuruṣa meaning "the king of kings of all-earth." 5. sarva and bhūmi, a karmadhāraya meaning "all the earth." The final meaning of the compound is "The shadow of the glory of the king of kings of all the earth." If the compound were interpreted as a bahuvrīhi rather than a tatpuruṣa, the meaning would be "whose shadow is the glory of the king of kings of all the earth." Of course when you actually encounter a compound such as the above, you need not go through such a long process to determine its meaning. It is generally possible simply to go from the back of the compound to the front and read it off. There are often several possible versions of a compound. In such cases, the version which best accords with common sense is the correct one. Another rule to be observed is that where elements within a long compound may reasonably be interpreted as dvandvas, it is generally best to do so.

VOCABULARY:

अ-, अन्-	In bahuvrīhis, this prefix means "without" "-less." In karmadhārayas, it means "un-". It has the form a- before consonants, an- before vowels. See lesson.
जीवितम्	life
दु:खम्	sorrow, pain
दुस्-	In bahuvrīhi: "having bad A," "having difficult A." See lesson. * In karmadhāraya: bad, hard.
निस्-	in bahuvrīhi: without, devoid of, lacking in. See lesson.*
स-, सह-	with, accompanied by (see lesson); a prefix
सु-	in bahuvrīhi: "having good A," "having easy A"; in karmadhāraya: easy, very good
सुखम्	happiness, well-being, comfort

EXERCISE: read the following compounds first as tatpuruṣas (if possible), then as bahuvrīhis. Note that endings are not given, so as not to prejudice the interpretation one way or another.

मघुवाक्	वीरमित्र	सगजाश्वनगर
पुष्पतीर	धर्मपत्नीक	रत्नधन
जलहस्त	कथाकीर्ति	सूर्यमित्रनामन्

*nis and dus follow the normal saṃdhi rules when prefixed to words, except that before k, kh, p, and ph, their final s becomes ṣ.

विषहस्त	अतिथिकीर्ति	पित्राचार्य
अधर्म	नदीमातृक	शत्रुकोप
दुष्कीर्ति	सूर्यचक्षुस्	शूद्राचार्य

TRANSLATE into English;

धनुर्हस्तो वीरो राजसकाशमागच्छन्निर्दुःखो भवेत्यवदच्च ॥१॥ ये मनुष्या अपुत्रास्तेषां जीवितं दुःखमेव ॥२॥ यस्मात्त्वद्राज्येऽधर्म एव वर्धते तस्मात्तन्निर्ब्राह्मणमिति ब्राह्मणोऽवदत् ॥३॥[1] कदा लोकोऽयं निर्युद्धो भवेदित्यमन्यत स वीरः ॥४॥ अयं लोकः सराज्यनगरग्रामो ममैव भवत्वित्यवदद्राजा ॥५॥ यद्यसूर्यो भवेदयं लोको यद्यप्यब्राह्मणो भवेल्लोको यद्यपि वा निर्जला भवेद्भूमिस्तथापि त्वमेवास्य लोकस्य राजेत्यपठत्कविः ॥६॥ सपुष्पवृक्षोद्यानेष्वक्रीडत्सभ्रातृपत्नीको राजराजनामा नृपः ॥७॥ न कुत्रापि निरग्निब्राह्मणगृहं मम राज्ये भवेदित्यमन्यत राजा ॥८॥[2] निर्धूममग्निमपश्यच्छिष्यः किमेतदित्यमन्यत च ॥९॥ स वीरो राजमित्रः ॥१०॥ स वीरो राजमित्रम् ॥११॥

Notes on translation:

[1]yasmāt/tasmāt: since/therefore

[2]agni in this sentence means the sacred fires which brāhmaṇas are supposed to keep.

TRANSLATE into Sanskrit, putting italicized phrases into compound: 1. The king *whose name was Harṣa* became *without enemies*. 2. Even though the Śūdra reads the Veda *in my presence*, I do not say that he is a Brāhmaṇa, said the king. 3. When the king became *without enemies*, then with happiness (sukha) even the *subjects of other kingdoms* praised him. 4. The teacher came *book in hand* and read the *story of the crows and horses*. 5. "May this world be *without Kṣatriyas*," thought Paraśurāma. 6. *In the shadows of the flowery* (*with-flower*) *trees*, the poets sat and read *stories of former times* (former is pūrva).

VERSES:

एकोऽहमसहायोऽहं कृशोऽहमपरिच्छदः ।
स्वप्नेऽप्येवंविधा चिन्ता मृगेन्द्रस्य न जायते ॥

सहाय	ally
कृश	thin
परिच्छद	garments, clothes; also, retinue
स्वप्नम्	sleep
एवंविध	of such a sort

चिन्ता	worry, anxiety
इन्द्र	king (The lion is the king of beasts in India as in the West)

राजा बन्धुरबन्धूनां राजा चक्षुरचक्षुषाम् ।
राजा पिता च माता च सर्वेषां न्यायवर्तिनाम् ॥

बन्धु friend, relative चक्षुस् eye
न्यायवर्तिन् (gen. pl. न्यायवर्तिनाम्) those who abide by the proper way

अयं निजः परो वेति गणना लघुचेतसाम् ।
उदारचरितानां तु वसुधैव कुटुम्बकम् ॥

निज	one's own, belonging to one
पर	belonging to someone else, alien
गणना	consideration
लघु	light, stupid, frivolous
चेतस्	mind
उदार	generous, noble
चरितम्	conduct
वसुधा	earth
कुटुम्बकम्	family

Lesson 19

ATHEMATIC VERBS, CLASS 2

In lesson 1, you learned to make the present stem of the various classes of thematic verbs, namely classes 1, 4, 6, and 10. In the next three lessons, athematic verbs will be treated—that is, those verbs which do not insert the thematic vowel -a- before the endings. These verbs are a bit complicated, and you need not memorize their forms. But you should learn the principles behind their formation and be able to identify any forms which may occur. In the following lessons, the present system is treated, that is, the present, imperfect, optative, and imperative. The principles concerning their formation which you should learn actively are italicized.

In all athematic classes, the following forms are strong: 1. *the 1st, 2nd, and 3rd persons singular active in the present;* 2. *the 1st, 2nd, and 3rd persons singular active in the imperfect; and* 3. *the 3rd person active singular imperative* [as well as all the 1st person imperative persons, active and middle—these are quite rare]. *All other forms are weak,* including all middle forms [except for 1st-person middle imperatives].

In class 2, the endings are added directly to the root of the verb, which is guṇated (if capable of it) in the strong forms. In the following paradigms, pay particular attention to the singular and plural (the dual forms are not used very often). Below are the paradigms of i, go, an active verb, and ās, sit, a middle verb.

Active Present:

	Singular	Dual	Plural
1st person	emi	ivaḥ	imaḥ

2nd person	eṣi	ithaḥ	itha
3rd person	eti	itaḥ	yānti

Note here the 3rd plural, where the initial i- becomes the semivowel y- before the vowel beginning the ending -anti.

Middle Present:

1st person	āse	āsvahe	āsmahe
2nd person	āsse	āsāthe	āddhve
3rd person	āste	āsāte	āsate

In the imperfect, the augment is used as for thematic verbs. Since many athematic verbs begin with a vowel, it is important that you know the following rule: *the augment a- added to the initial vowels i-, u- and ṛ- coalesces to make the vṛddhi (not the guṇa) of the second element, that is, ai-, au-, and ār-. The rule applies to both thematic and athematic verbs.* That is why the dual and plural of i in the imperfect look strong.

Imperfect Active:

	Singular	Dual	Plural
1st person	āyam	aiva	aima
2nd person	aiḥ	aitam	aita
3rd person	ait	aitām	āyan

Imperfect middle:

1st person	āsi	āsvahi	āsmahi
2nd person	āsthāḥ	āsāthām	āddhvam
3rd person	āsta	āsātām	āsata

For roots ending in a consonant, the imperfect 2nd and 3rd singular active is rather strange. For the word dviṣ, to hate, for example, the paradigm in the imperfect active is:

1st person	adveṣam	adviṣva	adviṣma
2nd person	adveṭ	adviṣṭam	adviṣṭa
3rd person	adveṭ	adviṣṭām	adviṣan

Here, the form in the 2nd and 3rd sg. is adveṣ plus -s and -t. Since a double consonant cannot stand alone at the end of a word, the last consonant is dropped, and the -ṣ reverts to -ṭ, as with the noun stems (see page 47). The list of consonant changes given on page 32 applies to verbs as well as nouns, as you will note in many athematic forms where an ending beginning in a consonant is added to a stem ending in a consonant.

. *The optative takes the sign -yā- in the active and -ī- in the middle in all athematic verbs.* All forms are weak. Note that the -ā- of -yā- disappears before vowels (i.e. before the -uḥ of the opt. active plural 3rd person).

Optative active:

	Singular	Dual	Plural
1st person	iyām	iyāva	iyāma
2nd person	iyāḥ	iyātam	iyāta
3rd person	iyāt	iyātām	iyuḥ
Optative middle:			
1st person	āsīya	āsīvahi	āsīmahi
2nd person	āsīthāḥ	āsīyāthām	āsīdhvam
3rd person	āsīta	āsīyātām	āsīran

In the imperative, all of the first person forms, both active and middle are strong, and the 3rd singular active is strong. The first persons are extremely rare. *The active second person singular ending (which is very common) is -hi if the root ends in a vowel and -dhi if it ends in a consonant for all athematic classes,* except classes 5 and 8 (which have -nu and -u), and stems of class 9 ending in a consonant (which have -āna). The only forms commonly encountered are the 2nd and 3rd person singular and plural:

Imperative active:

1st person	ayāni	ayāva	ayāma
2nd person	ihi	itam	ita
3rd person	etu	itām	yantu
Imperative middle:			
1st person	āsai	āsāvahai	āsāmahai
2nd person	āssva	āsāthām	āddhvam
3rd person	āstām	āsātām	āsatām

Note that the 2nd singular active imperative of duh, to milk, is dugdhi (-h changes to -k before a consonant—see page 32).

An especially important root belonging to this class is as, to be. Its strong forms begin with as-, while its weak forms begin with s-. Thus the present (it is an active verb):

	Singular	Dual	Plural
1st person	asmi	svaḥ	smaḥ
2nd person	asi	sthaḥ	stha
3rd person	asti	staḥ	santi

The imperfect of as has irregular forms in the 2nd and 3rd person sg., where the vowel -ī- is interposed before the endings (lest the form be āḥ):

1st person	āsam	āsva	āsma
2nd person	āsīḥ	āstam	āsta
3rd person	āsīt	āstām	āsan

Optative:

1st person	syām	syāva	syāma
2nd person	syāḥ	syātam	syāta
3rd person	syāt	syātām	syuḥ

Imperative (only the 3rd person is given—other forms are almost never encountered):

3rd person	astu	stām	santu

Note the present and imperfect of han, slay or strike, an active verb:

Present:

1st person	hanmi	hanvaḥ	hanmaḥ
2nd person	haṃsi	hathaḥ	hatha
3rd person	hanti	hataḥ	ghnanti

Imperfect:

1st person	ahanam	ahanva	ahanma
2nd person	ahan	ahatam	ahata
3rd person	ahan	ahatām	aghnan

VOCABULARY:

अस् (अस्ति)	to be
आस् (आस्ते)	sit; rest; dwell; continue or be in any state

इ (एति)	go
ए (ऐति)	come (from ā and i)
कस्मात्	why
किंतु	however
बन्धु	friend; relative
मार्ग	road, way, path
हन् (हन्ति)	kill, slay, strike

TRANSLATE into English:

अहं राजास्मि त्वं च मम बन्धुरसि । तस्माद्यो युद्धे त्वां हन्यात्स मामपि राजानं हन्तीत्यवदद्राजा ॥१॥ ये ब्राह्मणमित्रास्तान्राज्ञो न कोऽपि हन्यादित्यवदद्ब्राह्मणः ॥२॥ मम सकाशादिहि। यानि तव मित्राणीदानीं मृगमघ्नंस्तान्यत्रानयेति कोपेनावददृषिः ॥३॥ न धर्मं हन्तु मनुष्यः । यद्यपि पितरं हन्यान्मातरं वा न धर्मं हन्त्विति परशुरामो*ऽमन्यत ॥४॥ अस्मिन्राज्य आसीद्राजा कदा चित्स च सहवीरोऽरीनहन्युद्धे सदा कविभ्यो धनमयच्छच्चेत्यवदन्कवयः ॥५॥ अनेन मार्गेणायंस्ते देवा धर्मारीन्हन्म इत्यवदंश्च ॥६॥ अमार्गे वनेऽतिष्ठत्स कुत्रेदानी-मेमीत्यमन्यत च ॥७॥ स गजमुखो देवोऽत्रैद्ये मां सेवन्ते तेभ्योऽहं कीर्ति यच्छामीत्यवदच्च ॥८॥ यदाहं गृह आसं त्वं कुत्रासीरित्यपृच्छत्सभयां पत्नीं वीरः ॥९॥ आस्त स राजारिसकाशे यूयं कस्मादत्रैतेत्यपृच्छच्च ॥१०॥ मन्नगरे वनगजा आयन्तु क्रीडन्तु च वापीतीरे आसतां चेत्यवदद्राजा ॥११॥ ये स्वर्गलोक-मियुस्ते न किमपि हन्युः ॥१२॥

TRANSLATE into Sanskrit, putting the italicized phrases into compounds. 1. If I could be anyone at all (yaḥ ko 'pi), then I would be a king of the world with cities, villages, and kingdom. 2. The king killed the elephant in battle and then said, "Now whom may I kill ?" (Use optative for May I kill). 3. *They who have poets as friends* only sit in the presence of the king. 4. *The occean army* came and killed all who would offend (han) dharma. (Use e for came). 5. Come, sit there, and tell me what the *enemy king* said. (Use e for come, ās for sit. Translate " 'What...said' iti say.") 6. The man who came (e) to the presence of the god *named Śiva* said, "For your sake we will kill even our sons."

---

*A proper noun.

VERSES:

पदे पदे च रत्नानि योजने रसकूपिका ।
भाग्यहीना न पश्यन्ति बहुरत्ना वसुन्धरा ।।

पदम्	footstep. Repetition gives the sense of "every"
योजनम्	a yojana, about 7 miles
रस	taste. Here, good taste
कूपिका	a well
भाग्यम्	good fortune
हीन	devoid of
वसुन्धरा	earth

क्षणे क्षणे यन्नवतामुपैति तदेव रूपं रमणीयतायाः ।

क्षणम्	moment. Repetition gives the sense of "every"
नवता	newness
उपे (उपैति)	go. "Go to A-ness" means "to become A." From upa and i.
रूपम्	form
रमणीयता	loveliness; beauty

नास्ति कामसमो व्याधिर्नास्ति मोहसमो रिपुः ।
नास्ति क्रोधसमो वह्निर्नास्ति ज्ञानात्परं सुखम् ।।

काम	desire; lust
सम	equal (to)
व्याधि	disease
मोह	delusion
रिपु	enemy
क्रोध	anger
वह्नि	fire
ज्ञानम्	knowledge
पर	other (than)—plus the ablative

अतिरमणीये काव्ये पिशुनोऽन्वेषयति दूषणान्येव ।
अतिरमणीये वपुषि व्रणमेव हि मक्षिकानिकरः ।।

अति	very
रमणीय	beautiful; lovely
काव्यम्	a kāvyam, a long poem in an Indian language
पिशुन	low, contemptible. Here: a contemptible person

अन्वेष् (अन्वेषयति)	search out
दूषणम्	fault
वपुस्	form. Here: a woman's form
व्रणम्	wound
मक्षिका	a fly
निकर	treasure; also sap, pith

राजा पश्यति कर्णाभ्यां युक्त्या पश्यन्ति पण्डिताः ।
पशुः पश्यति गन्धेन भूतैः पश्यन्ति बर्बराः ॥

कर्ण	ear
युक्ति	stratagem, plan, scheme
पण्डित	wise person, clever person
पशु	cow
गन्धम्	scent
भूतम्	demon
बर्बर	barbarian, non-Aryan

Lesson 20

ATHEMATIC VERBS, CLASSES 5, 7, 8, AND 9

In classical Sanskrit, there are not many verbs which adhere to these classes, but those which do are fairly common. Learn to make the strong and weak form of each stem. Then you should have no trouble recognizing any forms you encounter.

I. Class 7. This class takes a nasal infix for both strong and weak forms. In the strong, the infix is -na-, while in the weak forms it is -n-. The infix is placed directly before the last consonant of the root. Thus for yuj, join, the strong form is yunaj-, the weak form is yuñj-. For rudh, obstruct, the strong form is ruṇadh-, and the weak form is rundh-

II. Classes 5 and 8. In class 5, -no- is added after the root to make the strong form, -nu- is added after the root to make the weak form. Thus the strong form of su, to press out, is suno-, while the weak form is sunu-. In class 8, -o- and -u- are added to the root to form the strong and weak forms respectively. Since all of the roots in this class (with the exception of kṛ, to do, given below) end in -n-, the forms actually look like those of class 5. Thus the root tan, stretch, makes the strong tano- and the weak tanu-. Note that the root śru, which belongs to class 5, makes the strong śṛṇo- and the weak śṛṇu (i.e. it makes its strong and weak forms from śṛ rather than śru). These classes take their imperative 2nd active sg. in -nu and -u.

III. Class 9. This class adds -nā- to make the strong forms, -nī- to make the weak forms. But the -ī- of -nī- disappears before endings beginning with a vowel. Thus krī, buy, makes strong krīṇā-, weak krīṇī-. Verbs of this class ending in a consonant take the 2nd imperative active sg. in -āna.

IV. The root kṛ. This very common root, which belongs to class 8, and means "to make," "to do" has the strong stem karo- and the weak stem kuru-. The final -u- of the weak stem is dropped before the initial -v- and -m- of the first dual and plural endings, and before the -yā- of the optative active.

In the following examples, the same verb is used to cite both active and middle forms, even though in classical Sanskrit most verbs may take only one set of endings. Note that as with consonant stems, -j becomes -k before endings beginning with a consonant. N becomes ñ before j, ṅ before k.

CLASS 7.

Present:	Active			Middle	
Singular	Dual	Plural	Singular	Dual	Plural
yunajmi	yuñjvaḥ	yuñjmaḥ	yuñje	yuñjvahe	yuñjmahe
yunakṣi	yuṅkthaḥ	yuṅktha	yuṅkṣe	yuñjāthe	yuṅgdhve
yunakti	yuṅktaḥ	yuñjanti	yuñkte	yuñjāte	yuñjate
Imperfect:					
ayunajam	ayuñjva	ayuñjma	ayuñji	ayuñjvahi	ayuñjmahi
ayunak	ayuṅktam	ayuṅkta	ayuṅkthāḥ	ayuñjāthām	ayuṅgdhvam
ayunak	ayuṅktām	ayuñjan	ayuṅkta	ayuñjātām	ayuñjata
Optative:					
yuñjyām	yuñjyāva	yuñjyāma	yuñjīya	yuñjīvahi	yuñjīmahi
etc. (see page 79)					
Imperative:					
yunajāni	yunajāva	yunajāma	yunajai	yunajāvahai	yunajāmahai
yuṅgdhi	yuṅktam	yuṅkta	yuṅkṣva	yuñjāthām	yuṅgdhvam
yunaktu	yuṅktām	yuñjantu	yuṅktām	yuñjātām	yuñjatām

CLASSES 5 and 8. In the present, imperfect, and imperative active 3rd pl., āp takes different forms than śru because it ends in a consonant.

Present:

śṛṇomi	śṛṇuvaḥ	śṛṇumaḥ	śṛṇve	śṛṇuvahe	śṛṇumahe
śṛṇoṣi	śṛṇuthaḥ	śṛṇutha	śṛṇuṣe	śṛṇvāthe	śṛṇudhve
śṛṇoti	śṛṇutaḥ	śṛṇvanti (āpnuvanti)	śṛṇute	śṛṇvāte	śṛṇvate

Imperfect:

aśṛṇavam	aśṛṇuva	aśṛṇuma	aśṛṇvi	aśṛṇuvahi	aśṛṇumahi
aśṛṇoḥ	aśṛṇutam	aśṛṇuta	aśṛṇuthāḥ	aśṛṇvāthām	aśṛṇudhvam
aśṛṇot	aśṛṇutām	aśṛṇvan (āpnuvan)	aśṛṇuta	aśṛṇvātām	aśṛṇvata

Optative:

śṛṇuyām	śṛṇuyāva	śṛṇuyāma	śṛṇvīya	śṛṇvīvahi	śṛṇvīmahi

etc. (see page 79)

Imperative:

śṛṇavāni	śṛṇavāva	śṛṇavāma	śṛṇavai	śṛṇavāvahai	śṛṇavāmahai
śṛṇu	śṛṇutam	śṛṇuta	śṛṇuṣva	śṛṇvāthām	śṛṇudhvam
śṛṇotu	śṛṇutām	śṛṇvantu (āpnuvantu)	śṛṇutām	śṛṇvātām	śṛṇvatām

CLASS 9:

Present:

krīṇāmi	krīṇīvaḥ	krīṇīmaḥ	krīṇe	krīṇīvahe	krīṇīmahe

krīṇāsi	krīṇīthaḥ	krīṇītha	krīṇīṣe	krīṇāthe	krīṇīdhve
krīṇāti	krīṇītaḥ	krīṇanti	krīṇīte	krīṇāte	kriṇate

Imperfect:

akrīṇām	akrīṇīva	akrīṇīma	akrīṇi	akrīṇīvahi	akrīṇīmahi
akrīṇāḥ	akrīṇītam	akrīṇīta	akrīṇīthāḥ	akrīṇāthām	akrīṇīdhvam
akrīṇāt	akrīṇītām	akrīṇan	akrīṇīta	akrīṇātām	akrīṇata

Optative:

krīṇīyām	krīṇīyāva	krīṇīyāma	krīṇīya	krīṇīvahi	krīṇīmahi

etc. (see page 79)

Imperative:

krīṇāni	krīṇāva	krīṇāma	krīṇai	krīṇāvahai	krīṇāmahai
krīṇīhi	krīṇītam	krīṇīta	krīṇīṣva	krīṇāthām	krīṇīdhvam
krīṇātu	krīṇītām	krīṇantu	krīṇītām	krīṇātām	krīṇatām

Conjugation of kṛ: (Strong stem karo-, weak stem kuru-. Kuru- loses final -u- before -v, -y, and -m, i.e. before semivowels and nasals).

karomi	kurvaḥ	kurmaḥ	kurve	kurvahe	kurmahe
karoṣi	kuruthaḥ	kurutha	kuruṣe	kurvāthe	kurudhve
karoti	kurutaḥ	kurvanti	kurute	kurvāte	kurvate

Imperfect:

akaravam	akurva	akurma	akurvi	akurvahi	akurmahi
akaroḥ	akurutam	akuruta	akuruthāḥ	akurvāthām	akurudhvam
akarot	akurutām	akurvan	akuruta	akurvātām	akurvata

Optative:

kuryām	kuryāva	kuryāma	kurvīya	kurvīvahi	kurvīmahi

etc. (see page 79)

Imperative:

karavāṇi	karavāva	karavāma	karavai	karavāvahai	karavāmahai
kuru	kurutam	kuruta	kuruṣva	kurvāthām	kurudhvam
karotu	kurutām	kurvantu	kurutām	kurvātām	kurvatām

Special note on the imperative of class 9 verbs. Roots of this class ending in a vowel take the ending -hi, *but* roots of this class ending in a consonant take the 2nd sg. active ending -āna. Thus the root grah, grasp, with the strong form gṛhṇā- and the weak form gṛhṇī- makes the 2nd sg. active imperative gṛhāṇa.

VOCABULARY:

आप् (आप्नोति)	obtain (class 5)
कृ (करोति)	do, make (class 8)
क्री (क्रीणाति)	buy (class 9)
ग्रह् (गृह्णाति)	grasp, hold, seize (class 9)
त्यज् (त्यजति)	abandon
विक्री (विक्रीणाति)	sell (class 9)
श्रु (शृणोति)	hear (class 5)

TRANSLATE into English:

यः स्वर्गमाप्नुयात्स कथमासीत किं वदेत्किं कुर्याच्च ॥१॥ यो वणिगन्यराज्ये पुस्तकान्यक्रीणात्स इदानीं तान्येव पुस्तकान्यस्मद्राज्ये विक्रीणाति ॥२॥ यस्मादेव त्वं मम बन्धुरसि तस्मादेवैतन्मधु तुभ्यं विक्रीणामि ॥३॥ य आचार्यवाचः शृण्वन्ति ते सदास्मिँल्लोके सुखमेवाप्नुवन्ति ॥४॥ ये युद्धवीरा धनुर्हस्ता मत्सकाशमधावंस्तैः सह युद्धमकरवं तानजयं चेत्यवदद्वीरः ॥५॥ तव गृहं विक्रीणीहि मया सह वनमेहि चेति राजानमृषिरवदत् ॥६॥ इदं पुस्तकं गृहाणेत्यवदच्छिष्यमाचार्यः ॥७॥ सूर्यो मां दहतु मम शत्रवः सर्वे मद्धनं गृह्णन्त्वन्यराजा अत्रासताम्। अहमिदं राज्यं न त्यजामीति राजावदत् ॥८॥ यदा तस्मिन्नगर आसं तदा त्वद्राज्यं सेनामानयेत्तन्नगरराज इत्यशृणवम् ॥९॥ या युद्धकाले पुष्पाणि व्यक्रीणात्तया सह गिरिनद्यामक्रीडद्वणिक् ॥१०॥ न शूद्रः कोऽपि मद्वाचः शृणोत्वित्यवदद्ब्राह्मणः ॥११॥ अयं लोको ब्राह्मणमुखो राजचक्षुश्चेत्यवददृषिः ॥१२॥

TRANSLATE into Sanskrit, rendering the italicized phrases into compounds. Use āp for attain and i for go. 1. Those who would do adharma attain only misfortune in this world. 2. Many friends heard the *words of the teacher*. 3. In our *lives of sorrow*, no one attains the happiness of paradise. 4. The king, well-disposed, did not kill his enemies. (well-disposed: sumanas) 5. "Grasp your bow and go into battle," said the king to the warrior. 6. The merchant bought the *horses, elephants, and chariots in our city* and sold them *in the city of the enemy king.*

VERSES:

यदैव भर्ता जानीयान्मन्त्रमूलपरां स्त्रियम् ।
उद्विजेत तदैवास्याः सर्पाद्वेश्मगतादिव ।

भर्तृ	husband
ज्ञा (जानति)	know (class 9; weak stem: jānī-). Here, learn, realize
मन्त्रम्	magic spell
मूल	root (used for working magic)
पर	(at end of compound) intent on, engaged in using
स्त्री	woman (acc. sg. striyam)
उद्विज (उद्विजते)	be afraid of (plus the ablative of the thing feared)
सर्प	snake
वेश्मन्	house
गत	situated in

मद्यपाः किं न जल्पन्ति किं न भक्षन्ति वायसाः ।
कवयः किं न पश्यन्ति किं न कुर्वन्ति योषितः ॥

मद्यप	liquor-drinker
जल्प् (जल्पति)	say
भक्ष् (भक्षति)	eat
वायस	crow
योषित्	woman

न यस्य चेष्टितं विद्यान्न कुलं न पराक्रमम् ।
न तस्य विश्वसेत्प्राज्ञो यदीच्छेच्छ्रेय आत्मनः ॥

चेष्टितम्	conduct; actions
विद् (वेत्ति)	know (weak stem vid-; class 2)
कुल	family, family background
पराक्रम	valor, enterprise, bravery

विश्वस् (विश्वसति)	have confidence in (here, with genitive of object of confidence)
प्राज्ञ	wise, wise person
इष् (इच्छति)	wish, desire
श्रेयस्	best, what is best, welfare (a neuter noun in -as)

Lesson 21

ATHEMATIC VERBS, CLASS 3; REDUPLICATION

I. Rules for reduplication. For those tenses of class 3 verbs formed on the present stem (the present, imperfect, etc.), and for the perfect, which you will learn later, the verbal root undergoes reduplication. There are a few other forms which undergo reduplication (the desiderative and intensative), for which the rules will be given later. Reduplication consists of repeating the root twice before adding the appropriate endings. However, the final consonant (if there is one) is omitted from the reduplicating syllable (i.e. the first syllable), and there are some rules governing changes which the root must undergo in the reduplicating syllable. In the second syllable, the root appears unchanged.

a. The consonant of the reduplicating syllable is in general the first consonant of the root. Thus paprach from prach; śiśri from śri; bubudh from budh.

b. A non-aspirate is substituted in reduplication for an aspirate. Thus dadhā from dhā; bibhṛ from bhṛ.

c. A palatal is substituted for a guttural or h. The palatal is either voiced or unvoiced as the letter it substitutes is voiced or unvoiced (remember that h is considered to be voiced in Sanskrit). Thus cakṛ from kṛ; cikhid from khid; jagrabh from grabh; jahṛ from hṛ.

d. If the root begins with a sibilant followed by a non-nasal stop (not a semivowel), then the consonant of the reduplicating syllable is the stop, modified according to rules b and c if necessary. Thus tasthā from sthā; caskand from skand; caskhal from skhal; cuścut from ścut; paspṛdh from spṛdh; pusphuṭ from sphuṭ. But if the root begins with a sibilant followed by a nasal or semivowel, then rule a applies. Thus sasnā from snā; sasmṛ from smṛ; śuśru from śru; śiśliṣ from śliṣ.

e. A long vowel is shortened in the reduplicating syllable. Thus dadā from dā; bibhī from bhī.

f. The vowel ṛ does not appear in the reduplicating syllable. Rather, it is replaced by -i- in the present system of reduplicating (class 3) verbs; and by -a- in the perfect of verbs. Thus class 3 present stems bibhṛ from bhṛ, pipṛc from pṛc. Perfect cakṛ from kṛ, cakṛṣ from kṛṣ.

II. The third class. The strong forms of this class have a guṇated root vowel (in the 2nd syllable of the reduplicated form), while the weak forms have a vowel without guṇa. Thus strong juho-, weak juhu- from hu, sacrifice. The root bhṛ, bear, makes the strong stem-form bibhar-, the weak bibhṛ.

(*contd. on pp.* 94, 95)

VOCABULARY:

ज्ञा (जानाति)	know (class 9. Strong jān..-, weak jānī-)
दा (ददाति)	give (class 3. Much more common than yam)
ब्रू (ब्रवीति)	say (class 2. Strong bravī-; weak brū-. 3rd pl. bruvanti, abruvan, bruvantu)
भृ (बिभर्ति)	bear, have, possess (class 3)
विधा (विदधाति or विधत्ते)	ordain; bring about, accomplish (class 3, from vi and dhā. This verb may be active or middle)
हा (जहाति)	leave, forsake, abandon (class 3. Strong jahā-; weak jahī- or jah- before vowel)

TRANSLATE into English:

राजकोपात्सर्वे क्षत्रियाः सपत्नीका नगरमजहुः ॥१॥ येभ्यो वीरेभ्यस्त्वं गजानश्वांश्च नाददास्ते कथं युद्धं कुर्युः ॥२॥ मां जहीहि । न हि कदापि मच्छत्रवो मत्सकाश आसीरन् ॥३॥ यज्जलं असौ कन्या हस्तयोरबिभस्तद्भूमावपतत् ॥४॥ यदा स नृपोऽस्मत्सेनामजयत्तदा तव नगरं तव धनानि सर्वाणि च देहि म इत्यब्रवीदस्मद्राजानम् ॥५॥ स ब्राह्मणः सर्वदेवनामानि न जानाति किं तु जानन्तीमे वणिजः ॥६॥ यद्यद्विदधाति देवस्तत्तन्मनुष्याणां लोके भवति ॥७॥ सर्वे मत्प्रजा रत्नानि मे ददत्विति व्यधत्त राजा ॥८॥ ये मद्राज्ये सुखजीवितमाप्नुयुस्ते यद्यदशृण्वन्यद्यद्वा जानन्ति तत्सर्वं मम वीरान्ब्रुवन्तु ॥९॥ ब्रूहि राजन् । किं कुर्यावावामित्यब्रूतां क्षत्रियौ ॥१०॥ स्वर्गे सदा वृक्षाः पुष्पफलानि बिभ्रतीत्य-

(*contd. on p.* 96)

The verbs of this third class lack the -n- in the 3rd plural endings of the present, and the imperative active. In the imperfect active 3rd plural, they take the ending -uḥ instead of -an, before which the final vowel is guṇated.* The conjugations of the root bhṛ, to bear, are given below:

	Active			Middle	
singular	dual	plural	singular	dual	plural
Present:					
bibharmi	bibhṛvaḥ	bibhṛmaḥ	bibhre	bibhṛvahe	bibhṛmahe
bibharṣi	bibhṛthaḥ	bibhṛtha	bibhṛṣe	bibhrāthe	bibhṛdhve
bibharti	bibhṛtaḥ	bibhrati	bibhṛte	bibhrāte	bibhrate
Imperfect:					
abibharam	abibhṛva	abibhṛma	abibhri	abibhṛvahi	abibhṛmahi
abibhar	abibhṛtam	abibhṛta	abibhṛthāḥ	abibhrāthām	abibhṛdhvam
abibhar	abibhṛtām	abibharuḥ	abibhṛta	abibhrātām	abibhrata
Optative:					
bibhṛyām	bibhṛyāva	bibhṛyāma	bibhrīya	bibhrīvahi	bibhrīmahi
etc. (see page 79)					
Imperative (Note the irregular 2nd imperative sg. active of this verb, which should, according to p. 79, be -hi. This is an irregularity of bhṛ, not of the class)					
bibharāṇi	bibharāva	bibharāma	bibharvai	bibharāvahai	bibharāmahai
bibhṛdhi	bibhṛtam	bibhṛta	bibhṛṣva	bibhrāthām	bibhṛdhvam
bibhartu	bibhṛtām	bibhratu	bibhṛtām	bibhrātām	bibhratām

*Note that all of the athematic classes lack -n- in the third person plural middle present, imperfect, and imperative.

The two roots dā and dhā, the commonest of the class, lose their radical vowel altogether in the weak forms, being shortened to dad and dadh. In the 2nd sg. imperative active, they form respectively dehi and dhehi. In combination with t, th, and s, the final d of dad and dh of dadh change to t. Before t, th, dh, and s, the aspiration of dadh is thrown back on the first syllable (see page 32 under Grassmann's law). The inflection of dhā, to place, follows:

Present:					
dadhāmi	dadhvaḥ	dadhmaḥ	dadhe	dadhvahe	dadhmahe
dadhāsi	dhatthaḥ	dhattha	dhatse	dadhāthe	dhaddhve
dadhāti	dhattaḥ	dadhati	dhatte	dadhāte	dadhate
Imperfect:					
adadhām	adadhva	adadhma	adadhi	adadhvahi	adadhmahi
adadhāḥ	adhattam	adhatta	adhatthāḥ	adadhāthām	adhaddhvam
adadhāt	adhattām	adadhuḥ	adhatta	adadhātām	adadhata
Optative:					
dadhyām	dadhyāva	dadhyāma	dadhīya	dadhīvahi	dadhīmahi
etc. (see page 79)					
Imperative:					
dadhāni	dadhāva	dadhāma	dadhai	dadhāvahai	dadhāmahai
dhehi	dhattam	dhatta	dhatsva	dadhāthām	dhaddhvam
dadhātu	dhattām	dadhatu	dhattām	dadhātām	dadhatām

ब्रवीत्कविः ॥११॥ यद्येतत्पुस्तकस्यार्थं जानीयास्तदाचार्यसकाशमिहि तं पृच्छ च ॥१२॥*

TRANSLATE into Sanskrit, using dā for give, brū for say, hā for leave, and āp for attain. Render italicized phrases by compounds. 1. Whatever Śiva may ordain, may that be (bhū). 2. The girl gave the water to her friend and said in fear, "Did anyone see me?" 3. When Rāma left the *city of Ayodhyā*, all the subjects attained sorrow. 4. Do you know the man to whom they gave the books? 5. "Even if you did not know all, I would do that which you have ordained," said the śūdra to the sage. 6. That man and his wife gave the jewels to the merchant in the *treeless, flowerless* garden. (render treeless and flowerless by separate compounds).

VERSES:

यद्ददासि विशिष्टेभ्यो यच्चाश्नासि दिने दिने ।
तत्ते वित्तमहं मन्ये शेषमन्यस्य रक्षसि ॥

विशिष्ट	set apart; distinguished (person)
अश् (अश्नाति)	eat (V)
दिन	day
वित्तम्	wealth
शेषम्	ther est
रक्ष् (रक्षति)	protect, keep charge of

यद्ददाति यदश्नाति तदेव धनिनो धनम् ।
अन्ये मृतस्य क्रीडन्ति दारैरपि धनैरपि ॥

अश् (अश्नाति)	eat
मृत	dead (person)
दार	wife (usually in plural, with singular meaning)

Note: this verse (yaddadāti...) is rather difficult to construe, though I find it a good verse. The key is to take anye as referring to those who do not conform to the model of the first half of the verse, and to take mṛta as meaning "someone who might as well be dead."

---

*The stem form of esa is etat.

सुलभं वस्तु सर्वस्य न यात्यादरणीयताम् ।
स्वदारपरिहारेण परदारार्थिनो जनाः ॥

सुलभ	easy to get
वस्तु	thing
या (याति)	go (II)
आदरणीयता	position of being valued (lit.: to-be-valued-ness. "Go to x-ness" means "to become x.")
स्व	one's own
दार	wife (usually in plural, with singular meaning)
परिहार	rejection, avoidance
पर	other, another (person)
अर्थिन्	desirous of (masc. nom. pl. arthinaḥ)
जन	people (in pl.)

वरमेको गुणी पुत्रो न च मूर्खशतान्यपि ।
एकश्चन्द्रस्तमो हन्ति न च तारागणोऽपि च ॥

वरम्	better
गुणिन	virtuous, excellent (nom. masc. sg. guṇī)
मूर्ख	fool
शतम्	hundred
चन्द्र	moon
तमस्	darkness (neuter)
तारा	star
गण	mass, collection, assemblage

LESSON 22

POSSESSIVES IN -IN, -VANT, -MANT; PRESENT ACTIVE PARTICIPLES

I. Possessives. Sanskrit has several suffixes which are added to nouns to form possessives. When a possessive suffix is added to a noun A, the meaning is "having A," "possessing A," though the best translation is often an English adjective. For example, dhanavant means "having money," but is best translated as "rich," "wealthy " The word could also be used as a noun, in which case it would mean "he who is wealthy," "a rich man," etc.

A. Possessives in -vant, -mant. The suffix -vant may be added to almost any noun to make a possessive. The suffix -mant is of less common occurrence, and is rarely affixed to a-stems (i.e. to words declined like deva, phalam, or senā). Before -mant and -vant, the stem form of the noun is used. The declension of these possessives is as follows:

Masculine:

	Singular	Dual	Plural
Nom.	dhanavān	dhanavantau	dhanavantaḥ
Acc.	dhanavantam	,,	dhanavataḥ
Inst.	dhanavatā	dhanavadbhyām	dhanavadbhiḥ

etc., as with pad.

Neuter:

Nom.	dhanavat	dhanavatī	dhanavanti
Acc.	,,	,,	,,

etc., as with pad.

Feminine:

Nom.	dhanavatī	dhanavatyau	dhanavatyaḥ

etc., as with nadī.

This declension can be easily remembered if you keep in mind that the strong form is in -ant, and the weak form is in -at, while the nom. masc. sg. is -ān, and the feminine is -atī, declined like nadī. Words in -mant are declined in the same way, except that they have -m- instead of -v-.

B. Possessives in -in. Most nouns in -a, -am, or -ā, make a possessive in -in, which is added after the -a, -am, and -ā, have been removed, The declension of sukhin, happy, (from sukha and -in) is as follows:

Masculine:

	Singular	Dual	Plural
Nom.	sukhī	sukhinau	sukhinaḥ
Acc.	sukhinam	,,	sukhinaḥ
Inst.	sukhinā	sukhibhyām	sukhibhiḥ

etc., with endings of pad. Weak endings are added to -in, pāda endings to -i.

Neuter:

Nom.	sukhi	sukhinī	sukhīni
Acc.	,,	,,	,,

etc., as in the masculine.

Feminine:

Nom.	sukhinī	sukhinyau	sukhinyaḥ

etc., as with nadī.

Remember that in this declension, both the strong and weak endings are added to -in, while the pāda endings are added to -i. The nom. mas. sg. is -ī; the nom. acc. neuter singular is -i, and the nom. acc. neuter plural is -īni. The feminine is -inī, declined like nadī.

II. Present active participles. These forms correspond to the English participle in -ing, as the man *going* to the city." Their use is explained below after their formation is discussed.

The present active participle is formed by removing the final -i of the 3rd person plural active present form of thc verb. As would be expected, it is made only from verbs which are active. All present active participles except those from class 3 verbs end in -ant, as is shown below. They are declined exactly like possessives in -vant and -mant, except that their nom. sg.

masculine is in -an rather than -ān. That is, weak endings and pāda endings are added to -at, while strong endings are added to -ant.

Rules for the formation of the feminine of present active participles: The thematic conjugations (classes 1, 4, 6, and 10) add -ī to the strong stem of the participle (i.e. end in -antī), while the athematic conjugations (classes 2, 3, 5, 7, and 9) add -ī to the weak stem of the participle (i.e. end in -atī). [But in class 6, the feminine to the present participle may be made optionally by adding -ī to the weak stem, while in class 2, verbs whose roots end in -ā may optionally make their feminine participle by adding -ī to the strong stem.] These participles are declined like nadī. It should be noted that the nom-acc. dual neuter of pres. act. part. 's is the same as the nom. sg. fem.

Note that participles of class 3 verbs end in -at, and do not differentiate between strong and weak stems (see below for an example of declension).

Study the following forms:

Class	Root	Present act. part.	Feminine
1	bhū	bhavant	bhavantī
1	sthā	tiṣṭhant	tiṣṭhantī
4	paś	paśyant	paśyantī
6	viś	viśant	viśantī [or viśatī]
6	pracch	pṛcchant	pṛcchantī [or pṛcchatī]
10	cur	corayant	corayantī
2	han	ghnant	ghnatī
2	as	sant	satī
2	snā (bathe)	snānt	snātī [or snāntī]
3	dhā	dadhat (N.B.)	dadhatī
3	dā	dadat (N.B.)	dadatī
3	bhṛ	bibhrat (N.B)	bibhratī
5	śru	śṛṇvant	śṛṇvatī
7	yuj	yuñjant	yuñjatī
8	kṛ	kurvant	kurvantī
9	krī	krīṇant	krīṇatī

With the exception of class 3, the present active participle is declined as follows (here, the root vad is used for the example):

Masculine:

	Singular	Dual	Plural
Nom.	vadan	vadantau	vadantaḥ
Acc.	vadantam	,,	vadataḥ
Inst.	vadatā	vadadbhyām	vadadbhiḥ

etc., with the endings of pad added to vadat-.

Neuter:

Nom.	vadat	vadantī*	vadanti
Acc.	,,	,,	,,

etc., with the endings of pad added to vadat-.

Feminine:

Nom.	vadantī	vadantyau	vadantyaḥ

etc., as with nadī.

Class 3 *present active participles.* Present active participles of class 3 end in -at, not -ant. This is so because they are derived from the 3rd active plural present form, which for class 3 verbs ends in -ati, not -anti like the corresponding form of other verbal classes. In this class, both strong and weak forms are in -at-. Thus from dā,

Masculine:

Nom.	dadat	dadatau	dadataḥ
Acc.	dadatam	dadatau	dadataḥ
Inst.	dadatā	dadadbhyām	dadadbhiḥ

etc., with the endings of pad added to dadat-.

Neuter:

Nom.	dadat	dadatī	dadati
Acc.	,,	,,	,,

etc., with the endings of pad added to dadat-.

---

*The -n- in this form is inserted or not depending on whether it is inserted in the feminine form. Thus the dual nom. -acc. neuter of as, an athematic verb, is satī, not santī.

Feminine:

Nom.	dadatī	dadatyau	dadatyaḥ

etc., as with nadī.

III. The Use of Present Participles. The present participle in Sanskrit corresponds to the participle in English ending in -ing (but *not* to the English gerund in -ing, which is used as a noun). All of the words construed with the participle must normally be placed before it in Sanskrit, while its antecedent normally immediately follows it. Thus, "the man running to the city" would be nagaraṃ dhāvan manuṣyaḥ. [In poetry, however, the normal order is not always followed.] Like other adjectives in Sanskrit, participles may also be used as nouns if their antecedent is not expressed. Thus dhāvan could mean "the running [man]."

The present participle is used when contemporaneity of action with the verb is indicated, as "speaking in this manner, he came into the city," that is, "iti bruvan sa nagara āgacchat," or "he gave the jewels to her as she carried the water," that is "jalam bibhratyai tasyai sa ratnāny adadāt." The present participle may also be used to denote an attendant circumstance or attribute, or cause of an action, as "dying in battle, he goes to heaven," that is, "yuddhe naśyan sa svargaṃ gacchati." The present participle may define the agent of an action, as "He is Devadatta who sits studying," that is, "yaḥ paṭhann āste sa devadattaḥ." Or it may be used to define a general truth, as "Men who die in battle go to paradise," that is, "yuddhe naśyanto [manuṣyāḥ] svargaṃ gacchanti." (Here, the word manuṣyāḥ may be either added or left out.) The present participle may not be used as a predicate noun—one may not say "sa kurvann asti" for "He is doing."

The prefix a-(an- before a vowel) may be added to a present participle to negate it. Thus "The king stands without entering battle" is "yuddham aviśan rājā tiṣṭhaty eva."

VOCABULARY:

जीव् (जीवति)	live
पति	lord, husband
भवन्त	you (used like German Sie, Italian Lei, Hindi

	āp, English "your excellency" with a 3rd person verb. Bhavant is declined like dhanavant. Its feminine is bhavatī. It is normally used when the speaker wishes to show respect to the person he is addressing.)
महन्त्	great (Compound stem mahā-. Masc. nom. sg. mahān; strong stem, mahānt-; weak stem mahat-. Fem. mahatī.)
स्नानम्	bathing, a bath
स्नानं कृ	bathe (literally, "make a bath.")

TRANSLATE into English:

पुस्तकं पठतः शिष्यानश्रृणवम् ॥१॥ यस्मिन्वीरे कोपेन दहतो राज्ञश्चक्षुषी अपततां स भयात्तस्य नृपस्य पादावस्पृशत् ॥२॥ साश्वान्पीडयतो वणिजः कोपेनापश्यद्यदि मम पतिरत्र स्यात्तदा भवन्तो न तथा कुर्युरित्यब्रवीच्च ॥३॥ केयमागच्छन्तीति पृच्छन्तीं पत्नीं मम स्वसेत्यवदत्स मनुष्यः ॥४॥ उपविशतु भवान्। इदं जलमिदं भोजनं चेत्यब्रवीदागच्छन्तमतिथिं वणिक् ॥५॥ उद्याने क्रीडन्तीं बालामपश्यद्वीरः किं करोति सेत्यमन्यत च ॥६॥ अयं ब्राह्मणो वेदं पठन्नपि न शूद्रं गच्छेति वदति ॥७॥ केयं जलं हस्ते बिभ्रतीत्यपृच्छद्वणिक् ॥८॥ अयं राजा सर्वं धनं ब्राह्मणेभ्यो ददतपि न कीर्तिं लभते ॥९॥ ये कविभ्योऽन्येभ्यो धनं ददतः शंसन्ति न तेषां कीर्तिर्वर्धत इति कविरब्रवीत् ॥१०॥ कोऽयं वृक्षच्छायायां तिष्ठन्निति पृच्छन्तं राजानं मम भ्रातेत्यवदद्वीरः ॥११॥ यस्य देवस्य नाम पठन्कविरागच्छत्तं वयमपि शंसेम ॥१२॥

TRANSLATE into Sanskrit, putting the italicized words and phrases into participial constructions. 1. The man *taking a bath in the tank* saw the king *coming* and ran to his house. 2. He came from his bath with his wife *as she carried water*. 3. The lives of those who are rich are happy. [Use possessives to translate "those who are rich" and "happy·" Be sure that the predicate adjective is in agreement with the subject.] 4. They *who attain* [*āp*] *glory in this life* are born again in paradise. 5. The wife of the merchant stood *without saying anything*. 6. The king whom the poet stood *praising* did not give any money.

VERSES:

पण्डिते चैव मूर्खे च बलवत्यपि दुर्जने ।
ईश्वरे च दरिद्रे च मृत्योः सर्वत्र तुल्यता ॥

पण्डित	wise, learned; a pundit
मूर्ख	fool
ईश्वर	lord
दरिद्र	poor
तुल्य	equal
-ता	-ness. Tulyatā means "even-handedness."

स्पृशन्नपि गजो हन्ति जिघ्रन्नपि भुजंगमः ।
हसन्नपि नृपो हन्ति मानयन्नपि दुर्जनः ॥

घ्रा (जिघ्रति)	smell
भुजंगम	snake
हस् (हसति)	laugh
मानयति	to honor

LESSON 23

THE PRESENT MIDDLE PARTICIPLE; THE LOCATIVE AND GENITIVE ABSOLUTES

I. Present middle participles. Thematic verbs (classes 1, 4, 6, and 10) make the present middle participle by adding -māna to the 3rd plural present middle minus -nte. Athematic verbs (classes 2, 3, 5, 7, 8, and 9) make it by adding -āna to the 3rd plural present middle minus -ate. These participles are declined like deva in the masculine, phalam in the neuter, and senā in the feminine. They may be made only from verbs which take the middle. Study the follawing list:

Thematic verbs, present middle participle:

	masculine	neuter	feminine
labh	labhamāna	labhamānam	labhamānā
man	manyamāna	manyamānam	manyamānā
vṛt	vartamāna	vartamānam	vartamānā
Athematic verbs, present middle participle:			
vidhā	vidadhāna	vidadhānam	vidadhānā
yuj	yuñjāna	yuñjānam	yuñjānā

Nota bene: the present middle of ās is irregular: āsīna, āsīnam, and āsīnā in the masculine, neuter, and feminine respectively.

The use of the present middle participle is the same as the use of the present active participle, treated in lesson 22. For example, the sentence, "Thinking in this manner, he came into the city" would be translated "iti manyamānaḥ sa nagara āgacchat."

II. The locative absolute and the genitive absolute. When a participle agrees with a subject *different* from the subject of the verb, the phrase is said to be an absolute construction.

An example in English is "The wind being favorable, the ship set sail." In Sanskrit, there are two types of absolute construction: the more common one, in which both the subject of the absolute and the participle, which agree in all respects, are in the locative, and a less common one, in which the subject of the absolute phrase and the participle are in the genitive. In both constructions, *the participle and its subject must agree in case, number, and gender.* It is important to remember that absolute constructions in Sanskrit may not be used if the subject of the absolute phrase and of the main verb are the same (in which case a continuative, given in lesson 27, or a simple participle agreeing with the subject of the main verb must be used). Thus, one may not use the locative absolute to translate the sentence, "Rāma, after he had taken Laṅkā, returned to Ayodhyā" since the subject of "had taken" and "returned" is the same. But in the sentence "Rāma after the monkeys had taken Laṅkā, returned to Ayodhyā," a locative absolute may be used for "after the monkeys had taken Laṅkā," since the subjects of "had taken" and "returned" are different.

The action expressed in the locative absolute specifies the time of the action of the main verb. That is, the time of the action expressed by the locative absolute is known, while the time of the action of the main verb is unknown and is determined with reference to the locative absolute. The English nominative absolute, exemplified above, is also used in this fashion. An example is "Who would conquer the earth while he is king ?" or "He being king, who would conquer the earth ?" In Sanskrit, both of these sentences would be translated "kas tasmin rājñi sati bhūmiṃ jayet?" (where sant is the present active participle of as, to be).

If the English verb in an absolute construction is "being," that verb may be omitted in Sanskrit. Thus "How could he fight when I am king" could be translated by "mayi rājñi sati sa kathaṃ yuddhaṃ kuryāt" or by "mayi rājñi sa kathaṃ yuddhaṃ kuryāt."

When contempt or disregard is to be shown, the genitive absolute is used. Such absolutes may generally be translated by prefacing them by the words "in spite of the fact that" or "even though." An example is "Even though the king was looking, the enemy killed the hero," that is, "paśyato rājñaḥ śatrur vīram ahan." The word api is often placed after a genitive absolute: "rājñaḥ paśyato 'pi śatrur vīram ahan."

When you translate an English phrase into an absolutive construction in Sanskrit, first put the subject of the construction into the locative or genitive, keeping its number and gender. Then make the participle agree with the subject. In general, the participle comes last in the absolutive construction, and is preceded by all that modifies it, though on occasion, the subject of the absolutive construction may immediately follow the participle. In addition to the present active and present middle participles, absolutive constructions may also be made from past passive and past active participles, to be given in lesson 26.

VOCABULARY:

कम्प् (कम्पते)	tremble, shake
मा	not, used with imperatives, as Greek μη, Hindi मत. E.g. mā kuru, "don't do it." The word na cannot be used with imperatives.*
सन्त्	(the present active participle of as) good (in addition to its primary meaning "being")

TRANSLATE into English:

सर्वरत्नानि लभमानोऽपि स वणिग्दुःखमेवाप्नोति ॥१॥ तस्यां मम पत्न्यां सत्यामहं कथमन्यया सह वाप्यां क्रीडेयम् ॥२॥ तस्य कीर्तिमतो राज्ञो धर्मं विदधानस्यापि सर्वाः प्रजा दुःखिन्य एवाभवन् ॥३॥ गच्छन्तस्तिष्ठन्तो भोजनं कुर्वन्त आसीना वा सदा विष्णुनामानं देवं स्मरन्तु धर्मवन्तो मनुष्याः ॥४॥ तस्मिन्राज्ञि धर्मं पीडयति भवान्कथं तत्रैवासीनो न किमपि करोति ॥५॥ भवति राज्ञि वयं कथं जीवेमेति भयात्कम्पमानो वणिगवदत् ॥६॥ मयि स्नानं कुर्वत्यां त्वं कस्मादत्रागच्छ इति ब्रुवाणां** राजपत्नीमहं किं वदेयम् ॥७॥ यद्यपि राजसकाशे-

*The word na, while never used before an imperative, may be used before an optative to form a negative command (which, however, has less force than mā plus the imperative). Mā may also be used before an augmentless aorist to make a negative command, and before a future or optative to mean "lest."

**Brū may be a middle verb as well as an active one.

ऽब्रुवन्स मृत्युमाप्नुयात्तथापि न किमपि वदति स वीरः ॥८॥ मत्सकाशे मा स क्षत्रिय ऐत्वित्यवदच्छूद्रराजः ॥९॥ पतौ मृत्युं लभमाने सा सत्यप्यग्निमविशत् ॥१०॥ मृत्युं विदधानं नृपं शत्रुः कम्पमानः सर्वं वदामीत्यवदत् ॥११॥ धर्मवद्राजराज्ये सन्तः सुखेन जीवन्त्यसन्तस्तु दुःखेनैव ॥१२॥

TRANSLATE into Sanskrit: 1. *While I am king* [locative absolute], no enemy may come into my kingdom. 2. *In spite of the fact that lions play in the forest* [genitive absolute], the sage enters there. 3. "Do not come here," said the good [woman] to the trembling merchant. 4. *Since the king killed dharma* [locative absolute], all good men left [his] kingdom. 5. *When the goddess entered the city* [locative absolute], all [men] trembled from fear. 6. "*Since you [bhavant] ordain dharma* [locative absolute], how could the wealth [artha] of men not grow?" said the poet.

VERSES:

वनानि दहतो वह्नेः सखा भवति मारुतः ।
स एव दीपनाशाय कृशे कस्यास्ति सौहृदम् ॥

वह्नि	fire
सखि	friend (nom. sg. sakhā)
मारुत	wind
दीप	lamp
नाश	destruction; (here) putting out
कृश	thin, wretched, small, poor (the locative gives the sense of "towards")
सौहृदम्	friendliness

स्वभावं नैव मुंचन्ति सन्तः संसर्गतोऽसताम् ।
न त्यजन्ति रुतं मञ्जु काकसंपर्कतः पिकाः ॥

स्वभाव	true nature, innate nature
संसर्ग	contact
-तः	an ablative suffix
रुतम्	calling, cooing
मञ्जु	sweet
संपर्क	contact
पिक	the Indian cuckoo

शून्येऽपि गुणवत्तामातन्वानः स्वकीयगुणजालैः ।
विवराणि मुद्रयन्द्रागूर्णायुरिव सज्जनो जयति ॥

शून्य	empty, void; an empty space
गुणवत्ता	excellence, virtue, goodness (from guṇa, [good] quality, plus -vant, the possessive suffix, plus -tā, a suffix meaning "ness." Thus literally "quality-possessing-ness.")
आतन् (आतन्वीते)	spread out, stretch (3rd pl. present ātanvate)
स्वकीय	one's own
जाल	net, web
विवरम्	hole, open place
मुद्रय् (मुद्रयति)	close, close over
द्राग्	quickly
ऊर्णायु	spider
जन	person

Lesson 24

THE PASSIVE

The passive in Sanskrit is made from a different stem from the finite forms you learned to make in lessons 1, 19, 20, and 21. The passive stem is formed by adding -y- to the root, which in some instances may be altered. *The passive may take only the middle endings* and it may be conjugated in all of the tenses you have studied so far: present, imperfect, optative, and imperative. The passive stem is treated like a thematic verb, that is, it is conjugated like labh. The use of the passive is treated after its formation is discussed.

I. Formation of the passive, In general, the passive is formed by adding -y- to the root and then affixing the endings you learned for labh. Thus from nī, the passive 3rd person singular present is nīyate; from labh, labhyate; from bhū, bhūyate. Some roots, however, are changed before the addition of the -y- of the passive according to the following rules.

1. Final -i and -u of roots are lengthened. Thus from ji, jīyate; from śru srūyate.

2. Roots ending in -ā change the -ā to -ī. [Similarly roots ending in -e, -ai, -o, and -au change those vowels to -ī.] Thus from sthā, dā, dhā, mā (measure), gai (sing), pā, hā, and so (complete), are formed sthīyate, dīyate, dhīyate, mīyate, gīyate, pīyate, hīyate and sīyate.

3. In some roots, y, r, or v is changed to the corresponding vowel i, ṛ, or u. This is called saṃprasāraṇa. When it takes place, the vowel following the y, r, or v in the original root is dropped. The most common roots in which saṃprasāraṇa occurs are: vas/uṣyate; grah/gṛhyate; vac (say)/ucyate; vad/udyate (rare); pracch/pṛcchyate; vah/uhyate; yaj (sacrifice)/

ijyate; and hve (call)/hūyate (here, the u is lengthened by rule 1); vap (sow)/upyate.

4. In some roots, a nasal is dropped. Thus from śaṃs, śasyate.

5. Roots in -ṛ and -ṝ.

a. Roots ending in -ṛ change -ṛ to -ri. Thus kriyate from kṛ. Exception:

Rootsending in -ṛ preceded by a conjunct consonant guṇate the -ṛ. Thus smaryate from smṛ.

b. -ṝ is changed to -īr, or, if preceded by a labial, to -ūr. Thus from tṝ, cross tīryate; from kṝ, scatter, kīryate; from pṝ, fill, pūryate.

6. Roots of the tenth class retain the guṇa or vṛddhi change that they take before the present stem, but the -ay- of the present stem is dropped before the passive is made. Thus from cur (whose present active 3rd sg. is corayati), the passive is coryate. From taḍ, strike (pres. act. 3 sg. tāḍayati) the passive is tāḍyate. [Note that this rule applies to causative stems, which you will learn in a future lesson, as well. Thus the causative active 3rd sg. of kṛ is kārayati; the causative passive of kṛ is kāryate.]

The present participle of passive verbs is formed regularly, by adding -māna to the passive stem. Thus from nī, nīyamāna. There follows a list of the verbs you have had with the passive 3rd sg. present and the present

Root	Present 3rd sg.	Passive pres. 3rd. sg.	Pass. pres. part.
adhī	adhīte	adhīyate	adhīyamāna
as	asti	none	
āp	āpnoti	āpyate	āpyamāna
ās	āste	āsyate	[āsyamāna]
i	eti	none	
kṛ	karoti	kriyate	kriyamāṇa
klp	kalpate	kḷpyate	kḷpyamāna
krī	krīṇāti	krīyate	krīyamāṇa

krīḍ	krīḍati	krīḍyate	[krīḍyamāna]
gam	gacchati	gamyate	gamyamāna
grah	gṛhṇāti	gṛhyate	gṛhyamāṇa
cur	corayati	coryate	coryamāṇa
jan	jāyate	none	
ji	jayati	jīyate	jīyamāna
jīv	jīvati	jīvyate	[jīvyamāna]
jñā	jānāti	jñāyate	jñāyamāna
tyaj	tyajati	tyajyate	tyajyamāna
dah	dahati	dahyate	dahyamāna
dā	dadāti	dīyate	dīyamāna
dhāv	dhāvati	dhāvyate	[dhāvyamāna]
naś	naśyati	naśyate	[naśyamāna]
nī	nayati	nīyate	nīyamāna
paṭh	paṭhati	paṭhyate	paṭhyamāna
paś	paśyati	dṛśyate	dṛśyamāna
pā	pibati	pīyate	pīyamāna
pīḍ	pīḍayati	pīḍyate	pīḍyamāna
pracch	pṛcchati	pṛcchyate	pṛcchyamāna
brū	bravīti	none	
bhū	bhavati	bhūyate	[bhūyamāna]
bhṛ	bibharti	bhriyate	bhriyamāṇa
man	manyate	manyate	manyamāna
muc	muñcati	mucyate	mucyamāna
yam	yacchati	yamyate	yamyamāna
labh	labhate	labhyate	labhyamāna
likh	likhati	likhyate	likhyamāna
vac	vakti	ucyate	ucyamāna
vad	vadati	udyate	udyamāna
vas	vasati	uṣyate	uṣyamāṇa
vah	vahati	uhyate	uyhamāna
vid	vidyate	none	
vidhā	vidadhāti/ vidhatte	vidhīyate	vidhīyamāna

viś	viśati	viśyate	viśyamāna
vṛt	vartate	vṛtyate	[vṛtyamāna]
vṛdh	vardhate	vṛdhyate	[vṛdhyamāna]
śaṃs	śaṃsati	śasyate	śasyamāna
śru	śṛṇoti	śrūyate	śrūyamāṇa
sev	sevate	sevyate	sevyamāna
sthā	tiṣṭhati	sthīyate	sthīyamāna
spṛś	spṛśati	spṛśyate	spṛśyamāna
smṛ	smarati	smriyate	smriyamāṇa
han	hanti	hanyate	hanyamāna
hā	jahāti	hīyate	hīyamāna

NOTE : The root used to form the present stem of see is paś, while the root used to form the passive stem (and other stems) is dṛś. While the root vad is generally used for the present stem of speak, the root vac (passive ucyate) is generally used for the passive stem. The stem brū cannot be used to form passives or any other stems except the present.

II. The use of the passive. There are two uses of the passive, of which the first is exactly analogous to the use of the passive in English, that is to say the passive use of transitive verbs. In this usage, when the transitive verb is put in the passive, then the word which was its subject as an active verb is placed in the instrumental case, while its former direct object is put into the nominative case. Other words (e.g. indirect object) retain their cases. For example, an active use of a verb is "The king kills the warrior." In the passive, the sentence is "The warrior is killed by the king." These two sentences in Sanskrit are rājā kṣatriyaṃ hanti and, in the passive, kṣatriyo rājñā hanyate. Another example is "He sees me," and "I am seen by him," that is sa māṃ paśyati and ahaṃ tena dṛśye. "He abandoned you" is sa tvām ajahāt, while "You were abandoned by him" is tvaṃ tenāhīyathāḥ,

[NOTE : When "say" is used in the passive, the person addressed is in the nom., while the thing said remains in the accusative. Thus sa na kim apy ucyate means "Nothing is said to him."]

The other use of the passive is called the bhāve construction, that is, the impersonal construction. In this usage, the verb used is generally intransitive, and the form is virtually always the third person singular. An example is the sentence "I stand in the house." This would be "ahaṃ gṛhe tiṣṭhāmi" in Sanskrit. The sentence cannot be made passive in English, but in Sanskrit it is possible to say "It is stood in the house by me," that is "gṛhe mayā sthīyate." Study the following examples of the bhāve construction. First, the active version is given, then the passive bhāve version is given.

I go to the forest
ahaṃ vanaṃ gacchāmi
vanaṃ mayā gamyate
He drank then.
tadā so 'pibat
tadā tenāpīyata
Let him go to the city.
sa nagaraṃ gacchatu
tena nagaraṃ gamyatām
"Sit down" (polite)
upaviśatu bhavān
upaviśyatām bhavatā
Note that with the bhāve use of bhū, the predicate noun may be put in the instrumental. This is called a predicative instrumental. Thus,
They should become our friends.
te 'smākaṃ mitrāṇi bhavantu
tair asmākaṃ mitrāṇi bhūyatām—or, more commonly,—tair asmākaṃ mitrair bhūyatām.

The present passive participle is normally formed only of transitive verbs (in the list above, it is given in brackets for intransitive verbs). It means "being—" —for example, hanyamāna means "being killed." Like other middle participles, it is declined like deva, phalam, and senā.

VOCABULARY :

अधी (अधीते)	study (from adhi, a verbal prefix, and i, go. Conjugated in the middle, unlike i).

काम	desire; sexual desire, lust
दृश्	see. Used for all but the present stem, for which paś is used. Thus the passive of see is dṛśyate.
लिख् (लिखति)	write
वच् (वक्ति)	say. Class 2. Used often in the passive, ucyate.
विद् (विद्यते)	to be, exist. Vidyate is used to mean "There is."
शब्द	sound, noise; word.

TRANSLATE into English :

भोजनं दीयतां ममातिथिभ्य इत्यौच्यत वणिजा ॥१॥ यस्य धनं न विद्यते तेन कथमस्मिँल् लोके जीव्यते ॥२॥ यन्मयालिख्यत तत्पुस्तकमिदानीं सर्वशिष्यैर-धीयत इत्यब्रवीदाचार्यः ॥३॥ यस्यां वाप्यामहं तया बालयाक्रीडं यस्यां वाप्यां च मम कामोऽवर्धत तस्यामिदानीमरिराजगजैः स्थीयते ॥४॥ तेन पुत्रकामेन महादेवो-ऽसेव्यत ॥५॥ आगम्यतां भवद्भिरिति धनवता शूद्रेणोच्यते ॥६॥ यद्यप्यहन्यथास्त-थापि त्वयैवाजीयत युद्ध इति कविरब्रवीत् ॥७॥ यत्र यत्र पती रामो विद्येत तत्र तत्र सीतायाश्चक्षुषी अपततां न तु तया सुखमलभ्यत ॥८॥ पुष्पमार्गेषु नगरेषु गम्यतां त्वया। यानि यानि सुखानि विद्यन्ते तानि सर्वाणि लभ्यन्तां त्वया। तथाप्यस्मिञ्जीविते न कोऽपि दुःखं नाप्नोति* ॥९॥ त्वमदीयथास्तस्मै वीराय मया। न कदापि पुनरागम्यतामत्रेत्युच्यते सकोपेन पित्रा ॥१०॥ शब्दः श्रूयते राज्ञा युद्धं क्रुत्रेति तेनोच्यते च ॥११॥ पिता माता वा हन्येत मया तथापि मा धर्मो हीयतामित्यमन्यत वीरः ॥१२॥

TRANSLATE into Sanskrit : 1. If there is poison in that honey, then you must not drink it [passive]. 2. Come, sir [bhavant with passive construction], and let the kingdom be seen by you. 3. He stands [use passive construction] in the water in which the king plays with his wives. 4. Burning with desire, he sees the girl playing in the forest [use passive construction]. 5. As the words of the merchant are heard [loc. absolute; use passive

---

*A double negative may be used in Sanskrit. The meaning then becomes positive, as in this sentence. The double negative may be kept in English by rendering the first "na" by "It cannot be said that. . . ."

present part.], the boys give the jewels to the king. 6. Let it be heard by all: the battle has been won by our king.

VERSES :

क्रतौ विवाहे व्यसने रिपुक्षये यशस्करे कर्मणि मित्रसङ्ग्रहे ।
प्रियासु नारीष्वधनेषु बन्धुषु धनव्ययस्तेषु न गण्यते बुधैः ॥

क्रतु	sacrifice
विवाह	marriage
व्यसनम्	crime
रिपु	enemy
क्षय	destruction
यशस्कर	conducive to fame
कर्मन्	act
सङ्ग्रह	favoring, help
प्रिय	pleasant, dear, loved
नारी	woman
व्यय	expense
गण् (गणयति)	consider; count
बुध	wise

सा भार्या या प्रियं ब्रूते स पुत्रो यत्र निर्वृतिः ।
तन्मित्रं यत्र विश्वासः स देशो यत्र जीव्यते ॥

भार्या	wife
प्रिय	pleasant. Here : pleasant thing
निर्वृति	happiness
विश्वास	confidence, trust
देश	country

दर्शने स्पर्शने वापि श्रवणे भाषणेऽपि वा ।
यत्र द्रवत्यन्तरङ्गं स स्नेह इति कथ्यते ॥

दर्शनम्	seeing
स्पर्शनम्	touching
श्रवणम्	hearing
भाषणम्	speaking
द्रु (द्रवति)	become liquid, melt
अन्तरङ्गम्	heart, soul
स्नेह	love, affection
कथ् (कथयति)	say

अजो नित्यः शाश्वतोऽयं पुराणो ।
न हन्यते हन्यमाने शरीरे ॥ (भगवद्गीता २, २०)

(The subject of hanyate is dehin, the embodied soul)

अज	unborn
नित्य	eternal
शाश्वत	eternal, everlasting
पुराण	primeval, ancient
शरीरम्	body

नवे वयसि यः शान्तः स शान्त इति मे मतिः ।
धातुषु क्षीयमाणेषु शान्तिः कस्य न जायते ॥

नव	new; here, young
वयस्	age
शान्त	at peace, peaceful, tranquil, serene (the second śāntaḥ is pregnant, and means "really at peace")
मति	opinion
धातु	essential ingredient of the body
क्षि	decay, waste away
शान्ति	peace, serenity

Lesson 25

THE CAUSATIVE

I. Formation of the Causative : The causative is formed by adding -ay- to the root, which is changed according to the rules given below. The causative of most verbs, whether middle or active, is active and hence is conjugated like bhū, though some causatives are middle [in which case, they may generally also be active.] The passive causative is always middle, like all passive verbs, and is conjugated like labh. The rules for changing the root before adding the -ay- of the causative are as follows :

1. A final vowel takes vṛddhi strengthening. Thus kārayati, from kṛ; bhāvayati from bhū.

2. Medial or initial (i.e. non-final) i, u, ṛ, and ḷ are guṇated unless the i, u, ṛ, or ḷ is followed by a double consonant, in which case it is unchanged. Medial or initial ī, ū and ṝ are unchanged. Thus darśayati from dṛś; vardhayati from vṛdh: but jīvayati from jīv; cintayati from cint, think.

3. A medial or initial a in a light syllable (i.e. not followed by a double consonant) is generally lengthened, the only exceptions among the verbs you have had being gam (gamayati), yam (yamayati), and jan (janayati). Thus pāṭhayati from paṭh.

4. Most roots ending in -ā add -p- before the -aya- of the causative. Thus dāpayati from dā; sthāpayati from sthā; jñāpayati from jñā; vidhāpayati from vidhā. But pāyayati from pā. [Some verbs in -i also follow this rule, as jāpayati from ji.]

5. If a nasal appears in any of the forms of the root, it appears in the causative. Thus yuñjayati from yuj, join, class 7 (strong form yunaj-); śaṃsayati from śaṃs.

6. Two important exceptions : adhyāpayati from adhī; ghātayati from han.

The passive of the causative is formed simply by taking the -ay- of the causative from the causative stem, and then adding the -y- of the passive, to which the appropriate endings are then affixed. Thus for the root jñā, the causative is jñāpayati and the causative passive is jñāpyate. Present participles may be formed from both the active and passive causative forms, using the rules you have learned. Thus the present participle causative of jñā is jñāpayant, causing to know; the present participle causative passive is jñāpyamāna, being caused to know. Examine the following list of the verbs you have had, with their causative and causative passive 3rd sg. forms.

Root	3 sg. pres.	3 sg. pres. caus.	3 sg. pres. caus. pass
adhī	adhīte	adhyāpayati	adhyāpyate
as	asti	none	
āp	āpnoti	āpayati	āpyate
ās	āste	āsayati	āsyate
i	eti	none	
kṛ	karoti	kārayati	kāryate
kṛṣ	karṣati	karṣayati	karṣyate
kḷp	kalpate	kalpayati	kalpyate
krī	krīṇāti	krāpayati	krāpyate
krīḍ	krīḍati	krīḍayati	krīḍyate
gam	gacchati	gamayati	gamyate
grah	gṛhṇāti	grāhayati	grāhyate
cur	corayati	corayati	coryate
jan	jāyate	janayati	janyate
ji	jayati	jāpayati	jāpyate
jīv	jīvati	jīvayati	jīvyate
jñā	jānāti	jñāpayati	jñāpyate
tyaj	tyajati	tyājayati	tyājyate
dah	dahati	dāhayati	dāhyate
dā	dadāti	dāpayati	dāpyate
dhāv	dhāvati	dhāvayati	dhāvyate
naś	naśyati	nāśayati	nāśyate
nī	nayati	nāyayati	nāyyate
paṭh	paṭhati	pāṭhayati	pāṭhyate
paś	paśyati	darśayati	darśyate

pā	pibati	pāyayati	pāyyate
pīḍ	pīḍayati	pīḍayati	pīḍyate
pracch	pṛcchati	pracchayati	pracchyate
brū	bravīti	none	
bhū	bhavati	bhāvayati	bhāvyate
bhṛ	bibharti	bhārayati	bhāryate
man	manyate	mānayati	mānyate
muc	muñcati	muñcayati	muñcyate
mṛ	mriyate	mārayati	māryate
yam	yacchati	yamayati	yamyate
labh	labhate	lambhayati	lambhyate
likh	likhati	lekhayati	lekhyate
vac	vakti	vācayati	vācyate
vad	vadati	vādayati	vādyate
vas	vasati	vāsayati	vāsyate
vah	vahati	vāhayati	vāhyate
vid	vidyate	none	
vidhā	vidadhāti/ vidhatte	vidhāpayati	vidhāpyate
viś	viśati	veśayati	veśyate
vṛt	vartate	vartayati	vartyate
vṛdh	vardhate	vardhayati	vardhyate
śaṃs	śaṃsati	śaṃsayati	śaṃsyate
śru	śṛṇoti	śrāvayati	śrāvyate
sev	sevate	sevayati	sevyate
sthā	tiṣṭhati	sthāpayati	sthāpyate
spṛś	spṛśati	sparśayati	sparśyate
smṛ	smarati	smārayati	smāryate
han	hanti	ghātayati	ghātyate
has	hasati	hāsayati	hāsyate
hā	jahāti	hāpayati	hāpyate

II. The use of the causative. The causative of a root conveys the notion that a person or thing causes or makes another person or thing to undergo the state denoted by the root. In other words, the causative changes the root from a simple one to one expressing "cause to—." We have a few causatives in English. The word "fell" in the sentence "He felled the tree" is a causative of "fall," for example.

1. The causative non-passive. There are two constructions used with the causative when it is not passive: one in which the agent caused to do the action is put in the instrumental, and one in which it is put in the accusative.

a. With instrumental of the agent caused to do the action. This construction is taken by all transitive verbs except those described in section b below. In this construction, the agent caused to do the action, that is the subject of the verb in its primitive, non-causative state, is put into the instrumental. It may help you to understand this construction if you consider the action expressed by the verb to be passive, that is, if you translate the English infinitive in "cause to—" as a passive (i.e. "cause to be—,") as this construction demands that the agent caused to do the action be put in the instrumental in English. Note that in this construction, as in all causative constructions, the direct object of the verb in its primitive state remains in the accusative. Study the following examples :

primitive	causative
rāmaḥ patnīṃ tyajati.	sa rāmeṇa patnīṃ tyājayati.
Rāma leaves his wife.	He causes his [Rāma's] wife to be left by Rāma i.e. he causes Rāma to leave his wife.
vīro'riṃ hanti.	rājā vīreṇāriṃ ghātayati.
The hero kills the enemy.	The king causes the enemy to be killed by the hero, i.e. causes the hero to kill the enemy.
śūdro brāhmaṇaṃ spṛśati	rājā śūdreṇa brāhmaṇaṃ sparśayati.
The Śudra touches the Brahmin.	The king causes the Brahmin to be touched by the Śudra, i.e. causes the Śudra to touch the Brahmin.

Note that while it helps in understanding the construction to translate the infinitive as a passive, it is always better style in English to translate it as an active, that is to use the second of the alternatives given above. The causative need not be rendered by "cause to" in English—there are several ways of translating it. The next-to-last sentence above, for example, might be translated "The king has the hero kill the enemy."

b. With accusative of the agent caused to do the action. This construction is taken by all intransitive verbs, i.e. by verbs which never take a direct object [but not by transitive verbs which happen to lack a direct object in the sentence at hand] as well as by verbs which imply any of the following categories of action : motion, knowledge, information, and eating. Thus all intransitive verbs are included under this category as well as such verbs as gam, paṭh, adhī, vad, vac, paś, jñā, pā. Study the following examples :

primitive	causative
śatravaḥ svargam agacchan.	śatrūn svargam agamayat.
The enemies went to heaven.	He caused the enemies to go to heaven.
sve vedārtham aviduḥ	svān vedārtham avedayat.
His own (sve) knew (vid) the meaning of the Vedas.	He caused his own to know the meaning of the Vedas.
devā amṛtam āśnan	devān amṛtam āśayat.
The gods ate (aś) nectar (amṛtam)	He caused the gods to eat nectar.
vidhir vedam adhyaita.	vidhiṃ vedam adhyāpayat.
Brahmā (vidhi) studied the Veda.	He caused Brahmā to study the Veda.
pṛthvī salila āsta	pṛthvīm salila āsayat.
The earth (pṛthvī) sat in the water (salilam).	He caused the earth to sit in the water.

These examples, which show the causative construction used respectively with verbs of going, knowing, eating, informing, and intransitive verbs, are summed up in the following verse, in which śrīhari means "Lord Viṣṇu," and gati means "refuge."

शत्रूनगमयत्स्वर्गं वेदार्थं स्वानवेदयत् ।
आशयच्चामृतं देवान्वेदमध्यापयद्विधिम् ।
आसयत्सलिले पृथ्वीं यः स मे श्रीहरिर्गतिः ॥

Note that if this construction is translated by making the infinitive after "cause" active, the agent caused to do the action is a direct object in English, and so corresponds to the accusative, which is used for it in Sanskrit.

[There are several exceptions to part b. Verbs which come under the categories of part b, but which nonetheless take the instrumental of the agent caused to act, are nī, vah (unless the agent caused to act is a word meaning "driver"); bhakṣ, eat; svāda, eat; ghrā, smell; and smṛ, unless it means "think of with regret." There are two words which take the agent caused to act in either the accusative or the instrumental : kṛ and hṛ, take.]

[The sentence "Rāma causes Govinda to go" would be "Rāmo govindam gamayati" in Sanskrit. The primitive sentence is simply "Govinda goes." It is also possible to say "Viṣṇumitra causes Rāma to cause Govinda to go." In Sanskrit, this sentence must be rendered as "Viṣṇumitra causes Govinda to go through Rāma," that is, "Viṣṇnmitro rāmeṇa govindaṃ gamayati."]

2. The causative passive. In this construction, the agent caused to act is put in the nominative, no matter whether the root belongs to category a or category b enumerated above, while the direct object in the primitive sentence remains in the accusative. In translating this construction, it is best to translate "cause" by a passive, i.e. "is [are] caused to—."*

Thus,

primitive	causative passive
rāmo grāmaṃ gacchati,	rāmo grāmaṃ gamyate.
Rāma goes to the village.	Rāma is caused to go to the village.
śūdraḥ kaṭam karoti.	śūdraḥ kaṭaṃ kāryate.
The Śudra makes a mat (kaṭa)	The Śudra is caused to make a mat.

In this construction, the agent who causes the action to be done

*There are also examples of the causative passive where it must be translated "caused to be—ed," even though this is not strictly correct. This usage is especially common with causative past passive participles (lesson 26).

is put in the instrumental, as indicated by the English translation. Thus, "The Śudra is caused to make the mat by the king" is "śūdro rājñā kaṭam kāryate."

[In the case of roots which imply knowledge, eating, and those which have a literary work for their object, the thing caused to be done is placed in the nominative and the agent caused to do is placed in the accusative or vice versa. Thus "The king is caused to know his duty" may be either "rājā dharmaṃ jñāpyate" or "dharmo rājānaṃ jñāpyate." "The boy is caused to eat food" is either "bālo bhojanaṃ bhojyate" or "bhojanaṃ bālaṃ bhojyate."]

Note that tenth-class verbs have the same causative and primitive forms—"corayati" could mean either "he steals" or "he causes to steal." In the passive, the causative and primitive forms are identical for many verbs—gamyate could mean either "he is caused to go" or "it is gone" (with the bhāve construction; [also, "it is traversed"]). In such cases, which form is meant must be decided from context.

VOCABULARY :

कृष् (कर्षति)	plow; pull, drag
क्षेत्रम्	field
दृश् in the caus.	(दर्शयति) show (with dat. or acc. of the person to whom the object is shown)
बाण	arrow
मन्त्रिन्	minister (of a king) (declined like a possessive in -in)
मृ (म्रियते)	die (note that mriyate, the present of mṛ, is actually a passive, used for the present in classical Sanskrit).
मृत्यु masc.	death
शस्त्रम्	weapon
हस् (हसति)	laugh

TRANSLATE into English :

येन शत्रुणा मार्यन्त ते वीराः स इदानीं युद्धभूमिं विशति ॥१॥ स आचार्यः शिष्या-

न्धर्मपुस्तकान्यध्यायपयद्धर्मकथास्तानश्रावयच्च ।।२।। यानि शस्त्राणि स राजा शूद्रैरकारयत्तैर्वीरा युद्धेऽमारयञ्छत्रून् ।।३।। तव कामं दर्शय म इति ग्रामबालाब्रवीद्वीरम् ।।४।। ये गजान्वनादगमयंस्तान्वणिजः सिंहा अगृह्णन्नमारयंश्च ।।५।। येऽस्मिन्राज्ये मम प्रजाभिः क्षेत्राणि कर्षयेयुस्ते मम सकाश आयन्त्विवत्यौच्यत राजदेवनाम्ना नृपेण ।।६।। स वीरः शूद्रैर्धनुर्बाणावानाययदरीनहंश्च ।।७।। अरिराजभी रथान्कर्षयतो राज्ञः कीर्तिरशस्यत प्रजाभिः ।।८।। ये मनुष्या अस्मिँल्लोके जायन्ते ते सर्वे म्रियन्ते । न कोऽपि जीवन्मृत्युं न गच्छतीत्यब्रवीदृषिः ।।९।। यो वणिग्रथानश्वांश्च मन्त्रिणानाय्यत स इदानीं नगरं विशतीत्यवदद्वीरं राजा ।।१०।। आचार्येण पुस्तकं पाठ्यमानं शिष्यं न कोऽपि किमपि ब्रूयात् ।।११।। राजानं मन्त्रिणश्च हासयन्कविर्धनवानभवत् ।।१२।।

TRANSLATE into Sanskrit : 1. The king caused his enemies to plow the fields with [their] weapons. 2. Mother saw the girls causing the boy to bring the flowers and laughed. 3. The god caused the girl to leave her husband in the forest. 4. The book was caused to be read by the student by the teacher. 5. The minister showed the king the merchant making elephants pull [vah] the chariot. 6. He made his sons steal the money of the merchant and then said, "I [will] give you nothing."

श्रमयति शरीरमधिकं भ्रमयति चेतः करोति सन्तापम् ।
मोहं मुहुश्च कुरुते विषविषमं वीक्षणं तस्याः ।।

श्रम् (श्राम्यति)	become tired, become weary
शरीरम्	body
अधिक	excessive, very much. Adhikam here is an adv., "excessively"
भ्रम् (भ्रमति)	whirl
चेतस्	mind, heart (figuratively)
सन्ताप	distress, anguish
मोह	delusion, confusion
मुहुस्	again, in addition
कृ	(this verb may be middle as well as active)
विषम	painful, troublesome
वीक्षणम्	eye(s), glance

न स्वल्पस्य कृते भूरि नाशयेन्मतिमान्नरः ।
एतदेव हि पाण्डित्यं न स्वल्पाद्भूरिनाशनम् ॥

स्वल्प	little; (as a neuter noun) a little
भूरि	much; (as a neuter noun) a lot
मति	judgment. Note the possessive suffix-mant is added
नर	man
पाण्डित्यम्	wisdom, cleverness
नाशनम्	destroying, getting rid of

The following two verses are by Jagannātha, a Telugu Brahmin who lived at the court of Shah Jahan. He is supposed to have written these verses to his mistress, a Moghul princess.

यवनी नवनीतकोमलाङ्गी शयनीये यदि नीयते कदापि ।
अवनीतलमेव साधु मन्ये न वनी माघवनी विनोदहेतुः ॥

न याचे गजालिं न वा वाजिराजं न वित्तेषु चित्तं मदीयं कदापि ।
इयं सुस्तनी मस्तकन्यस्तहस्ता लवङ्गी कुरङ्गीदृगङ्गीकरोतु ॥

यवनी	a non-Indian woman
नवनीत	butter
कोमल	soft, tender
अङ्ग	limb
शयनीयम्	bed
अवनी	earth
तल	surface
साधु	good, sufficient
वनी	grove
माघवन	which belongs to Indra
विनोद	pleasure
हेतु	cause. Vinodahetu means (non-literally) "necessary for enjoyment"
याच् (याचते)	ask for
आलि	line, row
वाजि	horse (note this is compounded with rājan)
वित्तम्	wealth
चित्तम्	mind, heart
मदीय	my
सुस्तनी	who (f.) has beautiful breasts

मस्तक	head, skull
न्यस्त	placed
हस्त	hand. Mastakanyastahastā "who (f.) holds her head in her hand"
लवङ्गी	name of an Apsaras, a kind of divine woman (compared here to the poet's mistress)
कुरङ्गी	doe
दृश्	eye (nom. sg. dṛk)
अङ्गीकृ	(अङ्गीकरोति) accept

Compare the second of these stanzas with Sappho's lines :

οἱ μὲν ἰππήων στρότον, οἱ δὲ πέσδων,
οἱ δὲ νάων φαῖσ' ἐπὶ γᾶν μέλαιναν
ἔμμεναι κάλλιστον, ἔγω δὲ κῆν ὄτ
τω τις ἔραται

LESSON 26

PAST PASSIVE PARTICIPLES; PAST ACTIVE PARTICIPLES

I. Saṃdhi Rules. The following two saṃdhi rules are used in forming many past passive participles and their derivatives.

a. A voiced aspirate plus an unvoiced non-aspirate or unvoiced aspirate becomes a voiced non-aspirate plus a voiced aspirate. Thus budh plus ta becomes buddha; labh plus ta becomes labdha; doh plus ti becomes dogdhi. Note that this rule explains the underlined forms found in the conjugation of duh, to milk (class 2), (-h becomes -gh before non-nasal stops) :

Present Active	Singular	Dual	plural
1st person	dohmi	duhvaḥ	duhmaḥ
2nd person	dhokṣi	<u>dugdhaḥ</u>	<u>dugdha</u>
3rd person	<u>dogdhi</u>	<u>dugdhaḥ</u>	duhanti

b. A dental t, when it immediately follows ṣ, is retroflexed. Thus tuṣ plus ta becomes tuṣṭa.

II. The past passive participle. The use of this participle is treated in part 2 below.

1. Formation of past passive participles. This form is made by adding -ta, -ita, or -na to the unstrengthened root. For each verb, only one of these endings may be used.

a. Verbs with -ta. Many verbs add -ta directly to the root. In such cases, final consonants of the roots change as follows (cf. changes of final consonants of nouns, p. 32) :

c becomes k. Thus sikta from sic, moisten.

ch becomes ṣ. Thus pṛṣṭa from pracch.

j becomes k or ṣ. Thus tyakta from tyaj; sṛṣṭa from sṛj, create.

ś becomes ṣ. Thus naṣṭa from naś, dṛṣṭa from dṛś.

ṣ is unchanged. Thus tuṣṭa from tuṣ, rejoice.

h becomes gh; or it may combine with the t to become ḍh, in which case the vowel preceding it is lengthened. Thus dugdha from duh, milk; dagdha from dah; but līḍha from lih, lick.

In general, the form of the root to which -ta is added is the same to which the passive affix -ya- is added. Thus, a penultimate nasal is dropped, as in śasta from śaṃs; saṃprasāraṇa takes place, as in ukta from vac, iṣṭa from yaj, sacrifice, ūḍha from vah, pṛṣṭa from pracch; final -ā, ai, etc. are weakened to -ī, as in pīta from pā, gīta from gai, sing. But there are some exceptions. In some verbs, -ā is weakened to -i, unlike the passive, as sthita from sthā, hita from dhā, place. From dā, datta is formed. In many roots, -am is weakened to -a. Thus gata from gam (Indo-European *gwṃto-), yata from yam, rata from ram, sport, nata from nam, bow. Final -an may also be weakened to -a, as in mata from man, hata from han. Some roots in -am make participles in -ānta, as kṣānta from kṣam, become weary. The root jan makes jāta.

b. Verbs with -ita. All verbs which make their present stem by adding -aya- make their past passive participles by adding -ita to the stem to which -aya- is added. Thus corita from cur, pīḍita from pīḍ. Note that this comprises all 10th class verbs *and all causative verbs*. Thus the causative of mṛ is mārayati. Its past passive participle causative is mārita.

Several other verbs also make their past passive participles in -ita. Thus patita from pat, uṣita from vas, likhita from likh, udita from vad. The verb grah makes gṛhīta. Roots ending in -kh. -ṭ, -ṭh, -ḍ, -th, and -ph make their past passive participles by adding -ita.

c. Verbs with -na. The following verbs make their past passive participles by adding -na :

Certain roots in -ā and in -ī, -ū, -ai. Thus hīna from hā; mlāna from mlai, wither; kṣīṇa from kṣi, destroy; lūna from lū, cut.

Roots in -ṛ add -na to the same stem used to form the passive. Thus kīrṇa from kṝ, scatter; tīrṇa from tṝ, cross; pūrṇa from pṝ, fill.

A few roots in -j, which becomes g before n. Thus bhagna from bhaj, share; bhugna from bhuj, bend; magna from majj, sink. Also lagna from lag, attach.

Some roots in -d, which becomes n before n. Thus sanna from sad, settle down; bhinna from bhid, cut.

The past passive participle is always declined like deva, phalam, and senā. In the following list, the past passive participle, the past causative passive participle, and the past active participle, described in section III below, are given. The past active participle is formed by adding -vant to the past passive participle. It is declined like dhanavant. The past active participle caus. is formed by adding -vant to the past passive participle caus.

Root	Past pass. part.	Past pass. part. caus.	Past act. part.
adhī	adhīta	adhyāpita	adhītavant
as	none	none	none
āp	āpta	āpita	āptavant
ās	āsita	āsita	āsitavant
i	ita	none	itavant
kṛ	kṛta	kārita	kṛtavant
kṛṣ	kṛṣṭa	karṣita	kṛṣṭavant
kḷp	kḷpta	kalpita	kḷptavant
krī	krīta	krāpita	krītavant
krīḍ	krīḍita	krīḍita	krīḍitavant
gam	gata	gamita	gatavant
grah	gṛhīta	grāhita	gṛhītavant
cur	corita	corita	coritavant
jan	jāta	janita	[jātavant]
ji	jita	jāpita	jitavant
jīv	jīvita	jīvita	jīvitavant
jñā	jñāta	jñapta (irreg.)	jñātavant
tyaj	tyakta	tyājita	tyaktavant
dah	dagdha	dāhita	dagdhavant
dā	datta	dāpita	dattavant
dhāv	dhāvita	dhāvita	dhāvitavant
naś	naṣṭa	nāśita	naṣṭavant
nī	nīta	nāyita	nītavant

paṭh	paṭhita	pāṭhita	paṭhitavant
paś	dṛṣṭa	darśita	dṛṣṭavant
pā	pīta	pāyita	pītavant
pīḍ	pīḍita	pīḍita	pīḍitavant
pracch	pṛṣṭa	pracchita	pṛṣṭavant
brū	none	none	none
bhū	bhūta	bhāvita	[bhūtavant]
bhṛ	bhṛta	bhārita	bhṛtavant
man	mata	mānita	matavant
muc	mukta	muñcita	muktavant
mṛ	mṛta	mārita	mṛtavant
yam	yata	yamita	yatavant
labh	labdha	lambhita	labdhavant
likh	likhita	lekhita	likhitavant
vac	ukta	vācita	uktavant
vad	udita	vādita	uditavant
vas	uṣita	vāsita	uṣitavant
vah	ūḍha	vāhita	ūḍhavant
vid	none		
vidhā	vihita	vidhāpita	vihitavant
viś	viṣṭa	veśita	viṣṭavant
vṛt	vṛtta	vartita	[vṛttavant]
vṛdh	vṛddha	vardhita	[vṛddhavant]
śaṃs	śasta	śaṃsita	śastavant
śru	śruta	śrāvita	śrutavant
sev	sevita	sevita	sevitavant
sthā	sthita	sthāpita	sthitavant
spṛś	spṛṣṭa	sparśita	spṛṣṭavant
smṛ	smṛta	smārita	smṛtavant
han	hata	ghātita	hatavant
has	hasita	hāsita	hasitavant
hā	hīna	hāpita	hīnavant

2. The use of the past passive participle. This form corresponds to the English past passive participle (to which it is related) in -ed or -en, as "received" or "broken". It may be used as a simple adjective. Thus rājñā dattaṃ dhanam means "the money given by the king" [though it could also mean "the money was given by the king," as explained immediately

below] "The money given by the king" could also be expressed by a compound, in which case there is no ambiguity as regards the function of the participle : rājadattaṃ dhanam.

The past passive participle is very often used to substitute for a finite verb, a usage which grows more and more common in time. There are two types of constructions which may be used : one in which the past passive participle modifies the subject, with which it agrees, and in which the word "is" must be supplied [rarely it may occur in the Sanskrit sentence]; and one which is impersonal and in which the past passive participle appears in the neuter singular nominative. An example of the first construction is "vīro rājñā hataḥ" [or, less commonly, vīro rājñā hata āsīt], "The hero was killed by the king." An example of the second is "iti tenoktam" [or, less commonly, iti tenoktam āsīt], "Thus it was said by him," or "jitam tena rājñā," "that king conquered." This second usage is equivalent to the bhāve use of the passive.

In general, the past passive participle must be translated as a passive; however, in the case of roots implying motion, in the case of sthā, ās, vas, jan, and most other intransitive verbs, as well as a few other verbs you have not had yet [śliṣ, embrace; śī, lie; ruh, climb; jṝ, grow old], the past passive participle may have an active sense. Thus "sa tatra gataḥ" means "he went there"; "sā tatrāsitā," "she sat there"; "putro jātaḥ," "a son has been born." Note that here, if the participle is used as a finite verb, it must agree with the subject.

Past passive participles ending in -ta sometimes are used in the sense of neuter abstract nouns, in which case they are declined like phalam. Thus "jīvitam." "life"; hasitam, "a laugh." Past passive participles with an active sense may be used as nouns, as "vṛddha" "an old person"; "mṛta," "a dead person."

When used as element a in a bahuvrīhi, the past passive participle gives the sense of "by whom [which] b is a' ed." Thus hatagaja means "by whom an elephant has been killed." Rarely it may also mean "on which b is a'ed," "for which b is a'ed," etc. If the past passive participle may have an active meaning, then it generally means "whose b are a." Thus vṛddhaputra, "whose sons are grown".

III. The past active participle. This participle is formed simply by adding -vant to the past passive participle, as shown in the list given above in section II. It is declined like dhanavant. A past active participle causative may also be formed by adding -vant to the past passive causative participle. Thus the past active participle of smṛ is smṛtavant, "he who remembered. The past active participle causative is smāritavant, "He who caused to remember."

There is no English participle to which the past active participle is equivalent, but it may be translated by an adjectival relative clause in which the verb is active and past. Like the past passive participle, it may be used as an adjective. It is often used for a noun, as "kṛtavān," "he who did." It rarely occurs in compounds, unlike the past passive participle. By far its most common use is to serve as a past active finite verb, as "sa tad uktavān," "He said that." Note that this usage is parallel to the use of the past passive participle, with which the same idea may be expressed as "tad uktaṃ tena," "that was said by him." In the case of verbs whose past passive participles may have an active meaning, the past active participle and the past passive participle may be used interchangeably. Thus "sā tatra sthitā" and "sā tatra sthitavatī" both mean "She stood there." For the past passive participle caus. "cause" is in the passive, while the infinitive may be active or passive in English. Thus "mārita" may mean "caused to kill" or "caused to be killed."

IV. Vocabulary Notes

1. vad, vac in the passive. As has been pointed out. vac. not vad, is generally used in the passive. Vad and vac take a double object, as has been seen : after them, both the thing said and the person addressed are placed in the accusative. In the passive, the thing said remains in the accusative, while the person addressed becomes the subject. It is often possible to translate vac and vad in the passive by "address" making the thing said the object of a "with" clause. Thus sa uktaḥ means "he was addressed." "Sa tāṃ vācam uktaḥ" means "He was addressed with those words."

2. Sva (stem form sva-). This is the reflexive 3rd person

pronoun, declined like sa, except that it does not lose final -s in the masculine nominative singular before consonants, and that its neuter singular nom. -acc. is svam. It is used when a 3rd person possessive pronoun (his, her, its, their) refers to the same person or thing as the subject of the sentence, as in "He gave his money to the poet," that is, "sa svaṃ dhanaṃ kavaye 'dadāt." Normally, this pronoun used in this way is omitted, unless it is strongly stressed. Sva may also be used to refer to the contextual, rather than the grammatical, subject, in which case it may be translated by "his own," "her own", "their own" "its own." For example, "He established the kings again in their own kingdoms" would be "sa punar nṛpān svarājyeṣv asthāpayat." See also sentence 4 in today's exercises.

3. The following words are used at the end of compounds in special ways :

a. -maya (fem. -mayī), placed at the end of a compound, means "consisting of," "entirely made of," "full of." Thus "jalamayo lokaḥ," "A world made of water," "a world full of water"

b. -prāya (fem. prāyī). At the end of a compound, this is translated as "almost," "nearly." Thus mṛtaprāya, "almost dead."

c. -mātra. This is translated as "mere," "only" when it comes at the end of a compound. Thus "dhanamātreṇa," "by mere wealth." When placed after a past passive participle, mātra means, "as soon as", "no sooner than," "just." Thus "sa hatamātro 'patat," "He, as soon as he was killed, fell." In this usage, -mātra agrees with the noun or pronoun which it modifies. This construction is often used in absolute constructions, as "teṣv āgatamātreṣu rājā dhanam adadāt," "As soon as they came, the king gave money."

VOCABULARY :

आत्मन्	(masc.) self; oneself
कुटुम्ब	family
-प्राय	almost—see b above on this page
भृत्य	servant

-मय	made of, consisting of, full of—see a, page 134.
-मात्र	mere, only—see c above on previous page.
सर्प	snake
स्व	one's own—see 2 on pages 133-34. (Stem form sva-)

TRANSLATE into English :

स वीरः ससर्पमृगं वनं गतस्तत्र च बहून्सर्पान्हितवानित्यश्रृणोद्राजा ॥१॥ यद्यपि न सा पत्नी कदापि कुटुम्बपतिना कोपेन हता तथापि सा यदा तमागच्छन्तमश्रृणोद्भयान्नात्मानं दर्शितवती ॥२॥ सीतया वृक्षमयं वनं दृष्टमत्र रामः कुत्र स्यादिति मतं च ॥३॥ स्वभृत्यसेवितः कविः किमन्यद्ददानि त इत्युक्तो राज्ञा ॥४॥ स वीरो मृतप्रायोऽपि शत्रवः कुत्रेति पृष्टवान् ॥५॥ गतमात्रे पत्यौ भृत्या गृहं त्यक्तवन्तो वाप्यां क्रीडितवन्तश्च ॥६॥ स सिंहो मारितगजोऽपि सभयो मनुष्यसकाशाद्धावितः ॥७॥ अस्मिन्वने काकमात्रा न्युषिता इत्युक्तवत्यृषौ ते वणिजो भयं त्यक्तवन्तस्तद्विष्टाश्च ॥८॥ ये राजानो दत्तरत्नास्तेषां सकाशे यूयं गच्छत ताञ्छंसत च ॥९॥ तस्मिन्राज्ञि ता वाच उक्ते कविना क्षत्रियास्तं कविं गृहीतवन्तः ॥१०॥ वृद्धच्छायेषु वृक्षेषु सा वणिक्पत्नी पतिमागच्छन्तं न दृष्टवती दुःखं गता च ॥११॥ तेऽरिराजा आनीयमाना नष्टप्राया वयमित्यवदन् ॥१२॥

TRANSLATE into Sanskrit, rendering the underlined verbs by past passive or past active participles. 1. The king by whom the enemies were slain [bahuvrīhi] came to our city. 2. As soon as the hero died [locative absolute with mātra construction], crows sat near him [in his presence]. 3. The teacher taught [adhī, causative] the students dharma. 4. The king, caused to remember Śakuntalā, went to happiness. 5. When he saw the Brahmin who had given [him] the money, the merchant thought, "Who is he ?" 6. "By whom was this world made," thus it is not known by anyone.

न द्विषन्ति न याचन्ते परनिन्दां न कुर्वते ।
अनाहूता न चायान्ति तेनाश्मानोऽपि देवताः ॥

द्विष् (द्वेष्टि)	hate, feel enmity for (class 2)
याच् (याचते)	ask, beg
पर	other. Here, other people
निन्दा	blame (note kṛ in this line is middle)

आह्वे	call, summon
आया (आयाति)	come (class II)
अश्मन्	rock, stone (masc.)
देवता	divinity, god

दैवं फलति सर्वत्र न विद्या न पौरुषम् ।
पाषाणस्य कुतो विद्या येन देवत्वमागतः ॥

दैवम्	fate, divinity
फल् (फलति)	bear fruit, come to fruition
सर्वत्र	everywhere
विद्या	knowledge
पौरुषम्	manliness
पाषाणम्	rock, stone
कुतः	where
-त्वम्	-ness. "Go to x-ness" means "to become x."

न तद्भुक्तं न तत्पीतं न तत्सुप्तं न तद्गतम् ।
यन्मांसमाहिषक्षीरललनावाजिवर्जितम् ॥

भुज्	eat
स्वप्	sleep
मांसम्	meat
माहिषक्षीरम्	buffalo yogurt
ललना	woman
वाजि	horse
वर्जित	without

एक एव पदार्थस्तु त्रिधा भवति वीक्षितः ।
कुणपः कामिनी मांसं योगिभिः कामिभिः श्वभिः ॥

पदार्थ	object, thing
त्रिधा	in three ways
वीक्ष्	consider
कुणप	corpse
कामिन	masc. : one who has desire. fem.: one who is the object of desire
मांसम्	meat
योगिन्	a yogi
श्वन्	dog

लालयेत्पञ्चवर्षाणि दशवर्षाणि ताडयेत् ।
प्राप्ते तु षोडशे वर्षे पुत्रं मित्रवदाचरेत् ॥

लल्	(in caus.) fondle, indulge	षोडश	sixteenth
पञ्च	five	-वत्	like (a suffix)
वर्षम्	year	आचर् (आचरति)	treat
दश	ten		

तड् (ताडयति) beat

प्राप् (प्राप्नोति) attain, reach (past passive participle prāpta)

LESSON 27

THE CONTINUATIVE; VERBAL PREFIXES

I. Formation of the continuative. In the following discussion, a prefixed root is a root to which a prefix, such as ā- in āgam, has been added. An unprefixed root is a root which lacks such a prefix, such as gam. (See III below.) *Note that the continuative, whether in -vā or -ya, is invariant and is not conjugated.*

1. Unprefixed roots. *For a root which has no prefix affixed to it, the continuative is formed by removing the final -a of the past passive participle and replacing it with -vā.* If, however, the past passive participle ends in -na, then the continuative is formed by adding -tvā to the root which is modified as follows: [a. roots in -ā, -ī, -ū̆ and -ai add -tvā to -ā, -ī, -ū̆, and -ā respectively. b, roots in -ṝ add -tvā to -īr or ūr, like the past passive participle ending -na. c. roots in -j add -itvā to the root. d. roots in -d change -d to -t before -tvā.] *Causatives and class* 10 *verbs are exceptions : their unprefixed continuatives are formed by inserting -i- after the appropriate pres. stem and then adding -tvā*, that is, they end in -ayitvā, not -itvā. See cur and the causative in the list below.

2. Prefixed roots. *If the root has a prefix, then the continuative is formed by adding -ya to the root. If ihe root ends in a short vowel, then -t- is inserted before the -ya.* Note that adhī forms adhītya because the root, i, ends in a short vowel, even though it is lengthened when it combines with the prefix. If the root undergoes saṃprasāraṇa or loss of a nasal in the formation of its passive stem, then it does so also before making the continuative in -ya (see vac, śaṃs in the list below). Roots in -ṝ add -ya to -īr or -ūr. Roots in -an add -ya to -at. while roots in -am may add -ya to either -am or -at (see man, upagam). Causatives and class 10 verbs make their prefixed continuatives by subtracting -aya- from the present stem and adding -ya. But

causatives from roots of a light syllable with a short -a- which is not lengthened in the causative make their continuatives by subtracting -aya- from the present stem and adding -ayya (i.e. by adding -ya to the caus. stem minus -a. See upagam).

Study the following list of continuatives of the roots you have had. For each root, the past passive participle, the unprefixed continuative, the unprefixed causative continuative, the prefixed continuative, and the prefixed causative continuative are given. In the case of the last two, the letter P represents a prefix which is affixed to the root.

II. Use of the Continuative. This form is used to denote an action prior in time to the action of the main verb. A series of continuatives may be used, but they must always be followed by a main verb, and each continuative must be prior in time to the continuative which immediately follows. For example, in the sentence, "She got up, washed her face, brushed her teeth, and went to school," all of the actions except "went" may be expressed by continuatives. A continuative may never come after the main verb with which it is construed, and in general, all elements (such as direct objects) construed with a continuative must precede it. The subject of the main verb, which must also be the subject of its continuatives, may come before the first continuative or between the last continuative and the main verb (rarely it may occur in other positions).

Occasionally, a continuative may be used whose action is not prior to the main verb, but rather is intimately connected with it (as adverbial participles in the Dravidian languages. This usage is especially conspicuous in the works of some South-Indian writers, Śaṅkara, for example). An example is muktvā, "having released," which may be used to mean "except," preceded by its object in the accusative.

In translating the continuative, it is best to use such words as "after," "after having," or "when," or to use a series of co-ordinated independent clauses, as in the example above "She got up, etc." It is extremely important to note that the continuative may be used *only* when the subject of the continuative is the same as that of the main verb, the only exception being

ROOT	P. PASS. PART.	CONT.	CONT. CAUS.	PREF. CONT.	PREF. CONT. CAUS.
adhī	adhīta	none	none	adhitya	adhyāpya
as	none	none	none	none	none
āp	āpta	āptvā	āpayitvā	Pāpya	Pāpya
ās	āsita	āsitvā	āsayitvā	Pāsya	Pāsya
āhve	āhūta	none	none	āhūya	āhvāpya
i	ita	itvā	none	Pitya	none (exc. adhī)
upagam	upagata	none	none	upagamya, upagatya	upagamayya
kṛ	kṛta	kṛtvā	kārayitvā	Pkṛtya	Pkārya
kṛṣ	kṛṣṭa	kṛṣṭvā	karṣayitvā	Pkṛṣya	Pkarṣya
kḷp	kḷpta	kḷptvā	kalpayitvā	Pkḷpya	Pkalpya
krī	krīta	krītvā	krāpayitvā	Pkrīya	Pkrāpya
krīḍ	krīḍita	krīḍitvā	krīḍayitvā	Pkrīḍya	Pkrīḍya
gam	gata	gatvā	gamitvā	Pgamya, Pgatya	Pgamayya
grah	gṛhīta	gṛhītvā	grāhayitvā	Pgṛhya	Pgrāhya
cur	corita	corayitvā	corayitvā	Pcorya	Pcorya
jan	jāta	none	janayitvā	none	Pjanayya
ji	jita	jitvā	jāpayitvā	Pjitya	Pjāpya
jīv	jīvita	jivitvā	jīvayitvā	Pjīvya	Pjivya
jñā	jñāta	jñātvā	jñāpayitvā	Pjñāya	Pjñāpya
tyaj	tyakta	tyaktvā	tyājayitvā	Ptyajya	Ptyājya

dah	dagdha	dagdhvā	dāhayitvā	Pdahya	Pdāhya
dā	datta	dattvā	dāpayitvā	Pdāya	Pdāpya
dhāv	dhāvita	dhāvitvā	dhāvayitvā	Pdhāvya	Pdhāvya
naś	naṣṭa	naṣṭvā	nāśayitvā	Pnaśya	Pnāśya
nigrah	nigṛhīta	none	none	nigṛhya	nigrāhya
nirdiś	nirdiṣṭa	none	none	nirdiśya	nirdeśya
nī	nīta	nītvā	nāyayitvā	Pnīya	Pnāyya
paṭh	paṭhita	paṭhitvā	pāṭhayitvā	Ppaṭhya	Ppāṭhya
paś	dṛṣṭa	dṛṣṭvā	darśayitvā	Pdṛśya	Pdarśya
pā	pīta	pītvā	pāyayitvā	Ppāya	Ppāyya
pīḍ	pīḍita	pīḍayitvā	pīḍayitvā	Ppīḍya	Ppīḍya
pracch	pṛṣṭa	pṛṣṭvā	pracchayitvā	Ppracchya	Ppracchya
pratīkṣ	pratīkṣita	none	none	pratīkṣya	pratīkṣya
prayuj	prayukta	none	none	prayujya	prayojya
brū	none	none	none	none	none
bhū	bhūta	bhūtvā	bhāvayitvā	Pbhūya	Pbhāvya
bhṛ	bhṛta	bhṛtvā	bhārayitvā	Pbhṛtya	Pbhārya
man	mata	matvā	mānayitvā	Pmatya	Pmānya
muc	mukta	muktvā	muñcayitvā	Pmucya	Pmuñcya
mṛ	mṛta	mṛtvā	mārayitvā	Pmṛtya	Pmārya
yam	yata	yatvā	yamayitvā	Pyamya, Pyatya	Pyamayya
labh	labdha	labdhvā	lambhayitvā	Plabhya	Plambhya
likh	likhita	likhitvā	lekhayitvā	Plikhya	Plekhya

vac	ukta	uktvā	vācayitvā	Pucya	Pvācya
vad	udita	uditvā	vādayitvā	Pudya	Pvādya
vas	uṣita	uṣitvā	vāsayitvā	Puṣya	Pvāsya
vah	ūḍha	ūḍhvā	vāhayitvā	Puhya	Pvāhya
vid	none	none	none	none	none
vidhā	vihita	none	none	vidhāya	vidhāpya
viś	viṣṭa	viṣṭvā	veśayitvā	Pviśya	Pveśya
vṛt	vṛtta	vṛttvā	vartayitvā	Pvṛtya	Pvartya
vṛdh	vṛddha	vṛddhvā	vardhayitvā	Pvṛdhya	Pvardhya
śaṃs	śasta	śastvā	śaṃsayitvā	Pśasya	Pśaṃsya
śru	śruta	śrutvā	śrāvayitvā	Pśrutya	Pśrāvya
sev	sevita	sevitvā	sevayitvā	Psevya	Psevya
sthā	sthita	sthitvā	sthāpayitvā	Psthāya	Psthāpya
spṛś	spṛṣṭa	spṛṣṭvā	sparśayitvā	Pspṛśya	Psparśya
smṛ	smṛta	smṛtvā	smārayitvā	Psmṛtya	Psmārya
han	hata	hatvā	ghātayitvā	Phatya	Pghātya
has	hasita	hasitvā	hāsayitvā	Phasya	Phāsya
hā	hīna	hātvā	hāpayitvā	Phāya	Phāpya

in the case of passive verbs, described below in the next paragraph. If a string of continuatives is used in a sentence, all must have the same subject, and that must be the subject of the main verb (again with the exception of passive verbs). If the subject is different, then an absolutive construction must be used. Thus in the sentence, "After he killed the enemy, I came," a continuative may not be used, as the subject of "killed" is different from that of "came." But in the sentence " I killed the enemy and came," a continuative may be used, that is "śatruṃ hatvāham āgaccham." The continuative may have only an active sense, never a passive one. Note that the tense of the continuative is determined by the main verb, the only requirement being that the action of the continuative be prior to that of the main verb. Thus if in the previous sentence, "āgaccham" is changed to the future (which you will soon have), so that the sentence reads, "śatruṃ hatvāham āgamiṣyāmi," then the meaning would be, "Having killed the enemy, I will come," so that the action of killing takes place in the future (but is still prior to the action of coming.) Note that in a series of continuatives, ca is normally not used.

If the main verb is passive, then the subject of the continuative is the doer of the action rather than the grammatical subject. In fact, if the main verb is passive, its grammatical subject *may not* be the subject of the continuative which precedes it. Rather, the subject of the continuative must be the doer of the action, which is placed in the instrumental before the passive verb. Thus in the sentence "The elephant was released by the king after he killed the warrior," that is, "vīraṃ hatvā rājñā gajo muktaḥ," the subject of the continuative is the instrumental agent, king. In some instances in which the main verb is passive, the subject of the continuative may even be omitted, so that it must be supplied by the reader, as in the sentence, "śiṣyān āhūya, idam pustakaṃ paṭhyatām," that is, "Let this book be read [by you] having summoned the students." (The saṃdhi between āhūya and idam has been omitted for clarity.)

If the continuative is causative, then it is construed like other causatives. Thus in the sentence, "Having caused the Śūdras to plow the fields, the Kṣatriya went to the city," is translated, "Śūdraiḥ kṣetrāṇi karṣayitvā, Kṣatriyo nagaram agacchat."

The prefix a/an may be placed before a continuative to negate it, usually in a way which may be translated by a "without" clause (similar to negative adverbial participles in the Dravidian languages). Thus "na tavārim ahatvā tasya rājyaṃ labhyethāḥ," "You will not get his kingdom without killing your enemy." Note that a/an does not count as a verbal prefix, and so the form is ahatvā, not ahatya. Before prayuj, the form would be aprayujya.

III. Verbal prefixes. Below are listed the common prefixes which are affixed to verbs in Sanskrit. Normally, the prefix quite changes the meaning of a verb, often in an unpredictable way. In general, it is only by hindsight that one can see why a certain prefix is used to modify the meaning of a root in a certain way; it is usually impossible to predict what prefixed verb will mean. In other words, you must learn each prefixed verb as a separate vocabulary item. Some prefixes (especially the ones marked intensative) scarcely change the meaning of the root at all. It is possible to add more than one prefix to a root (as upāgam, from upa plus ā plus gam, to approach, come up to). Even though they are not of great use in predicting meanings, it is nonetheless useful to be acquainted with the chief verbal prefixes and their primary meanings (though you need not memorize them):

ati : across, beyond, past, over, to excess.
adhi : above, over, on, onto.
anu : after, along, toward, in imitation of.
antar : between, among, within.
apa : away, forth, off.
abhi : to, unto, against (often with implied violence).
ava : down, off.
ā : to, unto, at.
ud : up, up out.
upa : to, toward.
ni : down; in, into.
nis : out, forth.
parā : to a distance, away, forth.
pari : round about, around; also, an intensative.
pra : forward, onward, forth, fore.

prati : in reversed direction, back to or against; in return.
vi : apart, asunder, away, out; also, an intensative.
sam : along, with, together; also, an intensative.

VOCABULARY :

(From now on, with each verb will be supplied its present 3rd person singular, its present 3rd person singular causative, and its past passive participle).

आह्वे (आह्वयति, आह्वापयति, आहूयते, आहूत)	call, summon (from ā and hve)
उपगम् (उपगच्छति, उपगमयति, उपगत)	go to, approach, attain (from upa and gam)
निग्रह् (निगृह्णाति, निग्राहयति, निगृहीत)	subdue, control (from ni and grah). Class 9.
निर्दिश् (निर्दिशति, निर्देशयति, निर्दिष्ट)	point out, indicate, show (from nir and diś)
पक्षिन्	bird (from pakṣa, wing, and -in)
प्रतीक्ष् (प्रतीक्षते, प्रतीक्षयति, प्रतीक्षित)	expect, await (from prati and īkṣ)
प्रयुज् (प्रयुङ्क्ते, प्रयोजयति, प्रयुक्त)	use, employ (from pra and yuj). Class 7.

TRANSLATE into English :

भोजनं कृत्वोद्याने क्रीडित्वा स्वसारमाहूयास्मद्गृहमेहि ॥१॥ स वीरोऽरीन्निर्दिश्य ये ये शस्त्रहस्ता आगच्छन्ति तान्सर्वान्हन्मीति राजानमुक्त्वा युद्धं विष्टः ॥२॥ स वणिग्भृत्यैः स्नानं कारयित्वा देवसकाश इदानीमितेत्यब्रवीत् ॥३॥ स राजारीन्निगृह्य पुनस्तान्स्वराज्येष्वस्थापयत् ॥४॥ यः शस्त्राणि प्रयुङ्क्ते स शस्त्रैरेव म्रियते ॥५॥ न युद्धमगत्वा केनापि कीर्तिर्लभ्येत ॥६॥ तस्मिन्वणिजि राजानमुपगच्छति कवयो यद्ददाति स तत्कथं वयमाप्नुयामेत्यमन्यन्त ॥७॥ बाणधनूंषि प्रयुञ्जानानरीन्घातयित्वा राज्ञाजीयत युद्धे ॥८॥ मन्त्रिण आनीय राज्ञा धर्मो विधीयते ॥९॥ तया दमयन्त्या पतिं त्यक्त्वा वनं गत्वा तत्रोषित्वागच्छतो मृगस्य शब्दोऽश्रूयत ॥१०॥ अरिगृहीतधेनूर्मुक्त्वा स वीरो राजसकाश आगतः किमन्यत्करवाणीत्युक्तवांश्च ॥११॥ कामेन दह्यमानानागतान्दृष्ट्वा के देवाः के च मनुष्या इति दमयन्ती नाजानात् ॥१२॥

TRANSLATE into Sanskrit, using continuatives wherever possible.

1. After playing in the waters of the river with his

wives, Rāma went to his house and ate [eat : bhojanaṃ kṛ]. 2. When Rāma won Laṅkā [use locative absolute with a past active participle], all the gods attained happiness. 3. The girl brought water from the tank, entered the house, and saw the boy burning with desire. 4. In this world, only the rich may live with happiness and die thinking, "Now I go to paradise." [Use continuatives for live, and think. Put die last]. 5. The boy ran from the tank in which the girls were bathing and summoned his friends. 6. After he bathed [continuative], the book was read by the teacher.

एकमप्यक्षरं यस्तु गुरुः शिष्यं निवेदयेत् ।
पृथिव्यां नास्ति तद्द्रव्यं यद्दत्त्वानृणी भवेत् ॥

अक्षर	syllable
गुरु	guru
निविद् (caus. निवेदयति)	impart to (with acc. of thing imparted and person imparted to)
पृथिवी	earth
द्रव्यं	thing, thing of value
अनृणिन्	debtless (ṛṇa means debt)

दुग्ध्वा हि भुज्यते क्षीरं गां विक्रीय न भुज्यते ।
तद्वद्दुग्धप्रयोगेन भोज्यं राष्ट्रं महीभृता ॥

दुह् (दोग्धि)	milk
भुज् (भुनक्ति)	eat
क्षीरम्	milk
विक्री (विक्रीणाति)	sell
तद्वत्	like that
दुग्धप्रयोगेन	in accord with the application of what is milked (i.e. of the milk), after the example of the milk
भोज्य	is to be enjoyed
राष्ट्रम्	kingdom
महीभृत	king

यस्य यस्य हि यो भावस्तस्य तस्य विभाव्य तत् ।
अनुप्रविश्य मेधावी तं तमात्मवशं नयेत् ॥

भाव	inclination, proclivity, nature
विभू	(caus., vibhāvayati). In the caus., think of, take into consideration
अनुप्रविश्	adapt oneself to
मेधाविन्	wise person, clever person
वश	power, control

Lesson 28

THE INFINITIVE; THE SIMPLE FUTURE; THE PERIPHRASTIC FUTURE

Each of these three forms is made from a verb stem strengthened by guṇating its vowel. As in most other cases in which the stem is strengthened by guṇation, the vowel is guṇated only if it is final, or if it is in a light syllable (i.e. is short and followed by no more than one consonant). If the vowel of the stem is non-final, and is in a heavy syllable, then it is unchanged.

I. The Infinitive

a. Formation. The infinitive is formed by adding -tum to the strong stem. In the list given later in this lesson, it is given for all verbs which you have had. In some cases, the union vowel -i- is inserted between the end of the root and the -tum of the infinitive.

b. Uses of the infinitive. The strict sense of the Sanskrit infinitive is motive or purpose of action, but there are a few cases in which it may be used with nouns and adjectives, as "fit to do," "able to go," "time to read." The most common words with which the infinitive is used are as follows :

1. With verbs and substantives meaning "to wish" or "to desire," provided that the agents of the infinitive and the verb are the same, as "I wish to go," that is, "ahaṃ gantum icchāmi." One cannot say, "I wish you to go" in Sanskrit. (For the roots exemplified in this section, such as iṣ, desire, see the vocabulary.)

2. With verbs meaning to be able, to make bold, to know, to be wearied, to strive, to begin, to get, to set about, to bear, to be pleased, and to be. For example, "sa rājānaṃ hantuṃ śaknoti," "He is able to kill the king"; "bhojanaṃ bhoktuṃ vidyate," "There is food to eat."

3. With words meaning sufficient, strong, able, and nouns meaning ability, power, or skill. For example, "tatra gantuṃ balaṃ na vidyate tasya," "He does not have the strength to go there."

4. With words meaning time. For example, "idānīm avasara ātmānaṃ darśayitum," Now is the time (avasaraḥ) to show yourself."

5. With arh, "ought," "should" (usually imparting a sense of deference). For example, "bhavān āgantum arhati," "You should come," i.e. "Please come."

The Sanskrit infinitive has no passive form, the same form being used to denote both active and passive senses. However, when the infinitive is to be translated in an active sense, the main verb of the sentence, with which the infinitive is construed, is active, while when it is to be translated by a passive, the main verb must be passive. Thus,

aham taṃ hantuṃ śaknomi, "I can kill him."

sa mayā hantuṃ śakyate, "He can be killed by me."

A passive bhāve construction may also be used with the infinitive, as sa pustakaṃ paṭhitum icchati, "He wishes to read the book." (primary, not bhāve); tena pustakaṃ paṭhitum iṣyate, "It is wished to read the book by him," i.e. "He wishes to read the book." (bhāve version)

The causative infinitive is formed simply by adding -itum to the causative stem in -ay. For example dā, give, forms the simple infinitive dātum, and the causative infinitive dāpayitum (adding -itum to the causative stem dāpay-). Its use is straightforward, as

sa kavibhiḥ kathāḥ kārayati, "He causes his poets to make stories."

sa kavibhiḥ kathāḥ kārayitum icchati, "He wishes to cause his poets to make stories."

II. The Simple Future

a. Formation. The simple future is formed by adding -sy- or -iṣy- to the strengthened root. It is given for all verbs which you have had in the list below. As you will notice, when -sy- is added, roots ending in consonants modify those consonants according to the rules given for finals in lesson 10. The future takes the present thematic active of middle endings, depending on whether the verb is active or middle. Thus the simple future of bhū and labh is as follows :

Active :	Singular	Dual	Plural
1st person	bhaviṣyāmi	bhaviṣyāvaḥ	bhaviṣyāmaḥ
2nd person	bhaviṣyasi	bhaviṣyathaḥ	bhaviṣyatha
3rd person	bhaviṣyati	bhaviṣyataḥ	bhaviṣyanti
Middle :			
1st person	labhiṣye	labhiṣyāvahe	labhiṣyāmahe
2nd person	labhiṣyase	labhiṣyethe	labhiṣyadhve
3rd person	labhiṣyate	labhiṣyete	labhiṣyante

Note that all roots in the future, even if they are athematic in the present, take the thematic endings. Thus dāsyāmi, dāsyasi, etc. from dā.

The future causative is formed by adding -iṣy- to the causative root in -ay, and by conjugating it in the active as above. Thus dāpayiṣyāmi, "I will cause to give."

The simple future passive is identical in form to the simple future middle. Thus labhiṣyate could mean either "will obtain" or "will be obtained."

Just as the simple future takes the present endings, it forms participles in the same way as the present tense, only from the future stem rather than the present stem. Thus bhaviṣyant, "which will be" and labhiṣyamāna, "which will obtain." If you reread the preceding paragraph, you will realize that labhiṣyamāṇa could also mean "which will be obtained."

A few examples. kariṣyati, "he will do." kariṣyate, "it will be done." kariṣyantī, "[she] who will do"; kariṣyamāṇa, "which will be done." kārayiṣyati, "he will cause to do"; kārayiṣyate, "it will be caused to do"; kārayiṣyan, "[he] who causes to do"; kārayiṣyamāṇaḥ, "[he] who will be caused to do." All of these forms are straightforward, even though they seem difficult at first glance. Study them until you are sure how and why they are formed as they are.

b. Uses of the simple future. This tense, which is far more common than the periphrastic future (given below), is employed to denote indefinite future time, today's future time, and recent and future continuous time, while the periphrastic future denotes a remote time not of today. In fact, most authors are not very careful in choosing which one to use, though the periphrastic future generally does have a sense of remoteness. When the close proximity of a future action is intended, the present or the simple future may be used, as "I will go to the city today," that is, "adya nagaraṃ gacchāmi" or "adya nagaraṃ gamiṣyāmi."

III. The Periphrastic Future. a. Formation. This form developed from the agent noun: "The king is a doer" came to mean "the king will do," that is, "rājā kartā." In the first and second persons, the appropriate forms of the verb as, to be, are added, while in the third person they are omitted. The agent noun which is the periphrastic future takes singular, dual, and plural in the third person, while in the first and second persons, it is always singular (the number then being indicated by the form of as). As is shown in the table below, in which the third singular active/middle periphrastic future is given for all verbs you have had, this form is made from the strengthened stem, to which -tā, -tārau, and -tāraḥ (the nominative singular, dual, and plural of the agent noun in -tṛ) are added. The periphrastic future of ji, conquer, and of vṛt are as follows (note the irregular first person singular middle) :

Active :	Singular	Dual	Plural
1st person	jetāsmi	jetāsvaḥ	jetāsmaḥ
2nd person	jetāsi	jetāsthaḥ	jetāstha
3rd person	jetā	jetārau	jetāraḥ
Middle :			
1st person	vartitāhe	vartitāsvahe	vartitāsmahe
2nd person	vartitāṣe	vartitāsāthe	vartitādhve
3rd person	vartitā	vartitārau	vartitāraḥ

The future periphrastic has no passive, and no participles. Its causative may be formed by adding -itā, etc., to the causative stem in -ay, as kārayitā, "he will cause to do," from kṛ.

b. Use of the periphrastic future. As explained above, the periphrastic future, which is far less common than the simple future, denotes a remote future action.

[There is, in addition to the simple and periphrastic future, a rare form called the conditional, made from the same base in -sy- as the simple future, but adding the augment and the thematic imperfect endings to that base. The conditional is used in those conditional sentences in which the non-performance of the action is implied, or where the falsity of the antecedent is implied as a ma ter of fact. It corresponds to English sentences of the form, "if—had," "if—had not." For example, "If the king had come there would have been no war" would be translated, "yadi rājāgamiṣyat tadā yuddhaṃ nābhaviṣyat." Note that in future conditional sentences, such as "if it rains, we will sow corn," both verbs may be placed in the present, the simple future, or the aorist (which will be given in the appendix), but not in the conditional.]

Root	Infinitive	Simple fut. 3rd singular	Periphrastic future 3rd singular
adhī	adhyetum	adhyeṣyate	adhyetā
as	none	none	none
āp	āptum	āpsyati	āptā
ās	āsitum	āsisyate	āsitā
āhve	āhvayitum	āhvayiṣyati	āhvātā
i	etum	eṣyati	etā
iṣ	eṣṭum	eṣiṣyati	eṣṭā
upagam	upagantum	upagamiṣyati	upagantā
kṛ	kartum	kariṣyati	kartā
kṛṣ	kraṣṭum	karkṣyati	karṣṭā
kḷp	kalpitum	kalpiṣyate	kalpitā
krī	kretum	kreṣyati	kretā
krīḍ	krīḍitum	krīḍiṣyati	krīḍitā
gam	gantum	gamiṣyati	gantā
grah	grahītum	grahīṣyati	grahītā
cur	corayitum	corayiṣyati	corayitā
jan	janitum	janiṣyate	janitā
ji	jetum	jeṣyati	jetā

jīv	jīvitum	jīviṣyati	jīvitā
jñā	jñātum	jñāsyati	jñātā
tyaj	tyaktum	tyakṣyati	tyaktā
dah	dagdhum	dhakṣyati	dagdhā
dā	dātum	dāsyati	dātā
dhāv	dhāvitum	dhāviṣyati	dhāvitā
naś	naṣṭum	naśiṣyati/naṅkṣyati	naśitā
nigrah	nigrahītum	nigrahīṣyati	nigrahītā
nirdiś	nirdeṣṭum	nirdekṣyati	nirdeṣṭā
nī	netum	neṣyati	netā
paṭh	paṭhitum	paṭhiṣyati	paṭhitā
paś	draṣṭum	drakṣyati	draṣṭā
pā	pātum	pāsyati	pātā
pīḍ	pīḍitum	pīḍiṣyati	pīḍitā
pracch	praṣṭum	prakṣyati	praṣṭā
pratīkṣ	pratīkṣitum	pratīkṣiṣyati	pratīkṣitā
prayuj	prayoktum	prayokṣye	prayoktā
brū	none	none	none
bhū	bhavitum	bhaviṣyati	bhavitā
bhṛ	bhartum	bhariṣyati	bhartā
man	mantum	maṃsyati	mantā
muc	moktum	mokṣyati	moktā
mṛ	martum	mariṣyate	martā
yam	yantum	yaṃsyati	yantā
labh	labdhum	lapsyate	labdhā
likh	likhitum/ lekhitum	lekhiṣyati	lekhitā
vac	vaktum	vakṣyati	vaktā
vad	vaditum	vadiṣyati	none
vas	vastum	vatsyati	vastā
vah	voḍhum	vakṣyati	voḍhā
vid	none	none	none
vidhā	vidhātum	vidhāsyati/te	vidhātā
viś	veṣṭum	vekṣyati	veṣṭā
vṛt	vartitum	vartiṣyate	vartitā
vṛdh	vardhitum	vardhiṣyate	vardhitā
śaṃs	śaṃsitum	śaṃsiṣyati	śaṃsitā
śak	none	śakṣyati	śaktā

śru	śrotum	śroṣyati	śrotā
sev	sevitum	seviṣyate	sevitā
sthā	sthātum	sthāsyati	sthātā
spṛś	spraṣṭum	sprakṣyati	spraṣṭā
smṛ	smartum	smariṣyati	smartā
han	hantum	haniṣyati	hantā
has	hasitum	hasiṣyati	hasitā
hā	hātum	hāsyati	hātā

VOCABULARY :

अर्ह् (अर्हति; deficient in other forms)	ought, should (followed by infinitive)
इष् (इच्छति, एषयति, इष्यते, इष्ट)	want, desire (followed by infinitive)
दरिद्र	poor, indigent
दूत	messenger, emissary
बलम्	power, strength, might
शक् (शक्नोति, शाकयति, शक्यते, शक्त)	be able, can (followed by infinitive)
स्वल्प	a little

TRANSLATE into English :

इदानीं ते दूता मामाह्वयिष्यन्तीति मन्यमानो राजा नगरमविशत् ।।१।। त्वदस्यां पत्न्यां जनिष्यमानः पुत्रस्त्वां हन्तेति क्षत्रियमृषिरवदत् ।।२।। मन्त्रिभिर्जनानाह्वापयितुमिच्छामीत्यृषिरब्रवीत् ।।३।। केन शत्रुणा मद्राज्य आगन्तुमिष्यते ।।४।। सर्वे इमे वणिजो धनं दातुं शक्नुवन्ति ।।५।। न मच्छत्रुभिर्मया सह युद्धं कर्तुं शक्यते ।।६।। न तथा विधातुमर्हति भवानिति मन्त्रिणमुक्त्वा दरिद्राः प्रजा नाददन्विहितं धनम् ।।७।। स्वल्पमपि कोपस्य मनुष्यं हन्तुं शक्नोति ।।८।। तेन राज्ञात्र सेनया सह गमिष्यत इति दूतेनारिराज उक्तः ।।९।। अत्र सदा धर्मवत्यः प्रजा भवितार इति दृष्टमृषिणा ।।१०।। अन्यान्निग्रहीतुं बलं प्रयुञ्जाना नंक्ष्यन्ति ।।११।। इयं कथोच्यमाना सर्वं दुःखं नाशयिष्यति ।।१२।।

TRANSLATE into Sanskrit : [Those who] use weapons to strike down others will die by weapons. [Use a present participle to translate *use.*] 2. Having said that he would give nothing to the poor, the merchant entered his house. [cf. sentence 7 above] 3. You should come to see my family. 4. Even if you give her everything, she will not be able to live without her husband. [Translate "without her husband" by patihīna, a compound from pati and hīna, the past passive participle of hā. The word patihīna must, of course, agree with its antecedent.] 5. Having remembered that the king would come after killing his foes, the girls ran to see him. 6. Having caused the deer to die, and having heard the words of the sage, the king, distressed [duḥkhin], said [use continuative], "Never again will I come here to kill," and went to the city.

VERSES :

यस्य चाप्रियमन्विच्छेत्तस्य कुर्यात्सदा प्रियम् ।
व्याधा मृगवधं कर्तुं सम्यग्गायन्ति सुस्वरम् ॥

प्रिय	pleasant, dear
अन्विष् (अन्विच्छति)	wish, desire something (acc.) for a person (gen.)
व्याध	hunter
वध	killing
सम्यक्	well
गै (गायति)	sing
सुस्वरम्	melodiously, sweetly

द्वाविमौ पुरुषौ लोके न भूतौ न भविष्यतः ।
प्रार्थितं यश्च कुरुते यश्च नार्थयते परम् ॥

द्वौ	two
पुरुष	man
प्रार्थ् (प्रार्थयते)	desire, ask, request
अर्थ् (अर्थयते)	ask (for a favor or help)
पर	other, another

Lesson 29

THE PERFECT; THE PERFECT PERIPHRASTIC; THE PERFECT PARTICIPLE

I. The formation of the simple perfect. Like the present tense stem of class 3 verbs, which you learned in lesson 21, the stem of the simple perfect is reduplicated. Reduplication consists of repeating the root twice before adding the appropriate endings. However, the final consonant (if there is one) is omitted from the reduplicating syllable (i.e. the first syllable), and there are some rules governing changes which the root must undergo in the reduplicating syllable, as you have learned in lesson 21. Those rules are repeated here, so that you may refresh your memory. In the second syllable, the root is unchanged.

a. The consonant of the reduplicating syllable is in general the first consonant of the root. Thus paprach from prach; śiśri from śri; bubudh from budh.

b. A non-aspirate is substituted in reduplication for an aspirate. Thus dadhā from dhā; perfect stem babhṛ from bhṛ (see f. below).

c. A palatal is substituted for a guttural or h. The palatal is either voiced or unvoiced as the letter for which it substitutes is voiced or unvoiced (remember that h is considered to be voiced in Sanskrit). Thus cakṛ from kṛ; cikhid from khid; jagrabh from grabh; jahṛ from hṛ.

d. If the root begins with a sibilant followed by a non-nasal stop (not a semivowel), then the consonant of the reduplicating syllable is the stop, modified according to rules b and c if necessary. Thus tasthā from sthā; caskand from skand; caskhal from skhal; cuścut from ścut; paspṛś from spṛś; pusphuṭ from sphuṭ. If the root begins with a sibilant followed by a nasal or semivowel, then rule a applies. Thus sasmṛ from smṛ; sasnā from snā; śuśru from śru; śiśliṣ from śliṣ.

e. A long vowel is shortened in the reduplicating syllable. Thus dadā from dā; bibhī from bhī.

f. The vowel ṛ does not appear in the reduplicating syllable. Rather, it is replaced by -i- in the present system of class 3 verbs (the class which is reduplicated to form the present stem); and by -a- in the perfect of verbs. Thus perfect babhṛ from bhṛ; papṛc from pṛc; cakṛ from kṛ; cakṛṣ from kṛṣ.

These rules, which you studied before in lesson 21, need to be amplified somewhat here for the perfect tense.

g. A root with initial a- before a single final consonant repeats the a-, which then fuses with the radical vowel to form ā-. Thus ās- from as.

h. Roots which may undergo saṃprasāraṇa do so in the reduplicating syllables in the strong forms (all 3 persons of the active singular), and in both the reduplicating and root syllables in the weak forms (all forms but the 3 persons of the singular). Thus for the strong perfect stem of grah, the reduplicating syllable is formed from gṛh, which grah becomes when it undergoes saṃprasāraṇa, and one gets jagrah- / jagrāh- (see rule b. below in the section on strengthening). The weak form is jagṛh-. From svap, sleep, the strong perfect stem is suṣvap- / suṣvāp-, the weak is suṣup-. For roots which begin in a vowel after they have undergone saṃprasāraṇa (e.g. vac), see rule i., immediately following.

i. A root with i- or u- before a single final consonant repeats the i- or u-, which then fuses with the radical vowel to form ī- or ū-, except in the strong forms. There, rule h applies if the initial i- or u- was the result of saṃprasāraṇa. If not, then the vowel of the root syllable is guṇated, while the reduplicated vowel is unstrengthened and is followed by its own semivowel before the guṇated root. Thus from iṣ, the strong perfect stem is iyeṣ-, the weak stem, īṣ- For vac, a root which undergoes saṃprasāraṇa, the strong perfect stem is uvac-/uvāc-, while the weak stem is ūc-.

j. Roots which begin with vowels long by nature or by position (i.e. followed directly by two consonants) do not make the simple perfect, but rather the perfect periphrastic, explained below. But āp is an exception and makes simple perfect forms (strong and weak forms āp-).

Like the athematic present classes in the present and imperfect, *the perfect takes strong forms in all three persons of the active singular, and weak forms elsewhere.* The rules for strengthening are as follows :

a. A final vowel takes either guṇa or vṛddhi in the first singular active, guṇa in the second singular active, and vṛddhi in the third singular active. Thus from kṛ, 1st active singular cakara or cakāra; 2nd active singular cakartha; 3rd active singular cakāra. Note that bhū is an exception and forms both strong and weak perfect forms from the stem babhūv-.

b. Medial -a- before a single final consonant follows the analogy of the final vowel—it is lengthened (vṛddhied) optionally in the first singular active, always in the third singular active.

c. *Roots having a medial -a- before a single final consonant, and beginning with a single consonant that is repeated unchanged in the reduplication (i.e. which is not an aspirate, an unvoiced guttural, or h) contract in the weak forms of the perfect their root and reduplication together into one syllable, having -e- as its vowel. Thus pat, fall, makes the weak perfect stem pet- (but the strong stem papat-/papāt-).*

d. The root vid, to know, has in the perfect the strong stem ved- and the weak stem vid-.

You will have noted that all of these rules are rather complex. It is emphasized at this point that you should not bother to memorize them. Rather, it is enough for you to be acquainted with the general principles involved, so that you can recognize those perfect forms which you encounter. In order to help you, the 3rd person singular and plural forms of all the verbs you have had are listed at the end of this lesson.

The personal endings of the perfect are as follows:

Active :	Singular	Dual	Plural
1st person	a	va	ma
2nd person	tha	athuḥ	a
3rd person	a	atuḥ	uḥ

Middle :	Singular	Dual	Plural
1st person	e	vahe	mahe
2nd person	se	āthe	dhve
3rd person	e	āte	re

In general, perfect stems which end in consonants take the union vowel -i- before those endings which begin with consonants.

For verb stems which end in -ā, -ai, o, and -au (e.g. dā, sthā, pā), the first and third singular active endings are -au. Thus tasthau, "I stood," "he stood."

As an example, the perfect conjugation of kṛ in both the middle and active is given below, even though kṛ is usually only active in classical Sanskrit :

Active :			
1st person	cakara/cakāra	cakṛva	cakṛma
2nd person	cakartha	cakrathuḥ	cakra
3rd person	cakāra	cakratuḥ	cakruḥ
Middle :			
1st person	cakre	cakṛvahe	cakṛmahe
2nd person	cakṛṣe	cakrāthe	cakṛdhve
3rd person	cakre	cakrāte	cakrire

You should memorize the third-person endings of the perfect, as they are commonly met with. The other forms, which are far less common, you need only look over.

In the chart below, the perfect 3rd singular and 3rd plural forms are given for all verbs you have had.

II. Formation of the Periphrastic Perfect. This is used instead of the simple perfect for all verbs beginning with a long vowel or with a short vowel followed directly by two consonants, for all causatives, for all verbs which make their present stems by adding -y or -ay (i.e. class 10 verbs and denominatives[1]), and for the desiderative and the intensative,[2] which, like the

1. The denominative class of verbs is formed from nouns, as senāyati "He treats like an army." It is described in the appendix.

2. The desiderative and the intensative, like the causative, are secondary conjugations. They are described in the appendix.

causative, are secondary conjugations which a verb may take. Note that a given verb stem forms *either the simple perfect or the periphrastic perfect, but never both.* The majority of verbs uses the simple perfect for the primary verb stem, and the periphrastic perfect for the causative stem.

The periphrastic perfect is formed by adding -ām to the present stem and then by affixing to that the perfect forms of kṛ or as (or rarely, bhū) in the active, and of kṛ in the middle. Of course, the form of kṛ etc. used will correspond to the mode (active or middle), person, and number into which the verb is placed. If you are making a causative perfect, then the causative present stem must be used. Thus for kṛ, the causative present stem is kāray-. "He caused to do" would be kārayāmāsa or kārayāṃ cakāra. From cur, the 3rd singular active perfect is corayāmāsa or corayāṃ cakāra. From ās, the 3rd singular perfect is āsāṃ cakre (note that ās must take the periphrastic perfect, as it begins with a long vowel.) In the list at the end of this lesson, the perfect causative 3rd singular (which must be a periphrastic perfect) is given for all verbs which you have had.

On the next page, the conjugations of dā in the causative perfect, and of ās in the perfect, are given.

Again it is stressed that you need memorize only the third person forms. The others, you should look over but not memorize.

III. Uses of the Perfect. In classical Sanskrit, the imperfect, the perfect, and the aorist (given in the appendix) are used interchangeably for any past action. Pāṇiṇi makes the following distinction, however, (which is not generally observed) : the *imperfect* denotes past action done previous to the current day (anadyatane laṅ); the *perfect* denotes past action done previous to the current day *and not witnessed by the speaker* (parokṣe liṭ); the *aorist* is used to refer to an indefinite past time (bhūtārthe luṅ). You might think, according to this scheme, that the perfect could never be used in the first person, as there could never be a 1st-person past action not witnessed by the speaker. The poet Māgha in his poem, *Śiśupālavadha*, has created such a situation, from which a verse is given at the end of this lesson.

Active :	Singular	Dual	Plural
1st person	dāpayām āsa/ dāpayāṃ cakāra	dāpayām āsiva/ dāpayāṃ cakṛva	dāpayām āsim dāpayāṃ cakṛma
2nd person	dāpayām āsitha/ dāpayāṃ cakartha	dāpayām āsathuḥ/ dāpayāṃ cakrathuḥ	dāpayām āsa dāpayāṃ cakra
3rd person	dāpayām āsa/ dāpayāṃ cakāra	dāpayām āsatuḥ dāpayāṃ cakratuḥ	dāpayām āsuḥ dāpayāṃ cakruḥ
Middle			
1st person	āsāṃ cakre	āsāṃ cakṛvahe	āsāṃ cakṛmahe
2nd person	āsāṃ cakṛṣe	āsāṃ cakrāthe	āsāṃ cakṛdhve
3rd person	āsāṃ cakre	āsāṃ cakrāte	āsāṃ cakrire

As with the future tense, the perfect passive is identical in form to the perfect middle. This is true for both the simple perfect and the periphrastic perfect.

IV. The Perfect Participle. a. The Active Participle. This participle is made by adding -vāṃs to the weak form of the perfect stem. It is similar in meaning to the past active participle, but it is far less common than that form, being encountered in classical Sanskrit with only a few verbs with any regularity. No perfect participle may be made from stems or conjugations which take the perfect periphrastic. The ending -vāṃs becomes -us in the weak forms, -vat before the pāda endings, -vān in the masculine nominative singular, and -uṣī in the feminine. Thus the declension of vidvāṃs, "someone who knows," "a learned person" is as follows:

Masculine	Singular	Dual	Plural
Nom.	vidvān	vidvāṃsau	vidvāṃsaḥ
Acc.	vidvāṃsam	vidvāṃsau	viduṣaḥ
Inst.	viduṣā	vidvadbhyām	vidvadbhiḥ

etc., with endings of pad.

Neuter :			
Nom.	vidvat	viduṣī	vidvāṃsi
Acc.	,,	,,	,,

etc., as in the masculine.

Feminine :			
Nom.	viduṣī	viduṣyau	viduṣyaḥ

etc., as with nadī.

[b. The Perfect Middle Participle. This participle, almost never encountered in classical Sanskrit, is made by adding -āna to the weak form of the perfect stem. It is declined like deva in the masculine, phalam in the neuter, and senā in the feminine.]

V. On the next few pages are given the 3rd person singular and plural perfect forms of all the verbs you have had, together with the 3rd person singular causative perfect form.

Root	3rd sg. perfect	3rd pl. perfect	3rd sg. perf. caus.
adhī	adhīye	adhīyire	adhyāpayām āsa
as	āsa	āsuḥ	none
avagam	avajagāma	avajagmuḥ	avagamayām āsa
ājñā	none	none	ājñāpayām āsa
ānī	ānināya	āninyuḥ	ānāyayām āsa
āp	āpa	āpuḥ	āpayām āsa
ās	āsāṃ cakre	āsāṃ cakrire	āsayām āsa
āhve	ājuhāva	ājuhuvuḥ	āhvāpayām āsa
i	iyāya	īyuḥ	āpayām āsa
iṣ	iyeṣa	īṣuḥ	eṣayām āsa
upagam	upajagāma	upajagmuḥ	upagamayām āsa
kṛ	cakāra	cakruḥ	kārayām āsa
kṛṣ	cakarṣa	cakṛṣuḥ	karṣayām āsa
kḷp	cakḷpe	cakḷpire	kalpayām āsa
krī	cikrāya	cikriyuḥ	krāpayām āsa
krīḍ	cikrīḍa	cikrīḍuḥ	krīḍayām āsa
gam	jagāma	jagmuḥ	gamayām āsa
grah	jagrāha	jagṛhuḥ	grāhayām āsa
cur	corayām āsa	corayām āsuḥ	corayām āsa
jan	jajñe	jajñire	janayām āsa
ji	jigāya	jigyuḥ	jāpayām āsa
jīv	jijīva	jijīvuḥ	jīvayām āsa
jñā	jajñau	jajñuḥ	jñāpayām āsa
tyaj	tatyāja	tatyajuḥ	tyājayām āsa
dah	dadāha	dehuḥ	dāhayām āsa
dā	dadau	daduḥ	dāpayām āsa
dhāv	dadhāva	dadhāvuḥ	dhāvayām āsa
naś	nanāśa	neśuḥ	nāśayām āsa
nigrah	nijagrāha	nijagṛhuḥ	nigrāhayām āsa
nirdiś	nirdideśa	nirdidiśuḥ	nirdeśayām āsa
nī	ninAya	ninyuḥ	nāyayām āsa
paṭh	papāṭha	papaṭhuḥ	pāṭhayām āsa
paś	dadarśa	dadṛśuḥ	darśayām āsa
pā	papau	papuḥ	pāyayām āsa
pīḍ	pipīḍa	pipīḍuḥ	pīḍayām āsa
pracch	papraccha	papracchuḥ	prachayām āsa
pratīkṣ	pratīkṣāṃ cakre	pratīkṣāṃ cakrire	pratīkṣayām āsa

prayuj	prayuyuje	prayuyujire	prayojayām āsa
brū	none	none	none
bhū	babhūva	babhūvuḥ	bhāvayām āsa
bhṛ	babhāra	babhruḥ	bhārayām āsa
man	mene	menire	mānayām āsa
muc	mumoca	mumucuḥ	mocayām āsa
mṛ	mamāra[1]	mamruḥ[1]	mārayām āsa
yaj	ije	ijire	yājayām āsa
yam	yayāma	yemuḥ	yāyayām āsa
labh	lebhe	lebhire	lambhayām āsa
likh	lilekha	lilikhuḥ	lekhayām āsa
vac	uvāca	ūcuḥ	vācayām āsa
vad	uvāda	ūduḥ	vādayām āsa
vas	uvāsa	ūṣuḥ	vāsayām āsa
vah	uvāha	ūhuḥ	vāhayām āsa
vid, to exist	none	none	none
vid, to know	veda	viduḥ	vedayām āsa
vidhā	vidadhau/ vidadhe	vidadhuḥ/ vidadhire	vidhāpayām āsa
viś	viveśa	viviśuḥ	veśayām āsa
vṛt	vavṛte	vavṛtire	vartayām āsa
vṛdh	vavṛdhe	vavṛdhire	vardhayām āsa
śaṃs	śaśaṃsa	śaśaṃsuḥ	śaṃsayām āsa
śak	śaśāka	śekuḥ	śākayām āsa
śru	śuśrāva	śuśruvuḥ	śrāvayām āsa
sev	siṣeve	siṣevire	sevayām āsa
sthā	tasthau	tasthuḥ	sthāpayām āsa
spṛś	pasparśa	paspṛśuḥ	sparśayām āsa
smṛ	sasmāra	sasmaruḥ	smārayām āsa
han	jaghāna	jaghnuḥ	ghātayām āsa
has	jahāsa	jahasuḥ	hāsayām āsa
hā	jahau	jahuḥ	hāpayām āsa

VOCABULARY :

अन्त	end
अवगम् (अवगमयति, अवगम्यते, अवगत)	understand
आज्ञा (causative only आज्ञापयति, आज्ञाप्यते, आज्ञप्त)	order, command

1. The root mṛ takes the middle throughout the present system, but the active in the perfect.

आनी (आनयति, आनाययति, आनीयते, आनीत) bring, lead to

ज्ञानम् knowledge

ब्रह्मन् masculine: the god Brahmā; neuter : Brahma, a formula, the Absolute, the principle underlying the univease. (Note the different nom. sg. of the masc. and neuter)

यज् (यजते, याजयति, इज्यते, इष्ट) sacrifice, with the accusative of the deity sacrificed to and the instrumental of what is sacrificed.

विद् (वेत्ति, वेदयति, विद्यते, विदित) (class 2) know. Found most commonly in the perfect (veda/viduḥ), which is translated as present.

विद्वांस् (the perfect active participle of vid) a learned person, a wise person

हविस् (neuter) an oblation or burnt offering. Most commonly, the oblation of ghee which is pouerd into the fire at the sacrifice.

TRANSLATE into English :

यं मन्त्रिणं राजाज्ञापयामास स एवागत्यामु ब्राह्मणमाह्वापयां चकार ।।१।। ब्रह्मणैवायं लोकश्चक्रे पुनश्च करिष्यते ।।२।। स ब्राह्मणोऽग्निमीजे हविषा ।।३।। अयं विद्वान्गृहमागत्यापठन्तं पुत्रं दृष्ट्वा तस्मै पुस्तकं ददौ पठ्यतां त्वयेत्युवाच च ।।४।। यस्य ज्ञानस्य नान्तो विद्यते स एव ब्रह्म वेद ।।५।। ब्राह्मणः पत्नी च नृपस्य पादौ पस्पृशतुरावयोरिष्टं दीयतां भवतेत्यूचतुश्च ।।६।। ब्रह्माणमिष्ट्वा सर्वकामैः स ऋषिर्यद्यदियेष तत्तदाप ।।७।। येषां विदुषां ज्ञानं विद्यते तेषां मृत्युर्नेतसकाशम् ।।८।। तेन राज्ञा स्वमन्त्रिण आनीत्य किं स मम शत्रुः कुर्यादिति पृष्टम् ।।९।। यस्य सेना बलवत्यास स एव मृतमरिं युद्धे ददर्श ।।१०।। स पिता बालैर्मित्राण्यानाययामास ।।११।। सोऽज्ञानी नृपः पुस्तकं पठित्वा न मया किं चनावगतमिति मन्त्रिणमुवाच ।।१२।।

TRANSLATE into Sanskrit, rendering all of the 3rd person past verbs in the perfect. 1. He saw his mother coming into the house. 2. The ministers asked what the king had heard in the city of the kṣatriyas. [use direct discourse.] 3. The two crows inhabited the woods in which the elephant was king. 4. While mother was bathing, I went to the house of that girl. 5. The Brahmins sacrificed the oblation to Indra. 6. While the Brahmins were sacrificing, which god's name did the kṣatriya recite ?

VERSES :

(See page 160, part III)

बहु जगद पुरस्तात्तस्य मत्ता किलाहं
चकर च किल चाटु प्रौढयोषिद्वदस्य ।
विदितमिति सखीभ्यो रात्रिवृत्तं विचिन्त्य
व्यपगतमदयाह्नि व्रीडितं मुग्धवध्वा ॥ (शिशुपालवधे ११।३६)

गद् say
पुरस्तात before, in front of
मत्त intoxicated
किल a particle indicating reported speech. Tamil -âm, Telugu aṭa
चाटु flattery, agreeable things
प्रौढ experienced, skilled
योषित् woman
-वत् like (a suffix)
सखी friend (fem.)
रात्रि night
वृत्तम् events, what happended
विचिन्त् think of
व्यपगम् leave, go from
मद intoxication
अहन् day
व्रीड् be ashamed (note passive bhāve construction)
मुग्ध innocent, naive
वधू woman

भोजनं देहि राजेन्द्र घृतसूपसमन्वितम् ।
माहिषं च शरच्चन्द्रचन्द्रिकाधवलं दधि ॥

(The first half of this verse is said to have been uttered by a Brahmin, his senses dulled from reciting the Vedas, to Kālidāsa, whom he wished to impress with his poetic skill. The second half is the poet's rejoinder)

इन्द्र king
घृतम् ghee
सूप soup
समन्वित accompanied by

(rājendra here is simply a polite mode of address)

माहिष	(adjective from mahiṣa) : of buffalo, "buffalo" as an adj.
शरत्	autumn
चन्द्र	moon
चन्द्रिका	moonlight
धवल	white
दधि	yogurt (eating buffalo yogurt is said to have a dulling effect on the intellect)

Lesson 30

THE THREE GERUNDIVES

The Sanskrit gerundive, which may be made in the three ways described below, is an adjective, corresponding in meaning to the Latin gerundive, and is to be translated literally by the phrase "to be—ed," though as shown below in the section on usage, other translations are often more felicitous in English. It is called by Apte, with justification, the potential passive participle, while Whitney erroneously calls it the future passive participle, a form which, as has been seen, can be made from the future stem in the middle, and therefore a quite separate form from the gerundive (see the 3rd paragraph on page 150).

I. Formation of the gerundives. Note that all of the gerundives are given at the end of this lesson for each verb which you have had. All of the gerundives are declined like deva in the masculine, phalam in the neuter, and like senā in the feminine.

1. The gerundive in -ya.

a. Before this suffix, final -ā of a stem becomes -e-, as deya from dā.

b. Other final vowels may remain unchanged, may be guṇated, may be vṛddhied, or may undergo optionally several of these processes depending on the verb. After guṇa or vṛddhi, the resulting -e or -ai sometimes becomes -ay or āy respectively before the -ya, while the resulting -o or -au always become respectively -av and -āv before -ya. If the root ends in a short vowel and is not guṇated or vṛddhied, then often -t- is inserted before -ya. Thus from ji, jeya or jayya; from śru śrutya, śravya, or śrāvya; from kṛ, kṛtya and kārya; and from bhū, bhavya and bhāvya.

c. For some verbs, medial -a- is unchanged, while for others it is lengthened. Thus from sad, sink, sadya; from vac, vācya.

d. Initial and medial i, u, and ṛ in a light syllable are sometimes unchanged, sometimes guṇated. Thus from guh, hide, guhya; from vid, know, vedya.

e. Causatives, class 10 verbs, and denominatives (see appendix) make the -ya gerundive on the present stem minus -ay. Thus from cur, corya. The causative gerundive of dā is dāpya.

2. The gerundive in -tavya. The gerundive suffix -tavya is added to the same stem to which the infinite in -tum is added. [The two forms are etymologically related, though in classical Sanskrit their meanings are quite different.]

3. The gerundive in -anīya. In general, radical vowels in light syllables are guṇated before this suffix. Final vowels are generally guṇated before this suffix. As with the -ya gerundive, class 10 verbs, causatives, and denominatives add this suffix to the present stem minus -ay.

II. The use of the gerundive. The gerundive can generally be translated literally by a "to be—'ed" phrase—simply "to be—ed," or "who is to be—ed," or, "the man who is to be—ed," etc. It denotes that the action or the state expressed by the root or derivative base must or ought to be done or undergone. For example, vācyam, vaktavyam, and vacanīyam all mean "that which ought to be said," literally, "that which is to be said." As in English, the Sanskrit implies either that it is fit to be said, that one is obliged to say it, or that it will inevitably be said. "Sa hantavyaḥ" means "he should be killed," literally, "he is to be killed." Note that as in this example, the gerundive is often used as a predicate adjective with the copula left out, thus in effect substituting for a finite verb.

The gerundive may be used in the neuter nominative singular to form a bhāve construction, like the past passive participle. Thus tena tatra gantavyam means literally "it is to be gone there by him," that is, "he must go there," "he should go there," or "he will certainly go there."

This last sense should be remarked upon. Occasionally, the gerundive is used to indicate that an action is inevitable in the future. Thus "tenāpi śabdaḥ kartavyah" means "he also will surely make a noise" (literally, "a noise is to be made by him also").

The gerundives of bhū in the neuter nominative singular, bhāvyam and bhavitavyam, are often used in a bhāve construction to mean "must be" or "in all probability is [are]." In both cases, both the subject and predicate of the English construction must be instrumental in the Sanskrit (cf. the note on the predicative instrumental on page 114). Thus "tena balavatā bhavitavyam" means "he is in all probability strong" or "he must be strong."

III. A list of gerundives of the verbs which you have had.

ROOT	-ya gerundive*	-tavya gerundive	-anīya gerundive
adhī	adhyeya	adhyetavya	none
arh	none	none	arhaṇīya
avagam	avagamya	avagantavya	avagamanīya
as	none	none	none
ājñā (caus.)	ājñāpya	ājñāpitavya	ājñāpanīya
ānī	āneya, ānayya	ānetavya	none
āp	āpya	āptavya	none
ās	none	āsitavya	none
āhve	āhavya	āhvayitavya	none
i	eya	etavya	none
iṣ	eṣya	eṣṭavya	eṣaṇīya
upagam	upagamya	upagantavya	upagamanīya
kṛ	kārya	kartavya	karaṇīya
kṛṣ	none	kraṣṭavya	karṣaṇīya
kḷp	kalpya	kalpitavya	kalpanīya
krī	kravya	kretavya	none
krīḍ	none	krīḍitavya	none
gam	gamya	gantavya	gamanīya
grah	grāhya	grahītavya	grahaṇīya
cur	corya	corayitavya	coraṇīya
jan	janya	janayitavya	none
ji	jeya	jetavya	none

*As has been seen in the lesson, some verbs take optionally more than one -ya gerundive. Here, only the ones commonly encountered are given.

jīv	jīvya	jīvitavya	jīvanīya
jñā	jñeya	jñātavya	none
tyaj	tyajya/tyājya	tyaktavya	none
dah	dāhya	dagdhavya	none
dā	deya	dātavya	none
dhāv	none	dhāvitavya	dhāvanīya
naś	none	naṣṭavya	none
nigrah	nigrāhya	nigrahītavya	nigrahaṇīya
nirdiś	nirdeśya	nirdeṣṭavya	none
nī	neya	netavya	none
paṭh	pāṭhya	paṭhitavya	paṭhanīya
paś	dṛśya	draṣṭavya	darśanīya
pā	peya	pātavya	pānīya
pīḍ	pīḍya	pīḍitavya	pīḍanīya
pracch	pṛcchya	praṣṭavya	none
pratīkṣ	pratīkṣya	pratīkṣitavya	pratīkṣaṇīya
prayuj	prayojya	prayoktavya	prayojanīya
brū	none	none	none
bhū	bhāvya	bhavitavya	none
bhṛ	bhṛtya/bhārya	bhartavya	bharaṇīya
man	mantavya	none	none
muc	mocya	moktavya	mocanīya
mṛ	none	martavya	none
yaj	yājya	yaṣṭavya	yājanīya
yam	yamya	yantavya	none
labh	labhya	labdhavya	none
likh	likhya/lekhya	likhitavya	lekhanīya
vac	vācya	vaktavya	vacanīya
vad	vādya	vaditavya	none
vas	vāsya	vastavya	none
vah	vāhya	voḍhavya	vāhanīya
vid, to exist	none	none	none
vid, to know	vedya	veditavya	vedanīya
vidhā	vidheya	vidhātavya	none
viś	veśya	veṣṭavya	none
vṛt	none	vartitavya	vartanīya
vṛdh	none	vardhitavya	vardhanīya
śaṃs	śaṃsya	none	śaṃsanīya
śak	śakya	none	none

śru	śravya/śrāvya	śrotavya	śravaṇīya
sev	sevya	sevitavya	sevanīya
sthā	stheya	sthātavya	none
spṛś	spṛśya	spraṣṭavya	sparśanīya
smṛ	smarya	smartavya	smaraṇīya
han	none	hantavya	none
has	hāsya	hasitavya	hasanīya
hā	heya	hātavya	none

Note that even those verbs for which -ya, -tavya, or -anīya gerundives are lacking usually have such forms in the causative For example, vidhā forms vidhāpanīya, "to be caused to ordain," "to be caused to be ordained," and śaṃs forms śaṃsayitavya, "to be caused to praise," "to be caused to be praised." Note here that as with the caus. of the past nassive part., the translated infinitive may be either active or passive.

A special note is in order on the use of the gerundive of śak, śakya. This form has lost its gerundive significance, and rather stands simply for the passive of śak. Thus "so 'rir hantuṃ śakyaḥ" means "that enemy can be killed." "Idaṃ pustakaṃ tvayā paṭhituṃ śakyam" means "this book can be read by you." The neuter nominative singular śakyam can be used similarly in bhāve constructions, as tatra gantuṃ śakyam, "It is possible to go there" (literally, "it can be goed there"). Such a construction can normally be rendered by "it is possible" followed by an infinitive.

VOCABULARY :

कारणम्	cause, reason
कार्यम्	effect, business, affair, matter, duty (a gerundive of kṛ)
भार्या	wife (gerundive of bhṛ, "she who is to be supported")
भृत्य	servant (gerundive of bhṛ, "to be supported")
माला	garland
स्वभाव	nature, natural constitution, innate disposition

TRANSLATE into English :

न त्वया जलं लब्धव्यम् । तया भृत्यया लभिष्यते ॥१॥ न कदाप्यरिः सन्नपि

दूतो हन्तव्यः ।।२।। न कदा चन स्वभावेन सह युद्धं कर्तुं शक्यम् ।।३।। त्वया साधवोऽश्वा आनाययितव्या इति मन्त्री राज्ञोक्तः ।।४।। कथमनया तव भार्यया न श्रुता भवेयुस्त्वत्पठिता वेदवाच इति ब्राह्मणमपृच्छद्राजा ।।५।। अस्मिंल्लोके दुःखमेव द्रष्टव्यं सर्वाभिर्जीवन्तीभिः प्रजाभिरिति महन्तं शब्दमकरोन्मृतपत्नीको वणिक् ।।६।। तन्नगरं गत्वा भवता स राजा द्रष्टव्यः कस्मादेते न मुक्ता इति प्रष्टव्यश्च ।।७।। त्वयैव प्रजानां सुखस्य कारणेन भवितव्यमित्यवदद्राजानं मन्त्री ।।८।। सर्वाणि कार्याणि कारणवन्ति न च किं चिदकारणकं जायते ।।९।। इयं माला त्वया ग्रहणीयेति यो वीरो बहूनरीन्हन्यात्स वक्तव्यः ।।१०।। केयं शिष्येभ्यः पुस्तकानि दर्शितवतीति पृष्ट आचार्यो मम भार्येत्यब्रवीत् ।।११।। सर्वभृत्या आहूय क्षेत्रं कर्षयतेति वक्तव्याः ।।१२।।

TRANSLATE into Sanskrit, rendering the underlined verbs by gerundives. Before translating such canstructions, rework them into a "to be—'ed" framework. 1. Since we must all live in the world, dharma must be performed (kṛ). 2. The lion will [certainly] come (continuative) and bathe. 3. Relatives, servants and wives of poets must be supported (bhṛ) by kings who give (use present active participle for "give"). 4. Even though the king said, "Flowers are not to be shown," his two wives came having grasped garlands. 5. Your servants are to be caused to make garlands. 6. The god should be sacrificed to with an oblation. After sacrificing [continuative], water should be drunk.

क्षन्तव्यो मन्दबुद्धीनामपराधो मनीषिणा ।
न हि सर्वत्र पाण्डित्यं सुलभं पुरुषे क्वचित् ।।

क्षम्	forgive
मन्द	slow, dense, stupid
बुद्धि	wit, judgment
अपराध	offense, sin
मनीषिन्	wise, intelligent
सर्वत्र	everywhere
पाण्डित्यम्	wisdom, intelligence, cleverness
सुलभ	easy to obtain, easy to find
पुरुष	man, person
क्व	where (interrogative)

पुष्पैरपि न योद्धव्यं किं पुनर्निशितैः शरैः ।
जये भवति सन्देहः प्रधानपुरुषक्षयः ॥

युध् (युध्यते)	fight
किं पुनर्	how much less
निशित	sharp
शर	arrow
जय	victory
सन्देह	doubt; risk; danger
प्रधान	chief, foremost
पुरुष	man
क्षय	loss

धन्यानां गिरिकन्दरे निवसतां ज्योतिः परं ध्यायताम् ।
आनन्दाश्रुजलं पिबन्ति शकुना निःशङ्कमङ्केशयाः ।
अस्माकं तु मनोरथपरिचितप्रासादवापीतट-
क्रीडाकाननकेलिकौतुकजुषामायुः परं क्षीयते ॥ (भर्तृहरिविरचितवैराग्यशतकात्)

धन्य	lucky, fortunate
कन्दर	cave
ज्योतिस्	light (neuter)
पर	highest
ध्यै (ध्यायति)	contemplate
आनन्द	joy
अश्रु	tear
शकुन	parrot
निःशङ्कम्	securely, without fear
अङ्केशय	sitting in (one's) lap
मनोरथ	wish (lit. thought-chariot)
परिचि (परिचिनोति)	assemble, put together, construct (V)
प्रासाद	palace
तट	shore, bank
क्रीडा	play
काननम्	grove. Krīḍākānanam : a pleasure grove
केलि	play, playing
कौतुकम्	elation, fun, joy
जुष्	experiencing, relishing
आयुस्	life, length of life
परम्	only
क्षि (क्षियति)	waste away, decay

APPENDIX 1

THE AORISTS, THE DESIDERATIVE, THE INTENSIVE, AND THE DENOMINATIVE

I. The Aorists. Theoretically, the aorist is used in classical Sanskrit to refer to indefinite past time (see page 160). In fact, however, it is used interchangably with the perfect and imperfect for all past actions, with the qualification that it is not remotely as common. The only other use of the aorist in classical Sanskrit is for negative commands with mā, in which case the augment is omitted before the aorist, and the aorist is placed in the correct number and person. With this exception, aorist forms always take the augment.

A. The simple aorists. These two aorists, the root aorist and the a- aorist, are formed simply from the unstrengthened verb stem.

1. The root aorist. This is formed simply by placing the augment before the verb stem, and then adding the imperfect athematic endings. It may be made in the active only, the middle using instead the s- aorist or the iṣ- aorist. The root aorist conjugation of bhū is as follows :

	Singular	Dual	Plural
1st person	abhūvam	abhūva	abhūma
2nd person	abhūḥ	abhūtam	abhūta
3rd person	abhūt	abhūtām	abhūvan

2. The a- aorist. This is formed by placing the augment before the verb stem, and then adding the imperfect thematic endings. It can be made in the active and middle, but the middle is rare. The a- aorist conjugation of gam is as follows:

1st person	agamam	agamāva	agamāma
2nd person	agamaḥ	agamatam	agamata
3rd person	agamat	agamatām	agaman

The middle is formed in the same way: by placing the augment before the verb stem and then adding to the stem the imperfect thematic mindle endings.

B. The sibilant aorists. These fall into two broad classes : the sibilant aorists which are conjugated like the athematic imperfect, and the sibilant aorist which is declined like the thematic imperfect. To the first group belong the s-, iṣ-, and siṣ-aorists, while to the second belongs the sa- aorist. The most common sibilant aorists are the s- aorist and the iṣ- aorist. The athematic sibilant aorists have several peculiarities in their conjugations: they end in -īḥ and -īt in the 2nd and 3rd persons sg. active respectively, and in -uḥ in the 3rd person plural active. In other respects they follow the athematic imperfect conjugation.

1. The s-aorist. This is made by adding s- to the strengthened and augmented root. A final vowel is vṛddhied in the active and guṇated in the middle, while a medial vowel is vṛddhied in the active and unchanged in the middle. The conjugation of nī in the active and middle is as follows :

Active :	Singular	Dual	Plural
1st person	anaiṣam	anaiṣva	anaiṣma
2nd person	anaiṣīḥ	anaiṣṭam	anaiṣṭa
3rd person	anaiṣīt	anaiṣṭām	anaiṣuḥ
Middle :			
1st person	aneṣi	aneṣvahi	aneṣmahi
2nd person	aneṣṭhāḥ	aneṣāthām	aneḍhvam
3rd person	aneṣṭa	aneṣātām	aneṣata

2. The iṣ-aorist. This is made by adding iṣ- to the strengthened and augmented root. A final vowel is vṛddhied in the active and guṇated in the middle, a medial vowel is guṇated in both voices, while a medial -a- is generally unchanged in both voices (though it may be lengthened in the active). The active

and middle iṣ- aorist conjugations of budh, wake, are as follows :

Active :	Singular	Dual	Plural
1st person	abodhiṣam	abodhiṣva	abodhiṣma
2nd person	abodhīḥ	abodhiṣṭam	abodhiṣṭa
3rd person	abodhīt	abodhiṣṭām	abodhiṣuḥ
Middle :			
1st person	abodhiṣi	abodhiṣvahi	abodhiṣmahi
2nd person	abodhiṣṭhāḥ	abodhiṣāthām	abodhiḍhvam
3rd person	abodhiṣṭa	abodhiṣātām	abodhiṣata

3. The siṣ- aorist. This aorist, which is rare, is made according to the grammarians from roots in -ā, and from nam, bow, yam, reach, and ram, be content. It is used only in the active, the corresponding middle being the s- aorist. It is conjugated like the iṣ- aorist. Thus the conjugation of yā, go, is as follows :

Active :			
1st person	ayāsiṣam	ayāsiṣva	ayāsiṣma
2nd person	ayāsīḥ	ayāsiṣṭam	ayāsiṣṭa
3rd person	ayāsīt	ayāsiṣṭām	ayāsiṣuḥ

4. The sa- aorist. This aorist takes the thematic imperfect endings. The roots allowed to form this aorist end in -ś, -ṣ, and -h, all of which sounds become in combination with the s- sign of the aorist -kṣ-. All roots which form this aorist have, furthermore, i, u, or ṛ as their radical vowels. The conjugation of diś, point, in the sa- aorist is as follows :

Active :			
1st person	adikṣam	adikṣāva	adikṣāma
2nd person	adikṣaḥ	adikṣatam	adikṣata
3rd person	adikṣat	adikṣatām	adikṣan

The middle is formed in the same way, but with the middle imperfect thematic endings.

C. The reduplicated aorist. This aorist, which is not common in classical Sanskrit, is attached to verbs which have been augmented by -ay, that is, to causatives, class 10 verbs, and denominatives. In other words, a reduplicated aorist, if it is not made from a class 10 verb or from a denominative, *is causative.* The rules for reduplication of the stem to make this aorist are somewhat complex, and are not given here. They can be found in Whitney's *Sanskrit Grammar*, 858-863. The reduplicated stem is augmented, and then the imperfect thematic endings are added to it. The conjugation in the active of the reduplicated aorist of jan, which has a causative signification and hence means "cause to be born," "give birth" is as follows :

Active :	Singular	Dual	Plural
1st person	ajījanam	ajījanāva	ajījanāma
2nd person	ajījanaḥ	ajījanatam	ajījanata
3rd person	ajījanat	ajījanatām	ajījanan

The middle is formed in the same way, but with the middle imperfect thematic endings.

D. The use of the aorists. As explained above, the aorists are generally used like the imperfect and perfect for past action. The one exceptional usage is as a negative imperative, in which case the augment is omitted and the verb is construed with mā. For example, mā yāsīḥ, "do not go"; tan mā bhūt, "may that not become."

E. The aorist passive 3rd person singular. In theory, the middle forms of the s-, iṣ-, and sa- aorists are used for the aorist passive, but such usage is extremely rare in classical Sanskrit. There is one form, however, which is common, and which is quite peculiar, having no conjugation and able to be construed only as an aorist passive 3rd singular. It is formed by adding -i to the augmented, strengthened root. In general, final vowels are vṛddhied and medial vowels guṇated before the -i. Thus from nī, anāyi, "it was led"; from vac, avāci, "it was said"; from dā, adāyi, "it was given."

II. The desiderative. The sense of this form is to indicate desire to perform the action of the verb. Thus from kṛ, cikīrṣati means "he desires to do"; from jīv, jijīviṣāmi means "I want to live." The desiderative stem is made by reduplicating the root and adding to it -s or -iṣ, *after which it is treated like a normal thematic verb stem, and takes the thematic present, imperfect, optative, and imperative endings, forms present participles, makes a causative stem, a passive stem, a future stem, and a periphrastic perfect, just like any other verb stem conjugated as a thematic verb.* Indeed, the only difference from a normal thematic verb is that it must take the periphrastic perfect, not the simple perfect.

The rules for reduplication are somewhat complex, and may be found in Whitney, 1026 ff. Here, it is enough to say that the consonant of the reduplication is determined by the usual rules, while the vowel of reduplication is -i- if the root has ā, ī, or ṝ, and -u- if the root has ū. Thus from yā, go, yiyāsati; from nī, ninīṣati; from bhū, bubhūṣati. Some common desideratives have abbreviated reduplication, as īpsati from āp, ditsati from dā.

As pointed out above, in addition to the present, imperfect, optative, and imperative, the desiderative may make a passive (īpsyate, "it is desired to be obtained"), a causative (īpsayati, "he causes to desire to obtain"), and a future, both simple (īpsiṣyati) and periphrastic (īpsitāsmi). It makes only the periphrastic perfect (īpsāṃ cakāra). It makes the past passive and active participles in -ita (īpsita) and -itavant (īpsitavant) respectively, while its present active and middle participles are regular (īpsant, īpsamāna). It may, like other verbs, make a future active and middle participle as well (īpsiṣyant, īpsiṣyamāna). It forms the -is aorist (aipsīt, "he desired to get").

It should be clear from all of the preceding that, once the desiderative stem has been formed, it can be treated like a normal thematic verb stem (with the proviso that it takes the periphrastic perfect). Therefore, since it is treated like the thematic verb stems which you have already studied, examples of its forms are not given in detail here. See Whitney 1032.

There are in addition to the forms of the desiderative described above two important forms not taken by normal verb stems. One is a present participle, formed by adding -u to the desiderative stem, and declined like śatru, dhenu, and madhu in the masculine, feminine, and neuter. Thus cikīrṣuḥ means "the man [or woman] desiring to do," "desiring to do." This form is quite common and should be remembered.

There is also an action noun formed by adding -ā to the desiderative stem and declined like senā. For example, from pā is formed pipāsā, "desire to drink," "thirst."

III. The intensive. This secondary form is not common in classical Sanskrit, except in a very few roots. While theoretically it can take all of the forms any other verbal root can take, it is very rarely encountered outside of the present. Its signification is the repetition or intensification of the action of the verb. It is inflected in the present like verbs of class 3, and its stem is formed by a strong and peculiar reduplication of the verb stem, for which see Whitney 1000 ff. For example from vid, the intensative 3rd singular present active is vevetti or vevidīti, "he knows indeed." See Whitney 1006 for further examples of inflection of this rare form.

IV. The denominative. This form is relatively common in classical Sanskrit. As its name implies, it consists of verbs made from nouns. If the noun from which the denominative is made is called A, then the meaning of the denominative verb is one of the following (though there are a few denominatives which do not fit any of these models) : be like A, act as A, play the part of A; regard or treat as A; cause to be A, make into A; use A, make application of A; desire A, wish for A, crave A.

In general, the denominative is formed by adding -y- to the noun stem, and then declining the resulting stem like a thematic verb. Thus amitrayati, "he plays the enemy" from amitram, enemy. But a few stems may be changed: final -a, while usually unchanged, may change to -ā or -ī before the -y-. final -ā is generally unchanged.

final -i, -ī and -u, -ū very rarely form denominatives. When they do, -i and -u become -ī and ū, or, more rarely, -a.

final -ṛ is changed to -rī before -y-.

most consonant stems are unchanged before -y-, but -an may change to -a-, -ā-, or -ī- before -y-, and -in may change to -ī-. For more particulars, see Whitney 1053 ff.

In classical Sanskrit, any noun or adjective stem may be compounded with any of the forms of kṛ or bhū, in which case -ā and -ī of the noun stem become -ī, and -ū becomes -ū, With kṛ, the meaning is "to make A," while with bhū, it is "to become A." For example stambhībhū means "become a post (stambha)"; surabhīkṛ means "to make fragrant (surabhi)." This form is not commonly made from the consonantal declensions, though occasionally -an and -as are changed to -ī to make this form (ātmīkṛ, to make into oneself).

APPENDIX 2

A REVIEW SHEET

The material below is based on a review sheet I made up when I taught this primer at the University of Wisconsin. The teacher may or may not wish to use it.

The following is the material from these lessons which should be memorized for the exam at the end of the first semester of study. If the entire primer has not been covered, then of course those parts not covered should be omitted from the review. In addition to memorizing the following, your review should consist in reading over the Sanskrit sentences at least three times.

I. Saṃdhi rules. Rules 1-27, pp. 13-20. It is not necessary to memorize the rules word for word; but you should be able to apply them. You do not need to know the numbers of the rules. Learn also rules I.a. and I.b. on page 128.

II. Nouns. The following declensions :

deva, p. 8.

phalam, p. 8.

agni, p. 22

senā, pp. 22-23

pad, p. 31

rājan, p. 35

dātṛ, p. 36

nadī, p. 30

Note that rājan, dātṛ, and pad, all masculine, are strong in the nominative singular, dual, and plural, and in the accusative singular and dual. All masculine nouns following the declension of rājan or of dātṛ exhibit this peculiarity, while pad is the only consonantal stem you have had to do so. In the neuter, only the plural nominative and accusative are strong—but you have been given no such words to memorize. Review what is said about the pāda endings on page 31.

III. Pronouns. Memorize the following declensions.

aham (sg., dual, plural), p. 39

tvam (sg., dual, plural), p. 39

sa (sg., dual, plural; masculine, neuter, feminine), pp. 39-40

ayaṁ (sg., dual, plural; masculine, neuter, feminine) p. 44

IV. Finite verb forms, present system : For bhū and labh, that is for active and middle thematic verbs, learn the following forms :

present, entire, p. 3, 11.

imperfect, entire, p. 24, 27

optative, singular and plural only, p. 51, 55

imperative, singular and plural only, p. 59, 64

For athematic verbs, you should learn how to form the strong and weak stems for each class, and you should know all of the italicized material on pages 77-97; but you need not memorize any conjugations. You should learn also the strong and weak stems of as, dhā, brū and jñā. Remember that the augment plus initial ī, ū, and ṛ gives the vṛddhi (not the guṇa) of the initial vowel.

V. Passive. This is made from the weakened stem plus -y- plus the middle thematic endings (the endings which labh takes). pages 110-114. Be sure you know what saṃprasāraṇa is (page 110).

VI. Causative. Strengthened stem plus -ay- plus active thematic endings. This strengthened stem plus -ay- is called the causative stem.

Passive causative : stem strengthened in the same way as for the active causative, (but without -ay) plus -y- plus middle thematic endings. Pages 118-122.

VII. The Future.

A. The Simple Future. Root plus -sy or -iṣy plus thematic present endings. The passive future is simply the future with the middle endings. The causative future is made by adding -iṣy to the causative stem. Page 150.

B. The periphrastic future. Strengthened root plus -tā in the 3rd person sg. -tārau in the 3rd person dual, and -tāraḥ in the 3rd person plural, for both active and middle. In the first two persons, strengthened root plus -tā plus requisite present form of as, to be. Pages 151-152.

VIII. The perfect. You need not learn all of the rules for reduplication. Reduplicated stem plus perfect endings. Memorize the 3rd person endings, all 3 numbers, active and middle. Memorize also the special ending in the 3rd person singular active for verbs in -ā (page 158), and the special weak reduplicated form for some verbs of the pattern CaC (page 158). Causatives and class 10 verbs take the perfect periphrastic, formed by adding -ām to the requisite present stem, and then adding the appropriate perfect form of as or kṛ in the active and of kṛ in the middle. You will not be asked to actually form any perfects, but you should be able to recognize and identify them. Remember that as with the future, the passive perfect is simply the perfect conjugated in the middle. Pages 156-160.

IX. Non-finite verb forms.

A. Present active participles. These are formed by taking -i from the 3rd person plural present active. The feminine is in -ī—in -antī for thematic verbs, -atī for athematic verbs. They may be formed from the simple or causative stem. Ex. kurvan, doing kārayan, causing to do (both masc. nom. sg.). Learn also about the special participle for class 3 verbs (page 101). Pages 98-104.

B. Present middle participles.

1. Thematic : take -nte from the 3rd plural present middle and add -māna. May be formed from the simple root, from the passive stem, and from the causative passive stem. Ex. labhamāna, obtaining; labhyamāna, being obtained; lambhyamāna, being caused to obtain. Page 105.

2. Athematic : take -ate from the 3rd plural present middle and add -āna. Note that since all passive and causative stems are thematic, this form may be made only from the simple root. Page 105. Review also the absolute constructions described on pages 105-107, and remember that they may only be used when

the subject of the absolute is different than the subject of the main verb.

C. Past passive participle. Weak root plus -ta, -ita, or -na. To form the causative past passive participle, remove -ay from the causative stem and add -ita. Ex. dṛṣṭa, seen; darśita, caused to be seen. Pages 126-131.

D. Past active participle. Past passive participle plus -vant. May be formed from the simple stem or the causative stem, like the past passive participle. Ex. kṛtavān, he who did; kāritavān, he who caused to do. Page 133.

E. The continuative.

1. Unprefixed verbs. Past passive participle plus -vā. But if the past passive participle ends in -na, then the weak root plus -tvā. May be formed from the simple stem or the causative stem, in which case -itvā is added to the causative stem. Ex. kṛtvā, having done; kārayitvā, having caused to do. Remember that the continuative can be used only when its subject is the same as that of the main verb, unless the main verb is passive, in which case its subject is the instrumental, actually present or implied, construed with the main verb. Pages 138-139.

2. Prefixed verbs. Weakened stem plua -ya. If the stem ends in a short vowel, -t- is inserted before -ya. May be made from the simple stem and the causative stem. Ex. vidhāya, having ordained; vidhāpya, having caused to ordain. Pages 138-139.

F. The Infinitive. The stem, strengthened by guṇa, plus -tum or -itum. For the causative, the causative stem plus -itum. Ex. kartum, to do; kārayitum, to cause to do. Pages 148-149.

G. The gerundives. Review the use of these forms, described on page 168-170.

1. The -ya gerundive. Root, sometimes strengthened plus -ya. Final -ā changes to -e before -ya. For causatives, the causative stem minus -ay plus -ya. Pages 168-170.

2. The -tavya gerundive. The gerundive ending -tavya is added to the same stem as the infinitive in -tum. Page 169.

3. The -anīya gerundive. The verb stem, generally guṇated, plus -anīya. To make the causative, add -anīya to the causative stem minus -ay. Page 169.

X. Compounds. Learn to form and construe tatpuruṣas (59-61), karmadhārayas (59-61), itaretara and samāhara dvandvas (64), and bahuvrīhis (68-73). Be sure that you can recognize and identify each type of compound.

XI. Vocabulary. You should know actively all the words given at the end of the lessons before the exercises. These words, and only these words, are included in the Sanskrit-English glossary (but not all are included in the English-Sanskrit glossary). You do not need to know the vocabulary of the verses given at the end of each lesson.

XII. Special notes. You should be able to recognize all of the forms which you have had (though you will not be asked to identify any utterly strange athematic verb forms). As far as actively making forms is concerned, you need only know the material outlined in this review sheet—you should not bother, for example, to memorize all of the rules for the formation of the passive given on pages 113-114. Be sure that you understand the meaning and the use of each form, so that you can translate it correctly. Pay especial heed to the uses of the forms given in the last lessons : absolutive constructions, the passive, the causative, the past passive and active participles, the continuative, the infinitive, and the gerundive. A sample final examination, given to a class at the University of Wisconsin, is reproduced on the next 2 pages. [The following exam covers lessons 1-27].

ELEMENTARY SANSKRIT
FINAL EXAM

Be sure to answer each question. It is to your advantage to spend only the time allotted on each question. It is especially important that you spend at least the allotted time on the last question, the sight passage.

I. 30 *minutes.* This section consists of the production of what you have memorized (as summed up in the review sheet).

1. Give the complete declensions of *phalam*, *dātṛ*, and *sa.*

2. Conjugate *bhū* and *labh* in the present and the optative. Give the entire conjugation of the present, but only the singular and plural of the optative. Give both active and middle forms.

3. Give the strong and weak present stems of the following athematic verbs : *i*, *āp*, *jñā*, *dā*. (classes 1, 5, 9 and 3 respectively).

4. Put the following words together, applying *saṃdhi*. Write in *devanāgarī.*

rathe / atiṣṭhat / nṛpaḥ / tatra / upaviśan / ca / ācāryau / āhūya / idam / ratnam / kasmāt / deśāt / hi / alabhyata / brūhi / iti / apṛcchat /

II. 20 *minutes*. The following sentences are to be translated from English into Sanskrit in *devanāgarī.*

1. Whoever would touch my feet, let him come into my presence.

2. The man taking a bath in the tank saw the king coming and ran to his house.

III. 35 *minutes*. Translate the following sentences into English, and identifiy the underlined forms as fully as possible. If a special construction is involved (e.g. a locative absolute), identify that as well. Be sure to fully identify all underlined compounds.

न पुनः कदापि सूर्यं पश्येत्स मम शत्रुरिति कोपादवदत्क्षत्रियः ॥१॥ त्वदर्थेऽहमागच्छं त्वदर्थेऽहं युद्धेऽजयमिदानीं तु गच्छेत्येव वदसीत्यवदद्वीरो राजानम् ॥२॥ निर्धूममग्निमपश्यच्छिष्यः किमेतदित्यमन्यत च ॥३॥ स्वर्गे सदा वृक्षाः पुष्पफलानि बिभ्रतीत्यब्रवीत्कविः ॥४॥ अस्मिन्वने काकमात्रा न्युषिता इत्युक्तवत्यृषौ ते वणिजो भयं त्यक्तवन्तस्तद्दिष्टाश्च ॥५॥ तया दमयन्त्या पतिं त्यक्त्वा वनं गत्वा तत्रोषित्वागच्छतो मृगस्य शब्दोऽश्रूयत ॥६॥

VI. 35 *minutes*. Translate the following story into English. Translate as quickly as you can, getting the gist of what is going on. Be as literal as possible—but do not linger over any construction which you cannot get immediately.

एकस्मिन्वने शृगाल उष्ट्रश्च न्यवसताम् । कदा चिच्छृगाल उष्ट्रम् "अस्ति नदीतीर उद्यानं । तत्रावयोरद्भुतं भोजनं विद्यत इत्युक्तवान् । उष्ट्र एवं भवत्वित्यवदत् । पृष्ठ आरोहिते शृगाल उष्ट्रो नदीं तीर्णः । तदोद्यानं गत्वा शृगाल अल्पजन्तूनभक्षयदुष्ट्रश्च यानि यानि फलानि पत्राणि चोद्याने विद्यन्ते तानि भक्षितवान् । शृगालो भोजनं कृत्वा महन्तं शब्दमकरोत् । तच्छ्रुत्वा ग्रामात्प्रजा "उद्याने शृगाल आगतः, तं हत्वापसारयाम" इत्यमन्यन्त । उद्यानमागत्य न शृगालमपश्यन् । किं तूष्ट्रमपश्यन् । उष्ट्रं हत्वा ग्राममगच्छन् । तदोष्ट्रः शृगालमाहूय, "इदानीं वनं गच्छेव । त्वं कस्मान्महन्तं शब्दमकरोः" इत्यपृच्छत् । "भोजनं कृत्वा सदा शब्दं करोमि । तदेव मम स्वभाव" इत्यवदच्छृगालः । तदोष्ट्रपृष्ठे पुनरारोहच्छृगालः । उष्ट्रश्च नद्यामगच्छत् । नदीमध्य उष्ट्रः पर्यवर्तत । किं

करोषीत्यपृच्छच्छृगालः । "एष एव मम स्वभावः । सदा ह्यहं परिवृत्य जले प्लोमि" इत्यवददुष्ट्रः । तदा शृगालो जले पतित्वाम्रियत ॥

शृगाल	fox, jackal
उष्ट्र	camel
अद्भुत	wonderful, marvelous
पृष्ठम्	back
आरुह् (आरोहति)	climb. Plus locative : climb onto
तॄ (तिरति)	cross over (here, by swimming). Past pass. part. *tīrṇa*
अल्प	small, little
जन्तु	creature, animal
भक्ष् (भक्षयति)	eat (class 10)
पत्रम्	leaf
अपसृ (अपसरति)	go away
हन् (हन्ति)	here : beat.
स्वभाव	innate nature
मध्यम्	middle
परिवृत् (परिवर्तते)	roll over
प्लु (प्लोमि)	swim (class 1)

SANSKRIT-ENGLISH GLOSSARY

The following glossary contains those words given at the end of each lesson before the exercises and used in Sanskrit-English sentences. It does not contain the words used in the verses. In addition to using this glossary as you translate the Sanskrit sentences, it is suggested that you use it at the end of the semester for review. If so, it is an easy matter to delete any words from lessons not covered. For verbs, 4 forms are given: the present 3rd singular, the causative 3rd singular, the passive 3rd singular, and the past passive participle. Classes of athematic verbs are indicated.

अ- un-, a prefix, In bahuvrīhi's, "without." See lesson 18

अग्नि fire

अतिथि guest

अत्र here

अधी (अधीते, अध्यापयति, अधीयते, अधीत) study (II, from adhi and i, go)

अन्- the form which a-takes before vowels. See a-.

अन्त end

अन्य other. Declined like sa—see lesson 13

अपि even, . also, although. (placed after the word it goes with) After an interrogative, a universalizing participle. Page 25.

अयम this, that. See lesson 13.

अरि enemy

अर्थ meaning, wealth, goal

अर्थे for the sake of (preceded by the gen. of the word governed)

अर्ह् (अर्हति deficient in other forms) ought, should (plus infinitive)

अवगम् (अवगच्छति, अवगमयति, अवगम्यते, अवगत) understand

अश्व horse

अस् (अस्ति, deficient in other forms) be (II)

असौ that (lesson 13)
अस्मत्- stem form of vayam, we
अहम् I (see lesson 12)
आगम् (आगच्छति, आगमयति, आगम्यते, आगत) come (ā plus gam)
आचार्य teacher, preceptor
आज्ञा (caus. only. आज्ञापयति, आज्ञप्यते, आज्ञप्त) order (from ā plus jñā)
आत्मन् m. self; oneself
आनी (आनयति, आनाययति, आनीयते, आनीत) bring. lead to (from ā plus nī)
आप् (आप्नोति, आपयति, आप्यते, आप्त) obtain (V)
आवाम् we, dual (nom-acc.)
आस् (आस्ते, आसयति, आस्यते, आसित) sit, rest, dwell, continue or be in any state. (II)
आह्वे (आह्वयति, आह्वापयति, आहूयते, आहूत) call, summon, invite (from ā plus hve)
इ (एति, —, ईयते, इत) go (II)
इति thus; particle marking end of direct discourse See pp 27-28.
इदानीम now
इव like (placed after word with which it is construed)
इष् (इच्छति, एषयति. इष्यते, इष्ट) desire, want (plus infinitive)
उद्यानम् garden
उपगम् (उपगच्छति, उपगमयति, उपगम्यते, उपगत) go to, approach, attain (upa plus gam)
उपविश् (उपविशति, उपवेशयति, उपविश्यते, उपविष्ट) sit, sit down (upa plus viś)
ऋषि sage, seer
ए ऐति, —, एयते, एत come (II) (ā plus i)
एक one, alone (declined like sa; neut sg. nom-acc ekam)
एतत् neuter singular nom-acc. of eṣa, q. v.
एतत्- stem form of eṣa
एव only (placed after word with which it is construed); indeed
एष this (from e plus sa, whose declension it follows)
क who (interrogative) (declined like sa; neut. sg. nom-acc kim)

कथम्	how (interrogative)
कथा	story
कदा	when (interrogative)
कन्या	girl, daughter; an unmarried girl; virgin, maiden
कम्प् (कम्पते, कम्पयति, कम्प्यते, कम्पित)	tremble, shake
कवि	poet
कस्मात्	why (interrogative) (the neuter ablative singular of ka)
काक	crow
काम	desire; sexual desire, lust
कारणम्	cause, reason
कार्यम	effect, business, affair, matter, duty (gerundive of kṛ)
काल	time
किंतु	however
कीर्ति f.	glory, renown
कुटुम्ब	family
कुत्र	where (interrogative)
कृ (करोति, कारयति, क्रियते, कृत)	make, do (VIII)
कृष् (कर्षति, कर्षयति, कृष्यते, कृष्ट)	plow, drag, pull
क्लृप् (कल्पते, कलपयति, क्लृप्यते, क्लृप्त)	be fit for (plus dative)
कोप	anger
क्री (क्रीणाति, क्रापयति, क्रीयते, क्रीत)	buy (IX)
क्षत्रिय	kṣatriya, a member of the second varṇa, a warrior
क्षेत्रम्	field
गज	elephant
गम् (गच्छति, गमयति, गम्यते, गत)	go
गिरि	mountain
गृहम्	house
ग्रह् (गृह्णाति, ग्राहयति, गृह्यते, गृहीत)	grasp, hold, seize (IX)
ग्राम	village
च	and (placed after the last member of the series, like Latin -que)
चक्षुस् n.	eye
चन	a universalizing particle placed after interrogative. P. 25.

चित् a universalizing particle placed after interrogatives. P. 25.

चुर् (चोरयति, चोरयति, चोर्यते, चोरित) steal

छाया shadow

जन् (जायते, जनयति, —, जात) be born. In causative, give birth to

जलम् water

जि (जयति, जापयति, जीयते, जित) vanquish, conquer

जीव् (जीवति, जीवयति, जीव्यते, जीवित) live

जीवितम् life

ज्ञा (जानाति, ज्ञापयति, ज्ञायते, ज्ञात) know (IX)

ज्ञानम् knowledge

तत्- the stem form of sa.

तत्र there

तथा so, in that way. Tathā ca means "moreover"

तथापि still, even so, nevertheless; correlative of yadyapi, yadāpi

तदा then; correlative of yadi, yadā

तस्मात् therefore (neuter ablative sg. of sa)

तीरम् shore

तु but (never used at the beginning of a clause; usually after first word)

त्यज् (त्यजति, त्याजयति, त्यज्यते, त्यक्त) abandon, give up

त्वच् f. skin (nom. sg. tvak)

त्वत्- stem form of tvam

त्वम् you, sg. See lesson 12

दरिद्र poor

दह् (दहति, दाहयति, दह्यते, दग्ध) burn; be painful; cause pain (both trans. and intransitive)

दा (ददाति, दापयति, दीयते, दत्त) give (class 3)

दातृ giver

दुःखम् sorrow, pain

दुस्- in bahuvrīhi: "having bad A," "having difficult A." in karmadhāraya, "bad" "hard"

दूत messenger, emissary

दृश् See paś. Used for all but the present system of paś, see. In the causative (darśayati),

	"show" with dative or accusative of person to whom object is shown.
देव	god
देवी	goddess
धनम्	money, wealth
धनुस	bow (weapon)
धर्म	dharma (untranslatable); law, religious or moral merit; duty: justice; piety; morality

धाव् (धावति, धावयति, धाव्यते, धावति) run

धूम	smoke
धेनु f.	cow
न	not (used like English not, except with imperatives, where mā is used)
नगरम्	city
नदी	river
न वा	or not

नश् (नश्यति, नाशयति, नश्यते, नष्ट) perish; be lost

नामन् n.	name

निग्रह् (निगृह्णाति, निग्राहयति, निगृह्यते, निगृहीत) subdue, control (IX)

निर्दिश् (निर्दिशति, निर्देशयति, निर्दिश्यते, निर्दिष्ट) point out, indicate, show

निवस् (निवसति, निवासयति, न्युष्यते, न्युषित) live, reside

निस्	in bahuvrīhis, "without" "devoid of" "lacking in"

नी (नयति, नाययति, नीयते, नीत) lead, convey

नृप	king
पक्षिन्	bird (from pakṣa, wing, and -in)

पठ् (पठति, पाठयति, पठ्यते, पठित) read, recite

पत (पतति, पातयति, पत्यते, पतित) fall, fly

पति	lord, husband
पत्नी	wife
पद्	foot (nom. sg. pāt. Strong stem pād-, weak stem pad-)
पयस् n.	milk

पश् (पश्यति, दर्शयति, दृश्यते, दृष्ट) see

पा (-पिबति, पाययति, पीयते, पीत) drink

पितृ	father; (dual) parents; (pl.) manes

पीड् (पीडयति, पीडयति, पीड्यते, पीडित) squeeze, afflict, hurt

पुत्र	son

पुनर् again
पुष्पम् flower
पुस्तकम् book
प्रच्छ् (पृच्छति, प्रच्छयति, पृच्छ्यते, पृष्ट) ask; ask (acc.) about (acc.)
प्रजा subject (of a king); offspring, progeny; creature
प्रतीक्ष् (प्रतीक्षते, प्रतीक्षयति, प्रतीक्ष्यते, प्रतीक्षित) await, expect (from prati and ikṣ)
प्रयुज् (प्रयुङ्क्ते, प्रयोजयति, प्रयुज्यते, प्रयुक्त) use, employ (from pra and yuj. VII)
-प्राय almost (see page 134)
फलम् fruit
बन्धु friend, relative
बलम् power, might, strength
बहु (f. बह्वी) many, much
बाण arrow
बाल boy; fool
बाला girl
ब्रह्मन् masculine : the god Brahmā; neut.: brahma a verbal formula, the absolute, the principle underlying the universe (note the different nom. sg. of the masculine and neuter)
ब्राह्मण a Brahmin, a member of the varṇa of priests
ब्रू (ब्रवीति, —, —, —) say (strong present stem bravī-; weak, brū-, 3rd pl. bruvanti, abruvan, bruvanti. Deficient outside present) II
भयम् fear
भवन्त् you (used with 3rd-person verb. See lesson 22)
भार्या wife (a feminine gerundive of bhṛ, support)
भू (भवति, भावयति, भूयते, भूत) become
भूमि f. earth
भृ (बिभर्ति, भारयति, भ्रियते, भृत) bear, support (III)
भृत्य servant (a gerundive of bhṛ, support)
भोजनम् food
भ्रातृ brother
मत्- stem form of aham
मधु n. honey

मन् (मन्यते, मानयति, मन्यते, मत) think
मनुष्य man
मन्त्रिन् minister (of a king) (Declined like a possessive in -in)
-मय made of, consisting of, full of. See a, page 134
महन्त् great (see lesson 22)
मा not (used with imperatives, like Greek $\mu\eta$, Hindi mat)
मातृ f. mother
-मात्र mere, only (see c. on page 134)
मार्ग road, path, way
माला garland
मित्रम् friend
मुखम् face; mouth
मुच् (मुञ्चति, मोचयति, मुच्यते, मुक्त) loose, release, free
मृ (म्रियते, मारयति, म्रियते, मृत) die (note: the form used for the present, mriyate, is actually a passive).
मृग deer; any wild beast
मृत्यु f. death
य who (relative. Declined like sa—see lesson 13)
यज् (यजते, याजयति, इज्यते, इष्ट) sacrifice (w. acc. of deity sacrificed to and inst. of what is sacrificed)
यत्र where (relative)
यदा when, since (relative)
यदापि even though (from yadā and api)
यदि if
यद्यपि even if, even though (from yadi and api)
यम् (यच्छति, यमयति, यम्यते, यत) yield, give, bestow
युद्धम् war, fight, battle
युवाम् dual of tvam, q. v.
युष्मत्- stem form of yūyam, the plural of tvam, you
यूयम् you, pl.
रथ chariot
राजन् king
राज्यम् kingdom

लभ् (लभते, लम्भयति, लभ्यते, लब्ध) obtain

लिख् (लिखति, लेखयति, लिख्यते, लिखित) write

लोक people, world (in the meaning of people, used as collective in the singular and in the plural)

वच् (वक्ति, वाचयति, उच्यते, उक्त) say (II). Used most often in the passive, when it generally means "address."

वणिज् m. merchant (nom. sg. vaṇik)

वद् (वदति, वादयति, उद्यते, उदित) say (with double accusative, of thing said and person addressed.)

वनम् forest

वस् (वसति, वासयति, उष्यते, उषित) live, dwell

वह् (वहति, वाहयति, उह्यते, ऊढ) pull, drag, carry

वा or (like ca, placed after last member of series)

वाच् f. speech; words. Often plural (nom. sg. vāk)

वापी tank (Indian usage—i.e. artificial pond)

विक्री (विक्रीणाति, विक्रापयति, विक्रीयते, विक्रीत) sell (IX)

विद् (विद्यते, —, —, —) be, exist. Vidyate means "there is"

विद् (वेत्ति, वेदयति, विद्यते, विदित) know (II). Often used in the perfect (veda/viduḥ) with present meaning, as Greek οιδα

विद्वांस् a learned person, a wise person (perfect act. part. of vid)

विधा (विदधाति/विधत्ते, विधापयति, विधीयते, विहित) ordain, bring about, accomplish (III)

विश् (विशति, वेशयति, विश्यते, विष्ट) enter

विषम् poison

वीर fighting man, warrior; virile man

वृक्ष tree

वृत् (वर्तते, वर्तयति, वृत्यते, वृत्त) be, exist

वृध् (वर्धते, वर्धयति, वृध्यते, वृद्ध) grow

शंस् (शंसति, शंसयति, शस्यते, शस्त) praise

शक् (शक्नोति, शाकयति, शक्यते, शक्त) be able, can (with infinitive) (V)

शत्रु m. enemy

शब्द sound, noise; word

शस्त्रम् weapon

शिष्य pupil, chela

शूद्र a Śūdra, a member of the 4th, or servile varṇa

श्रु (शृणोति, श्रावयति, श्रूयते, श्रुत) hear (V)

स he, she, it, they. See declensions on pages 39-40.

स- (in bahuvrīhi) with, accompanied by (see lesson 18)

सकाश vicinity, nearness, proximity, presence (see lesson 12)

सदा always

सन्त् good (the pres. act, part. of as. This meaning is in addition to its primary meaning "being").

समुद्र ocean

सर्प snake

सर्व all, each (declined like sa—lesson 13)

सह with, in the company of. Follows instrumental of word governed.

सह- (in bahuvrīhi) with, accompanied by (see lesson 18)

सिंह lion

सु- in bahuvrīhi: having good A, having easy A. In karmadhāraya, easy, very

सुखम् happiness, well-being, comfort

सूर्य sun

सेना army

सेव् (सेवते, सेवयति, सेव्यते, सेवित) serve, honor, frequent (as animals a woods)

स्था (तिष्ठति, स्थापयति, स्थीयते, स्थित) stand

स्नानम् bath

स्नानं कृ bathe (see kṛ for forms)

स्पृश् (स्पर्शति, स्पर्शयति, स्पृश्यते, स्पृष्ट) touch

स्मृ (स्मरति, स्मारयति, स्म्रियते, स्मृत) remember

स्व one's own. (See 2 on page 133)

स्वभाव nature, natural constitution, innate disposition

स्वर्ग heaven, paradise,

स्वल्प a little

स्वसृ f. sister

हन् (हन्ति, घातयति, हन्यते, हत) kill, slay; strike, hit

हविस् n. oblation, burnt offering. Usually the oblation of ghee poured on the fire at the sacrifice

हस् (हसति, हासयति, हस्यते, हसित) laugh

हस्त hand; the trunk of an elephant

हा (जहाति, हापयति, हीयते, हीन) leave, forsake, abandon (III. jahā-/, jahī-, jah-)

हि for (the conjunction). Placed after word, like tu.

हृदयम् heart

ENGLISH-SANSKRIT GLOSSARY

In this glossary, only those words which appear in the English sentences to be translated into Sanskrit at the end of the lessons are given. For verbs, the 3rd singular present, the 3rd singular present causative, the 3rd singular present passive, and the past passive participle are given. When you know more than one Sanskrit equivalent of an English word, the Sanskrit word which appears in the later lesson has in parenthesis after it the lesson in which it appears, so that you will not use it before that lesson.

able	see be able
afflict	पीड्, पीडयति, पीडयते, पीड्यते, पीडित
again	पुनर्
all	सर्व (declined like स, except in nom. masc. sg. which is always सर्वः and in nom-acc. neut. sg., सर्वम्)
also	अपि (placed after word with which it is construed)
always	सदा
and	च (like Latin -que, placed after last word in co-ordinated series. If 2 sentences are co-ordinated, then च is usually placed after the first or last word of the second sentence)
anger	कोप
animal	मृग
any	(in a negative sentence): omit, or use कोऽपि (which must, of course, agree with its antecedent)
anyone	कोऽपि, in proper gender, number, case
are	see be
army	सेना

as	(in the sense of like) इव (placed after word with which it is construed)
ask	प्रच्छ् (पृच्छति, प्रच्छयति, पृच्छ्यते पृष्ट). With acc. of person asked and acc. of thing inquired about)
attain	लभ् (लभते, लम्भयति, लभ्यते, लब्ध)
	आप् (20 आप्नोति, आपयति, आप्यते, आप्त. V)
bath	स्नानम्
bathe	स्नानम् कृ. (see make for forms)
battle	युद्धम्
be	वृत् (वर्तते, वर्तयति, वृत्यते, वृत्त) (in sense of become)
	भू (भवति, भावयति, भूयते, भूत) as
	(19. अस्ति —, —,—. II.)
	(there is, there are) विद् (24. विद्यते, —, —, —)
be able	शक् (शक्नोति, शाकयते, शक्यते शक्त. (V)
be born	जन् (जायते, जनयति, —, जात)
be fit	क्लृप् (कल्पते, कल्पयति, क्लृप्यते, क्लृप्त)
become	भू (भवति, भावयति, भूयते, भूत)
book	पुस्तकम्
born	see be born
bow	धनुस्
boy	पुत्र; बाल (16)
Brahmin	ब्राह्मण
bring	आनी (आ and नी. आनयति, आनाययति, आनीयते, आनीत)
brother	भ्रातृ
burn	दह् (दहति, दाहयति, दह्यते, दग्ध)
but	तु (never used at the beginning of a clause; usually after the first word)
buy	क्री (क्रीणाति, क्रापयति, क्रीयते, क्रीत. IX.)
carry	see lead.
	in sense of bear, भृ (बिभर्ति, भारयति, भ्रियते, भृत. III. Lesson 21)
chariot	रथ
citizen	प्रजा
city	नगरम्
come	आगम् (आ and गम्. आगच्छति, आगमयति, आगम्यते, आगत)
	ए (आ and इ. ऐति —, एयते, एत. II. Lesson 19)
conquer	जि (जयति, जापयति, जीयते, जित)
cow	धेनु f.

crow	काक
daughter	दुहितृ
deer	मृग
defeat	जि (जयति, जापयति, जीयते, जित)
desire	काम
die	मृ (म्रियते, मारयति, म्रियते, मृत)
distressed	दुःखिन्
do	कृ (करोति, कारयति, क्रियते, कृत. VIII)
drink	पा (पिबति, पाययति, पीयते, पीत)
earth	भूमि f.
eat	भोजनम् कृ (see make for forms of कृ)
elephant	गज
enemy	अरि, शत्रु (lesson 14)
enter	विश् (विशति, वेशयति, विश्यते, विष्ट)
every	सर्व (see all for forms)
even if	यद्यपि (correlative : तथापि
even though	यदापि (correlative : तदापि)
everything	सर्व, in the neuter singular
fall	पत् (पतति, पातयति, पत्यते, पतित)
fame	कीर्ति f.
family	कुटुम्ब
father	पितृ
fear	भयम्
field	क्षेत्रम्
fight	युद्धम्
fire	अग्नि
fit	see be fit
flourish	वृध् (वर्धते, वर्धयति, वृध्यते, वृद्ध)
flower	पुष्पम्
foe	अरि, शत्रु (lesson 14)
food	भोजनम्
foot	पद् (nom. sg. पात्. Masculine)
for the sake of	अर्थे (after the genitive of the word governed)
forest	वनम्
free	मुच् (मुञ्चति, मोचयति, मुच्यते, मुक्त)
frequent	सेव् (सेवते, सेवयति, सेव्यते, सेवित)
friend	मित्रम्
fruit	फलम्

garden	उद्यानम्
garland	माला
get	see obtain
girl	कन्या, बाला (lesson 16)
give	यम् (यच्छति, यमयति, यम्यते, यत)
	दा (ददाति, दापयति, दीयते, दत्त. III. Lesson 21. दा is much more common than यम्, and should be used for give after lesson 21)
giver	दातृ
glory	कीर्ति, f.
go	गम् (गच्छति, गमयति, गम्यते, गत)
	इ (एति, —, ईयते, इत Lesson 19. II)
god	देव
goddess	देवी
good	साधु (f. साध्वी). As noun : good man, good woman
grasp	ग्रह् (गृह्णाति, ग्राहयति, गृह्यते, गृहीत. IX)
grow	वृध् (वर्धते, वर्धयति, वृध्यते, वृद्ध)
guest	अतिथि
hand	हस्त
happiness	सुखम्
happy	सुखिन्
he	स
hear	श्रु (शृणोति, श्रावयति, श्रूयते, श्रुत, V)
heart	हृदयम्
her (possessive)	leave out, if same as subject
here	अत्र
hero	वीर
his	leave out, if same as subject
honey	मधु, n.
horse	अश्व
house	गृहम्
how	कथम्
husband	पति
I	अहम्
if	यदि (correlative: तदा)
in no way	न कथमपि
inhabit	सेव् (सेवते, सेवयति, सेव्यते, सेवित)

is	see be
it	स in the neuter singular
jewel	रत्नम्
kill	हन् (हन्ति, घातयति, हन्यते, हत. II)
king	नृप, राजन् (lesson 11)
kingdom	राज्यम्
know	ज्ञा (जानाति, ज्ञापयति, ज्ञायते, ज्ञात. IX)
kṣatriya	क्षत्रिय
laugh	हस् (हसति, हासयति, हस्यते, हसित)
lead	नी (नयति, नाययति, नीयते, नीत) (in the sense of lead to, take to) आनी (आ and नी) (आनयति, आनाययति, आनीयते, आनीत)
leave	त्यज् (त्यजति, त्याजयति, त्याज्यते, त्यक्त) हा (जहाति, हापयति, हीयते, हीन. Lesson 21. III)
-less	निस् (first element of बहुव्रीहि. निस् follows the usual सन्धि rules, except that it becomes निष् before क्, ख्, प् and फ्).
life	जीवितम्
like	इव (after word with which it is construed)
lion	सिंह
live	(in sense of dwell) वस् (वसति, वासयति, उष्यते, उषित) (in sense of dwell) निवस् (निवसति, निवासयति, न्युष्यते, न्युषित) (in sense of be alive) जीव् (जीवति, जीवयति, जीव्यते जीवित)
look at	पश् (पश्यति, दर्शयति, दृश्यते, दृष्ट)
make	कृ (करोति, कारयति, क्रियते, कृत. VIII)
man	मनुष्य
merchant	वणिज् (nom. sg. वणिक्), m.
minister	मन्त्रिन् (declined like -इन् possessive), m.
misfortune	दुःखम्
money	धनम्
mountain	गिरि
mouth	मुखम्
my	use genitive of अहम्
my	leave out if same as subject
name	नामन्, n.
never	न कदापि, न कदाचन, न कदाचित्

no one	न कोऽपि (कोऽपि must, of course, be in the proper gender, case and number). Also न कश्चित्, न कश्चन
not	न
nothing	न किं चित् (किं चित् the neuter nom. sg. of कश्चित् must be in the proper case). Also न किमपि, न किं चन
now	इदानीम्
oblation	हविस्
obtain	लभ् (लभते, लम्भयति, लभ्यते, लब्ध)
	आप् (आप्नोति, आपयति, आप्यते, आप्त. Lesson 20, V)
ocean	समुद्र
offend	हन् (हन्ति, घातयति, हन्यते, हत II)
once	कदाचित्
only	एव (placed after word with which it is construed)
or not ?	न वा
ordain	विधा (विदधाति, विधत्ते, विधापयति, विधीयते, विहित III)
other	अन्य (declined like स but does not lose -ḥ in the nom. masc. sg. and takes nom-acc neut. sg. अन्यम्. "Other than is translated by the ablative of the word of comparison followed by the requisite form of अन्य)
our	use genitive of we. Do not translate if same as subject.
paradise	स्वर्ग
perform	कृ (करोति, कारयति, क्रियते, कृत. VIII)
perish	नश् (नश्यति, नाशयति, नश्यते, नष्ट)
play	क्रीड् (क्रीडति, क्रीडयति, क्रीड्यते, क्रीडित)
plow	कृश् (कर्शति, कर्शयति, कृश्यते, कृष्ट)
poet	कवि
poison	विषम्
poor	दरिद्र
praise	शंस् (शंसति, शंसयति, शस्यते, शस्त)
presence	सकाश (see lesson 12 for use)
pull	पठ् (पठति, पाठयति, पठ्यते, पठित)
pupil	शिष्य
read	पठ्, (पठति, पाठयति, पठ्यते, पठित)

recite	पठ् (पठति, पाठयति, पठ्यते, पठित)
relative	बन्धु
remember	स्मृ (स्मरति, स्मारयति, स्मर्यते, स्मृत)
rich	धनिन्
river	नदी
run	धाव् (धावति, धावयति, धाव्यते, धावित)
sacrifice	यज् (यजति, याजयति, इज्यते इष्ट. Takes the accusative of the deity sacrificed to and the instrumental of the thing sacrificed)
sage	ऋषि
sake	see for the sake of
say	(all 3 verbs take a double accusative in the active. ब्रू has no passive, while वद् is not commonly used in the passive. वद् and वच् in the passive take the nominative of the person addressed and the accusative of the speech said, or, if the person addressed is not specified, the nominative of what is said)
	वद (वदति, वादयति, उद्यते, उदित)
	ब्रू (ब्रवीति, —, —, — Lesson 21. II. ब्रू has the strong stem ब्रवी, weak, stem ब्रू, 3rd pl. ब्रुवन्ति)
	वच् (वक्ति, वाचयति, उच्यते, उक्त. Lesson 24. II)
sea	समुद्र
see	पश् (पश्यति, दर्शयति, दृश्यते, दृष्ट)
seer	ऋषि
sell	विक्री (विक्रीणाति, विक्रापयति, विक्रीयते, विक्रीत IX)
shadow	छाया
she	feminine of स
shore	तीरम्
show	use causative of see, with accusative or dative of person to whom object is shown
sit	उपविश् (उपविशति, उपवेशयति, उपविश्यते, उपविष्ट)
	आस् (आस्ते, आसयति, आस्यते, आसित. Lesson 19 II)
slay	हन् (हन्ति, घातयति, हन्यते, हत)

smoke	धूम
some	कश्चित (कश्चित्) in proper case, gender, number
somehow	कथं चित्
son	पुत्र
sorrow	दुःखम्
stand	स्था (तिष्ठति, स्थापयति, स्थीयते, स्थित)
steal	चुर् (चोरयति, चोरयते, चुर्यते, चोरित)
still	(in the sense of nevertheless) तथापि
story	कथा
strike down	हन् (हन्ति, घातयति, हन्यते, हत)
student	शिष्य
subject	(meaning a royal subject, a citizen) प्रजा
Śūdra	शूद्र
summon	आह्वे (आह्वयति, आह्वापयति, आहूयते, आहूत. From आ and ह्वे)
sun	सूर्य
support	भृ (बिभर्ति, भारयति, भ्रियते, भृत)
take a bath	स्नानम् कृ (see make for conjugation of कृ)
tank	वापी
teach	अधी in caus. (—, अध्यापयति, अध्याप्यते, अध्यापित From अधि and ई)
teacher.	आचार्य
that	for indirect discourse, use इति construction (lesson 9)
	adj: असौ, अयम्, स
	noun: स in neuter
their	leave out, if same as subject
then	तदा
there	तत्र
there is	see be
they	स in the plural
think	मन् (मन्यते, मानयति, मन्यते, मत)
this	(adj. or noun) अयम्
this one	see this
touch	स्पर्श् (स्पर्शति, स्पर्शयति, स्पृश्यते, स्पृष्ट)
town	नगरम्

tree	वृक्ष
tremble	कम्प् (कम्पते, कम्पयति, कम्प्यते, कम्पित)
use	प्रयुज् (प्रयुङ्क्ते, प्रयोजयति, प्रयुज्यते, प्रयुक्त. from प्र and युज्. VII)
vanquish	जि (जयति, जापयति, जीयते, जित)
village	ग्राम
war	युद्धम्
warrior	क्षत्रिय, वीर (lesson 16)
water	जलम्
we	वयम् (plural of अहम्)
wealth	धनम् (often in plural)
weapon	शस्त्रम्
well-disposed	सुमनस्
went	see go
whatever	यद् यत् (correlative: तत् तत्. The neuter of य, repeated)
when	(relative) यदा (correlative, तदा) (interrogative) कदा
where	(relative) यत्र (correlative: तत्र) (interrogative) कुत्र
which	(relative) य (correlative स) (declined like स, but does not lose -ḥ in masc. nom. sg.) (interrogative) क (must agree with antecedent) (declined like स, but does not lose-ḥ: in masc. nom. sg., and has nom-acc. neut. sg. किम्)
who	(relative) य (correlative: स) (declined like स, but does not lose-ḥ: in masc. nom. sg.) (interrogative) क (declined like स, but does not lose -ḥ in nom. sg. masc., and has nom-acc., neut. sg. किम्)
whoever	यो यः (correlative, स सः. The masculine of य repeated. See who)
whose	genitive, in proper gender and number, of य. (Correlative requisite form of स)
wife	पत्नी; भार्या (lesson 30)
win	जि (जयति, जापयति, जीयते, जित)

with	(meaning in the company of) सह (placed after instrumental of word it governs) (translated by बहुव्रीहि) स-, सह-
without	(translated by बहुव्रीहि) निस् (follows regular सन्धि rules, except that -स् becomes -ष् before क्, ख्, प्, फ्)
woods	वनम्
words	वाच् (nom. sg. वाक्), f. (may be used in singular or plural)
world	लोक
you	त्वम् (singular); यूयम् (plural).